CIMA Exam Practice Kit

Management Accounting Business Strategy

CIMA Exam Practice Kit

Management Accounting Business Strategy

Tony Graham

Amsterdam • Boston • Heidelberg • London • New York • Oxford
Paris • San Diego • San Francisco • Singapore • Sydney • Tokyo

CIMA Publishing
An imprint of Elsevier
Linacre House, Jordan Hill, Oxford OX2 8DP
30 Corporate Drive, Burlington, MA 01803

First published 2007

Copyright © 2007, Elsevier Ltd. All rights reserved

No part of this publication may be reproduced in any material form (including
photocopying or storing in any medium by electronic means and whether
or not transiently or incidentally to some other use of this publication) without
the written permission of the copyright holder except in accordance with the provisions
of the Copyright, Designs and Patents Act 1988 or under the terms of a licence issued by
the Copyright Licensing Agency Ltd, 90 Tottenham Court Road, London, England
W1T 4LP. Applications for the copyright holder's written permission to reproduce any
part of this publication should be addressed to the publisher

Permissions may be sought directly from Elsevier's Science and Technology Rights
Department in Oxford, UK: phone: (+44) (0) 1865 843830; fax: (+44) (0) 1865 853333;
e-mail: permissions@elsevier.com. You may also complete your request on-line via
the Elsevier homepage (http://www.elsevier.com), by selecting 'Customer Support'
and then 'Obtaining Permissions'

Notice
No responsibility is assumed by the publisher for any injury and/or damage to persons
or property as a matter of products liability, negligence or otherwise, or from any use
or operation of any methods, products, instructions or ideas contained in the material
herein.

British Library Cataloguing in Publication Data
A catalogue record for this book is available from the British Library

Library of Congress Cataloguing in Publication Data
A catalogue record for this book is available from the Library of Congress

ISBN 13: 978 07506 8400 2
ISBN 10: 0 7506 8400 3

For information on all CIMA Publishing Publications
visit our website at www.cimapublishing.com

Typeset by Integra Software Services Pvt. Ltd, Pondicherry, India
www.integra-india.com
Printed and bound by Krips, Holland

Working together to grow
libraries in developing countries

www.elsevier.com | www.bookaid.org | www.sabre.org

ELSEVIER   BOOK AID International   Sabre Foundation

Contents

Syllabus Guidance, Learning Objectives and Verbs	x
Learning Outcomes, Syllabus Content and Examination Format	xiii
Examination Techniques	xvii

1 Strategic Management — 1
- Rational strategic planning — 1
- Emergent strategies — 2
- Incrementalism — 2
- Freewheeling opportunism — 2
- Questions — 2
    - Question 1 Strategy development (Practice question) — 2
    - Question 2 N strategic management — 3
    - Question 3 Strategic management accounting — 4
    - Question 4 Strategy formulation — 4
    - Question 5 Environmental uncertainty — 4
- Answers — 5
    - Question 1 Strategy development — 5
    - Question 2 N strategic management — 5
    - Question 3 Strategic management accounting — 6
    - Question 4 Strategy formulation — 7
    - Question 5 Environmental uncertainty — 8

2 Mission and Objectives — 10
- Mission — 10
- Objectives — 10
- Stakeholders — 11
- Not-for-profit organisations — 11
- Questions — 12
    - Question 1 Library missions (Practice question) — 12
    - Question 2 Possible objectives (Practice question) — 13
    - Question 3 Hospital stakeholders (Practice question) — 13
    - Question 4 BZ — 13
    - Question 5 Publicly funded — 14
    - Question 6 Objectives — 15
    - Question 7 School stakeholders — 15
    - Question 8 Genetic code — 16
    - Question 9 Eastborough — 16
    - Question 10 Doctors with Wings — 17

vi Contents

Answers	18
Question 1 Library missions	18
Question 2 Possible objectives	18
Question 3 Hospital stakeholders	19
Question 4 BZ	19
Question 5 Publicly funded	21
Question 6 Objectives	22
Question 7 School stakeholders	23
Question 8 Genetic code	24
Question 9 Eastborough	25
Question 10 Doctors with Wings	27

3 External Analysis — **29**

PEST	29
Porter's Five Forces model	30
Scenario analysis	30
Porter's Diamond	31
Questions	32
Question 1 Clothing company	32
Question 2 PD	32
Question 3 E	32
Question 4 Five forces	33
Question 5 Competitor analysis	33
Question 6 Don Mac	34
Question 7 Breakland	35
Question 8 Budget Airlines	35
Answers	36
Question 1 Clothing company	36
Question 2 PD	37
Question 3 E	39
Question 4 Five forces	40
Question 5 Competitor analysis	41
Question 6 Don Mac	43
Question 7 Breakland	44
Question 8 Budget Airlines	46

4 Position Analysis — **48**

The resource audit – the nine M's	48
Porter's value chain	49
Questions	50
Question 1 R	50
Question 2 University	50
Question 3 PA	51
Question 4 Supermarket	52
Question 5 Competitor benchmarking	52
Answers	53
Question 1 R	53
Question 2 University	54
Question 3 PA	55
Question 4 Supermarket	57
Question 5 Competitor benchmarking	58

5	**Corporate Appraisal**		**61**
	Gap analysis		62
	Questions		62
		Question 1 T plc	62
		Question 2 SWOTs	64
		Question 3 Gap analysis	65
	Answers		65
		Question 1 T plc	65
		Question 2 SWOTs	68
		Question 3 Gap analysis	69
6	**Strategic Options and Evaluation**		**70**
	Porter's generic strategies		70
	Strategic direction – Ansoff's matrix		71
	Methods of strategic development		72
	Strategy evaluation		73
	Questions		73
		Question 1 S and L	73
		Question 2 Qualispecs	74
	Answers		75
		Question 1 S and L	75
		Question 2 Qualispecs	76
7	**Strategy in Marketing**		**78**
	The marketing concept		78
	Boston consulting group matrix		78
	Strategies to achieve a competitive position		79
	Product life cycle		79
	Possible strategies for stages of product life cycle		80
	Questions		81
		Question 1 Sports centre	81
		Question 2 Marketing orientation	81
		Question 3 Brand strategy	82
		Question 4 GC conglomerate	82
	Answers		84
		Question 1 Sports centre	84
		Question 2 Marketing orientation	85
		Question 3 Brand strategy	86
		Question 4 GC conglomerate	87
8	**Strategy in IT**		**90**
	Critical success factors		91
	Data warehousing and data mining		91
	Questions		92
		Question 1 A and B strategies	92
		Question 2 RR university	93
		Question 3 SI organisation	93
		Question 4 SDW	95
	Answers		96
		Question 1 A and B strategies	96
		Question 2 RR university	97
		Question 3 SI organisation	98
		Question 4 SDW	99

9 Impact on the Organisation — 101
Types of organisational structure — 101
Centralisation — 103
Business process re-engineering — 103
Questions — 104
    Question 1   X restructuring — 104
    Question 2   Outsourcing — 104
    Question 3   J organisation — 105
Answers — 105
    Question 1   X restructuring — 105
    Question 2   Outsourcing — 106
    Question 3   J organisation — 107

10 Control and Performance Measurement — 109
Shareholder value analysis — 109
Financial assessment of divisions — 110
The dimensions of a service business — 111
Performance pyramid — 111
Questions — 112
    Question 1   Division X — 112
    Question 2   Destroying value — 114
    Question 3   M-HK — 116
    Question 4   Scorecard — 116
    Question 5   PAL — 117
    Question 6   RP manufacturing — 117
    Question 7   Financial scandals — 118
    Question 8   Royal Botanical Gardens — 119
Answers — 120
    Question 1   Division X — 120
    Question 2   Destroying value — 122
    Question 3   M-HK — 124
    Question 4   Scorecard — 126
    Question 5   PAL — 126
    Question 6   RP manufacturing — 128
    Question 7   Financial scandals — 129
    Question 8   Royal Botanical Gardens — 131

11 Case Study Questions — 133
Questions — 134
    Question 1   G — 134
    Question 2   FNJ and WT — 136
    Question 3   Y-Land FE — 139
    Question 4   ICS — 141
    Question 5   C — 144
    Question 6   PC airlines — 147
    Question 7   CG — 150
    Question 8   MW and FS — 153
    Question 9   ACEP — 155

		Contents	**ix**

	Answers	158
	Question 1 G	158
	Question 2 FNJ and WT	161
	Question 3 Y-Land FE	163
	Question 4 ICS	165
	Question 5 C	168
	Question 6 PC airlines	170
	Question 7 CG	173
	Question 8 MW and FS	175
	Question 9 ACEP	178
12	**May 2006 Questions and Answers**	**184**
13	**November 2006 Questions and Answers**	**208**

Syllabus Guidance, Learning Objectives and Verbs

A The syllabus

The syllabus for the CIMA Professional Chartered Management Accounting qualification 2005 comprises three learning pillars:

- Management Accounting pillar
- Business Management pillar
- Financial Management pillar

Within each learning pillar there are three syllabus subjects. Two of these subjects are set at the lower "Managerial" level, with the third subject positioned at the higher "Strategic" level. All subject examinations have a duration of three hours and the pass mark is 50%.

Note: In addition to these nine examinations, students are required to gain 3 years relevant practical experience and successfully sit for the Test of Professional Competence in Management Accounting (TOPCIMA).

B Aims of the syllabus

The aims of the syllabus are:

- To provide for the Institute, together with the practical experience requirements, an adequate basis for assuring society that those admitted to membership are competent to act as management accountants for entities, whether in manufacturing, commercial or service organisations, in the public or private sectors of the economy.
- To enable the Institute to examine whether prospective members have an adequate knowledge, understanding and mastery of the stated body of knowledge and skills.
- To complement the Institute's practical experience and skills development requirements.

C Study weightings

A percentage weighting is shown against each topic in the syllabus. This is intended as a guide to the proportion of study time each topic requires.

All topics in the syllabus must be studied, since any single examination question may examine more than one topic, or carry a higher proportion of marks than the percentage study time suggested.

The weightings *do not* specify the number of marks that will be allocated to topics in the examination.

D Learning outcomes

Each topic within the syllabus contains a list of learning outcomes, which should be read in conjunction with the knowledge content for the syllabus. A learning outcome has two main purposes:

1. to define the skill or ability that a well-prepared candidate should be able to exhibit in the examination;
2. to demonstrate the approach likely to be taken by examiners in examination questions.

The learning outcomes are part of a hierarchy of learning objectives. The verbs used at the beginning of each learning outcome relate to a specific learning objective, for example, evaluate alternative approaches to budgeting.

The verb "evaluate" indicates a high-level learning objective. As learning objectives are hierarchical, it is expected that at this level, students will have knowledge of different budgeting systems and methodologies and be able to apply them.

A list of the learning objectives and the verbs that appear in the syllabus learning outcomes and examinations, follows:

Learning objective	Verbs used	Definition
1 Knowledge *What you are expected to know*	List	Make a list of
	State	Express, fully or clearly, the details of/facts of
	Define	Give the exact meaning of
2 Comprehension *What you are expected to understand*	Describe	Communicate the key features of
	Distinguish	Highlight the differences between
	Explain	Make clear or intelligible/State the meaning of
	Identify	Recognise, establish or select after consideration
	Illustrate	Use an example to describe or explain something

3 Application

How you are expected to apply your knowledge

Apply	To put to practical use
Calculate/compute	To ascertain or reckon mathematically
Demonstrate	To prove with certainty or to exhibit by practical means
Prepare	To make or get ready for use
Reconcile	To make or prove consistent/compatible
Solve	Find an answer to
Tabulate	Arrange in a table

4 Analysis

How you are expected to analyse the detail of what you have learned

Analyse	Examine in detail the structure of
Categorise	Place into a defined class or division
Compare and contrast	Show the similarities and/or differences between
Construct	To build up or compile
Discuss	To examine in detail by argument
Interpret	To translate into intelligible or familiar terms
Produce	To create or bring into existence

5 Evaluation

How you are expected to use your learning to evaluate, make decisions or recommendations

Advise	To counsel, inform or notify
Evaluate	To appraise or assess the value of
Recommend	To advise on a course of action

Key to Icons

- Exam focus
- Key points
- Questions
- Answers

Learning Outcomes, Syllabus Content and Examination Format

Paper P6 – Management accounting business strategy

Syllabus outline

The syllabus comprises:

Topic and study weighting

- A Assessing the Competitive Environment   20%
- B Interacting with the Competitive Environment 20%
- C Evaluation of Options, Planning and Appraisal 30%
- D Implementation of Strategic Plans   30%

Learning aims

Students should be able to:

- identify and evaluate approaches to strategic management; explain the place of the enterprise in the broader economic and social environment;
- apply contemporary thinking on strategic management;
- identify and utilise appropriate tools for strategic analysis;
- evaluate appropriate strategic options and make recommendations;
- evaluate the linkages between strategic planning and the implementation of those plans;
- design and recommend appropriate performance measurement systems.

Assessment strategy

There will be a written examination paper of three hours, with the following sections.

Section A – 50 marks
A maximum of four compulsory questions, totalling 50 marks, all relating to a single scenario.

Section B – 50 marks
Two questions, from a choice of four, each worth 25 marks. Short scenarios will be given, to which some or all questions relate.

A – Assessing the competitive environment – 20%

Learning outcomes

On completion of their studies students should be able to:

 (i) identify relevant stakeholders in respect of an organisation;
 (ii) evaluate the impact of regulatory regimes on strategic planning and implementation;
 (iii) evaluate the nature of competitive environments, distinguishing between simple and complicated competitive environments;
 (iv) distinguish the difference between static and dynamic competitive environments;
 (v) evaluate strategies for response to competition.

Syllabus content

- PEST analysis.
- SWOT analysis.
- Interacting with stakeholders and the use of stakeholder mapping.
- Regulation in major markets (WTO, EU, NAFTA, Asia-Pacific). Country analysis and political risk.
- Porter's Diamond and its use for assessing the competitive advantage of nations.
- Porter's Five Forces model and its use for assessing the external environment.
- Qualitative approaches to competitive analysis.
- Competitor analysis and competitive strategies (both qualitative and quantitative tools of competitor analysis will be used).
- Sources, availability and quality of data for environmental analysis.

B – Interacting with the competitive environment – 20%

Learning outcomes

On completion of their studies students should be able to:

 (i) evaluate the impact and influence of the external environment on an organisation and its strategy;
 (ii) recommend pro-active and reactive approaches to business/government relations and to relations with civil society;
 (iii) discuss how stakeholder groups work and how they affect the organisation;
 (iv) discuss how suppliers and customers influence the strategy process and recommend how to interact with them;
 (v) evaluate the impact of electronic commerce on the way business is conducted and recommend an appropriate strategy;
 (vi) evaluate the strategic and competitive benefits of IS/IT and advise on the development of appropriate strategies.

Syllabus content

- Derivatives of PEST such as STEEP (Social, Technological, Environmental, Economic and Political factors) and PESTEL (Political, Economic, Socio-cultural, Technological and Legal factors).
- Approaches to business-government relations and with civil society (Braithwaite and Drahos).

- Stakeholder management (stakeholders to include government and regulatory agencies, non-governmental organisations and civil society, industry associations, customers and suppliers).
- The customer portfolio: Customer analysis and behaviour, including the marketing audit and customer profitability analysis as well as customer retention and loyalty.
- Negotiating with customers and suppliers and managing these relationships.
- The impact of IT (including electronic commerce) on an industry (utilising frameworks such as Porter's Five Forces and the Value Chain) and how organisations can use IT (including the Internet) to enhance competitive position.
- Competing through exploiting information (rather than technology), for example, use of databases to identify potential customers or market segments, and the management of data warehousing and mining.
- The relationship between current and predicted strategic importance of IS/IT (the applications portfolio).
- Implications of these interactions for Chartered Management Accountants and the management accounting system.

C – Evaluation of options, planning and appraisal – 30%

Learning outcomes

On completion of their studies students should be able to:

(i) evaluate strategic options;
(ii) evaluate the product portfolio of an organisation and recommend appropriate changes to support the organisation's strategic goals;
(iii) prepare a benchmarking exercise and evaluate the results;
(iv) identify an organisation's value chain;
(v) evaluate the importance of process innovation and re-engineering;
(vi) discuss and apply both qualitative and quantitative techniques in the support of the strategic decision-making function;
(vii) discuss the role and responsibilities of directors in the strategy development process.

Syllabus content

- Mission statements and their use in orientating the organisation's strategy.
- Forecasting and the various techniques used: trend analysis, system modelling, in-depth consultation with experts (Delphi method).
- Scenario planning and long range planning as tools in strategic decision-making (including gap analysis).
- Strategic options generation (e.g. using Ansoff's product/market matrix and Porter's generic strategies).
- Audit of resources and the analysis of this for use in strategic decision-making.
- Management of the product portfolio.
- Benchmarking performance with the best organisations.
- Value chain analysis.
- Acquisition and divestment strategies and their place in the strategic plan.
- The role of IT in innovation and Business Process Re-engineering.
- The role and responsibilities of directors in making strategic decisions (including issues of due diligence, fiduciary responsibilities).

D – Implementation of strategic plans – 30%

Learning outcomes

On completion of their studies students should be able to:

(i) evaluate and recommend appropriate control measures;
(ii) prepare and evaluate multidimensional models of performance measurement;
(iii) identify problems in performance measurement and recommend solutions;
(iv) evaluate and advise managers on the development of strategies for knowledge management, IM, IS and IT that support the organisation's strategic requirements;
(v) identify and evaluate IS/IT systems appropriate to the organisation's strategic requirements, and recommend changes where necessary;
(vi) discuss the role of change management in a strategic context.

Syllabus content

- Assessing strategic performance (i.e. the use and development of appropriate measures that are sensitive to industry characteristics and environmental factors).
- Non-financial measures and their interaction with financial ones. (Note: Candidates will be expected to use both qualitative and quantitative techniques.)
- Multidimensional models of performance (e.g. the balanced scorecard, the results and determinants framework, the performance pyramid).
- Business unit performance and appraisal, including transfer pricing, reward systems and incentives and agency theory. (Note: Details of agency theory will not be tested.)
- Project management: monitoring the implementation of plans.
- The implementation of lean systems across an organisation.
- Change management in a strategic context.
- Marketing in a strategic context.
- The purpose and contents of IM, IS and IT strategies, and the need for strategy complementary to the corporate and individual business strategies.
- The concept of knowledge management and its role as a key element in an organisation's success.
- Critical success factors: links to performance indicators and corporate strategy, and their use as a basis for defining an organisation's information needs.
- The role of research and development in an organisation, particularly the need to integrate product and process development.

Examination Techniques

Essay questions

Your essay should have a clear structure, that is, an introduction, a middle and an end. Think in terms of 1 mark for each relevant point made.

Numerical questions

It is essential to show workings in your answer. If you come up with the wrong answer and no workings, the examiner cannot award any marks. However, if you get the wrong answer but apply the correct technique then you will be given some marks.

Reports and memorandum

Where you are asked to produce an answer in a report type format you will be given easy marks for style and presentation.

- A *report* is a document from an individual or group in one organisation sent to an individual or group in another.
- A *memorandum* is an informal report going from one individual or group to another individual or group in the same organisation.

You should start a report as follows:

To: J. SMITH, CEO, ABC plc

From: M ACCOUNTANT

Date: 31st December 2000

Terms of Reference: Financial Strategy of ABC plc

Strategic Management

📝 Exam focus

You need to have a clear idea of the strategic process as it underlies much of the syllabus and it can form the basis of questions asking for advice on how to introduce strategic planning.

🔑 Key points

Corporate strategy looks at the organisation as a whole.
Business strategy looks at each individual business unit.
Operational strategy looks at each function or operational area.

Rational strategic planning

Also known as position-based strategy, this is the assumed strategic process for most of the syllabus. It considers the objectives of the organisation, looks at the environment to identify threats and opportunities and assesses the organisation's current position in order to develop a strategic plan.

It therefore involves:

Defining the direction, mission and objectives

Strategic analysis	External analysis of the environment
	Internal analysis of the firm
	Corporate appraisal
Strategic choice	Selecting strategic options
	Choosing options the firm is going to take
Strategic implementation	Policies and strategies for marketing, finance, R&D, IT, human resources and structure
Strategy evaluation and control	

However, this method takes some time to develop and an organisation's actions may then be constrained by the plan.

Emergent strategies

Emergent strategies are strategies which emerge out of the course of the business rather than having been formally planned. They could perhaps be due to opportunities which present themselves (e.g. a competitor comes up for sale) or threats which need to be addressed (e.g. a competitor develops a new product and the company must follow suit to remain competitive).

Emergent strategies can be combined with the successful elements of the planned strategy to define the way forward for the business. The process of bringing these together is called crafting a strategy. This is more appropriate for businesses in a changing environment, where restriction to one planned strategy may be a competitive weakness.

Incrementalism

In fast-changing environments it may be unrealistic to effectively undertake the full strategic planning process. Instead it is more practical to develop a short-term strategy based on the consensus of opinion of major stakeholders. The strategy is then developed regularly using a series of small-scale changes as dictated by the changing environment.

Freewheeling opportunism

In this model there is no formal approach to strategy development. Directors dictate the business direction through taking whatever opportunities are available at a particular point in time. This allows the business to be very flexible and take opportunities that companies using a more formal approach to strategy development would be slow to take.

Questions

Question 1 Strategy development (Practice question)

In the following situations, which form of strategy development is being followed?

Company A

Company A is in a high-tech industry where new innovation is important to the success of the business. They have been highly successful over recent years by ensuring good long-term investment in Research and Development coupled with the ability to be flexible to changing technologies. They have a good record of taking advantage of new opportunities and over recent years they have made significant profits from the Internet and mobile telephone booms.

Company B

Company B is run by Virginia Richards a dynamic entrepreneur. Over recent years she has set up businesses in the cosmetics, lingerie and coffee shop fields. She is an expert in setting up new businesses, developing them and selling them off for a big profit.

Company C

Company C is a large supermarket chain. They have developed a successful long-term strategy by maintaining low prices, creating good customer service and developing new sites in excellent locations.

Company D

Company D is in a manufacturing industry. It has produced the same building material for the last 50 years and was always highly profitable due to the patent on the product, until a new innovative and cheaper product came on to the market 3 years ago. It is now loss making and the directors have not yet made any major changes to the business.

Company E

Company E is a local doctors' surgery. Decisions are made at group meetings of the eight doctors who own the practice. The practice has successfully grown over recent years as new services have been gradually developed. Overall progress has been slower than it may have been as the doctors are reticent to build the new building the practice really needs.

Question 2 N strategic management

N Ltd is a small family controlled manufacturing company. In its 40-year history, the company has grown to the extent that it now employs 35 staff, producing a wide and diverse range of household goods and utensils. The company has increased in size from its small original base. However, it has never employed a strategic management approach for its development and has relied on operational decision-making to determine priorities. N Ltd has never gathered any information relating to its markets. In recent years, the company has experienced a reduction in turnover and profitability and is assessing how it might redress the situation.

Requirements

(a) Explain how strategic management differs from operational management.

(10 marks)

(b) The directors of N Ltd have now decided to introduce a strategic management approach which will assist in the selection of appropriate strategies for future development of the company.

Requirement

Discuss the cultural and organisational changes which N Ltd will need to implement in order to successfully introduce strategic management.

(15 marks)
(Total = 25 marks)

Question 3 Strategic management accounting

Management accountancy has been criticised for being inward-looking and focusing too much on internal organisational efficiency. Keith Ward, in 1992, stated that Strategic Management Accounting is concerned with providing "management accounting in the context of business strategies being planned and implemented by an organisation".

Requirements

(a) Discuss the above statement and explain the aims of Strategic Management Accounting.

(8 marks)

(b) Discuss whether Strategic Management Accounting serves any useful purpose in assisting organisations in their strategic development.

(12 marks)
(Total = 20 marks)

Question 4 Strategy formulation

Different approaches to strategy formulation were developed throughout the 20th century. These approaches have included the rational strategy process, emergent strategies and logical incrementalism. The rational strategy approach may be classified as a formal method of strategy formulation. Emergent strategies and logical incrementalism are regarded as informal approaches to strategy formulation.

Requirement

Compare and contrast the rational strategy approach with emergent strategies and logical incrementalism within the private sector environment.

(25 marks)

Question 5 Environmental uncertainty

Strategy involves planning ways in which the long-term objectives of the organisation can be achieved. An important part of such a process is the analysis of the external environment to determine future potential factors that are most relevant to the organisation.

Some believe that the external environment within which organisations operate has become increasingly uncertain and therefore wholly unpredictable. This raises important issues for strategy development, with some questioning the value of past approaches.

Requirements

(a) Discuss how environmental uncertainty might affect strategic thinking within organisations.

(12 marks)

(b) Assess the usefulness of scenario planning in strategy formulation, particularly under conditions of extreme uncertainty.

(13 marks)
(Total = 25 marks)

✓ Answers

Question 1 Strategy development

Company A

Crafting a strategy using a mixture of emergent and planned strategies.

Company B

Freewheeling opportunism

Company C

Planned strategy

Company D

No strategy

Company E

Incrementalism

Question 2 N strategic management

(a) Strategic vs operational management

Strategic management differs from operational management in the following respects:

Strategic management is concerned with the longer term, whereas operations look at the shorter term. How far into the future the strategic management looks depends on the extent to which the external environment is predictable by management.

In using strategic management, the managers will need to assess the external environment and make predictions about the future environment. This will be compared with the internal position before designing and implementing strategy; operational management will focus on the internal resources and the management of them.

While strategic management will review the resources available and assess them in the light of the objectives set, accessing more when necessary, operational management will be concerned with managing those resources which the company has.

(b) Cultural and organisational changes

In the past, N has continued its small family business approach by managing the business at an operational level, but has made no attempt to take a longer-term strategic view. This will entail a number of changes, which will need to be handled carefully:

Cultural changes

N will need to ensure that managers are aware of the different approach being taken and are alert to changes in the environment in which the company operates. This may involve some training in strategic planning so that managers understand the importance and relevance of a changing environment. There may also need to be a change in the general culture of management, as N will want managers to be innovative and participate so that they take a proactive role in recognising important changes in the company's position.

However, it is notoriously difficult to change a long-established culture, and much of the process described in (a) will have to be enforced through imposed routines and controls, reinforcing acceptable behaviour and penalising the unacceptable. After managers and staff start to see some benefits from a more strategic approach, the attitudes of staff and culture within the company might start to change.

Organisational changes

N will need to formalise its approach to strategic planning by setting formal objectives, conducting environmental screening and then using these to allocate resources, along with targets consistent with the objectives, to different areas, of the business. It is likely that the board in a small company will undertake these tasks, using a strategic planning approach. While this gives the family more control and ensures consistency, it means that the employees are less likely to be convinced of the benefits. As a result, the board will need to monitor the operations carefully to ensure that targets are being met.

N will need to ensure that its information systems are appropriate for the style of management it implements. These systems may need to be improved or possibly replaced so that it focuses on those areas which relate to the strategic objectives. This may mean developing performance indicates for activities of key importance.

The organisational structure may need to be adjusted, as it is likely the company operates on a functional structure. It is important that resources are assessed across the whole organisation so that they can be made available where they have most strategic impact.

N will probably have to redesign the control and review systems so that progress towards strategic objectives can be assessed. It is possible that in a strategic review, certain products are discontinued; this will clearly impact on the organisational structure and mean that some employees will have their jobs redefined. There may be the need for new skills, such as strategic planning or a greater emphasis on marketing, which could be set up as separate departments.

Question 3 Strategic management accounting

(a) Strategic management accounting

Strategic Management Accounting (SMA) looks not only at the internal position of the company in terms of its resources, but more importantly on the external business environment. SMA will therefore focus on customers, competitors and suppliers so that it can monitor and assess the changes in the environment in which the company operates.

Traditionally, management accounting has focused on managing the resources within the organisation, and is backward-looking. SMA looks to the future by assessing the likely trends in the external environment and helps management to make positive longer-term decisions rather than reactive short-term ones.

This approach will be more in line with the areas of the various stakeholders, as these will be reflected in the strategic objectives of the organisation. SMA will not only look externally but will measure progress towards these longer-term objectives.

For an organisation to be successful, it is important for it to maintain or improve its competitive advantage; this will be helped by the information collected by SMA so that the company can judge the actions of its customers and competitors.

(b) Accounting system

A strategic management accounting system needs to provide suitable information for management to take strategic decisions. As with all management accounting systems, it needs to:

- provide relevant information for managers. SMA must therefore report on appropriate performance measures, which will need to be identified. The SMA itself in giving feedback on the environment can help in the selection of these measures.
- provide selective information for managers so that they have sufficient, accurate and relevant information for planning, decision-making and control without overwhelming the managers with information.
- be capable of coping with changes, as the environment will change and so might the information requirements of the managers. As the environment changes, the system needs to detect them quickly and report them so that action can be taken and strategic plans adjusted.

Such a system should help the organisation to assess and monitor changes to its strengths and weaknesses and to the threats and opportunities it faces. This will enable it to plan strategically so that it has a better chance of achieving its objectives.

Question 4 Strategy formulation

All approaches to strategy formulation are trying to achieve the long-term objectives of a company and increase shareholder value. The company must therefore examine its environment and its current resources and skills.

Strategy encompasses corporate strategy (what markets to be in, what acquisitions to undertake), business strategy (how to obtain competitive advantage in a market) and operational strategy (managing the various functions of the business). The strategies discussed below are mostly applied to business strategy.

Rational strategy

This gives a formal approach to derive a strategy. The company sets its mission statement and objectives which are quantifiable. The company then undertakes corporate appraisal, which assesses the organisation's resources and skills and classifies them as strengths or weaknesses, and then the likely or possible changes in the environment in which it operates (including changes in competition) – these form opportunities and threats.

Strategic options are then derived by using the results of the corporate appraisal to identify ways in which it could achieve its objectives while minimising any weaknesses or potential threats. The options generated are then reviewed for suitability, feasibility and acceptability to assess how practical it really is to implement and how closely it will help to achieve its objectives. Strategies chosen are then implemented, which may involve acquiring new skills and resources, and progress towards the objectives carefully monitored.

This is a time-consuming process and is more suitable for large organisations; being very formal, it can be slow to react to changes in the environment and is therefore less suitable when there is a highly volatile environment. Smaller organisations often respond faster to changes but have limited scope for entering new markets or developing new products.

Emergent strategies

This suggests that strategies followed are not only those planned, but a mixture of those planned and those that emerged as time went by. These arise as a company takes advantage of any unforeseen opportunity (which is more likely in a faster reacting small company).

To encourage such flexible behaviour, a flatter structure and more entrepreneurial culture need to be encouraged, and management need a very clear understanding of the business and which situations would present opportunities. Again, this is more likely in smaller organisations.

Logical incrementalism

This says that most strategy is gradual in its development and implementation, even if management use the rational approach to give the overall direction of the strategy. This is partly because it takes time to persuade people to accept any major changes and partly because major changes may require finance which is not available.

Both emergent strategies and logical incrementalism show how in practice strategic planning often does not follow the logical, but theoretical, approach of rational strategy.

Question 5 Environmental uncertainty

(a) Impact of environmental uncertainty

The rational planning model sets objectives and then analyses the external environment and internal position so that a strategic plan can be put together. The external environment obviously changes, so managers need to make an educated guess as to the likely direction it will take and monitor the environment for changes.

When the environment is very uncertain, it becomes very difficult for managers to predict the future opportunities and threats and any strategy which results may not be appropriate. In addition, the changing environment will need to be constantly monitored which may lead to the strategy being regularly revised. When there is such uncertainty, organisations may, at the very least, decide there is too much risk in making long-term investment decisions. They may reduce their planning horizons and only plan for a shorter term, with smaller incremental steps. Organisations may follow low-risk strategies and lead to a trend to follow the leader.

Some organisations may decide that any logical strategic planning process is pointless and have no long-term strategy at all. However, this is an extreme reaction and companies should generally reduce their planning horizon to that which they can reasonably predict. This will lead to them being more risk-averse and unwilling to attempt innovation.

(b) Scenario planning

An organisation can use scenario planning as a method to assess future possible situations and consider the likely consequences for the organisation. These include well-established scenarios such as disaster recovery plans and hazard management. Public bodies may look at flooding, other natural disasters and major transport incidents.

When an organisation faces a very uncertain future, it can be difficult to decide on appropriate likely scenarios. However, in having to decide on those which are most likely, it will force organisations to identify the key uncertainties. It can then consider how it may influence these key uncertainties or mitigate their influence. There are various possibilities for dealing with a number of uncertain scenarios. The organisation could rank them according to likelihood and plan a course of action in response to the most likely ones. Alternatively, the organisation can try to develop core competencies which would sustain the organisation whichever scenario materialises. As the key uncertainties become clearer, the organisation can gradually make its strategy more specific and appropriate.

Scenario planning can therefore be very useful, particularly when there is extreme uncertainty as it will help the organisation think carefully about the key uncertainties. However, there are some difficulties in that:

- the scenarios may take considerable time and cost to construct
- they may be regarded as rather unreal and hypothetical
- they may still be ignored or down-played by decision-makers if they are unpalatable or would mean making unpopular decisions
- they might provoke disputes among managers.

Mission and Objectives

2

✏ Exam focus

You need to be able to write about objectives and stakeholders for organisations, including those in the public as well as the private sector.

🗝 Key points

Mission

A mission helps to:

- Provide a common purpose for all stakeholders
- Focus the strategy
- Focus the objectives
- Communicate the organisation's purpose.

A good mission statement is clear and unambiguous, concise, covers the whole organisation, and is open ended (not quantifiable). It should also give the purpose, strategy, values and policies of the organisation.

Objectives

Objectives are set at different levels within the organisation to motivate and focus performance in each major part of the business. This goes right down to the individuals who are set objectives as part of their appraisal.

To be effective objectives should have the following qualities:

– Specific
– Measurable

- **A**chievable
- **R**elevant (to the person/division who has been set the objective)
- **T**ime-bound.

Stakeholders

Stakeholders of an organisation are groups who have an interest in what the organisation does.

Stakeholders include:

- Internal such as employees, including directors and managers.
- Connected such as shareholders, customers, suppliers, financiers.
- External such as government, pressure groups, local community, wider community.

The degree to which stakeholder needs are considered as part of the objective setting process depends on the level of power they have to impact the organisation and its results. The needs of powerful groups will tend to be prioritised. For example large customers have significant power and products, prices, location of production facilities and so on may be impacted by their needs. Small customers have far less power and less consideration will be paid to their individual needs.

Not-for-profit organisations

Not-for profit organisations include government departments, councils, schools, hospitals and charities.

A profit-orientated organisation always has the measure of profit, derived from sales income less costs, which can then be supplemented with other measures.

A not-for-profit organisation is likely to have a large number of stakeholders. It is not that easy to reduce them down to a few key stakeholders, but even then they are likely to have very different, possibly conflicting views on what the organisation's key objectives should be.

This clearly makes it difficult to set objectives and tends to result in organisations such as councils publishing a very wide range of performance measures, often under government guidance.

A not-for-profit organisation will often have no sales revenue (e.g. a hospital or school) and therefore has to rely entirely on non-financial indicators for judging its service levels.

In addition, the non-financial inputs, such as use of land, employee's, time and the opportunity cost of other services foregone in a fixed budget organisation such as a council may be more important than in a profit-orientated organisation.

The three "E"s of economy, effectiveness and efficiency look at:

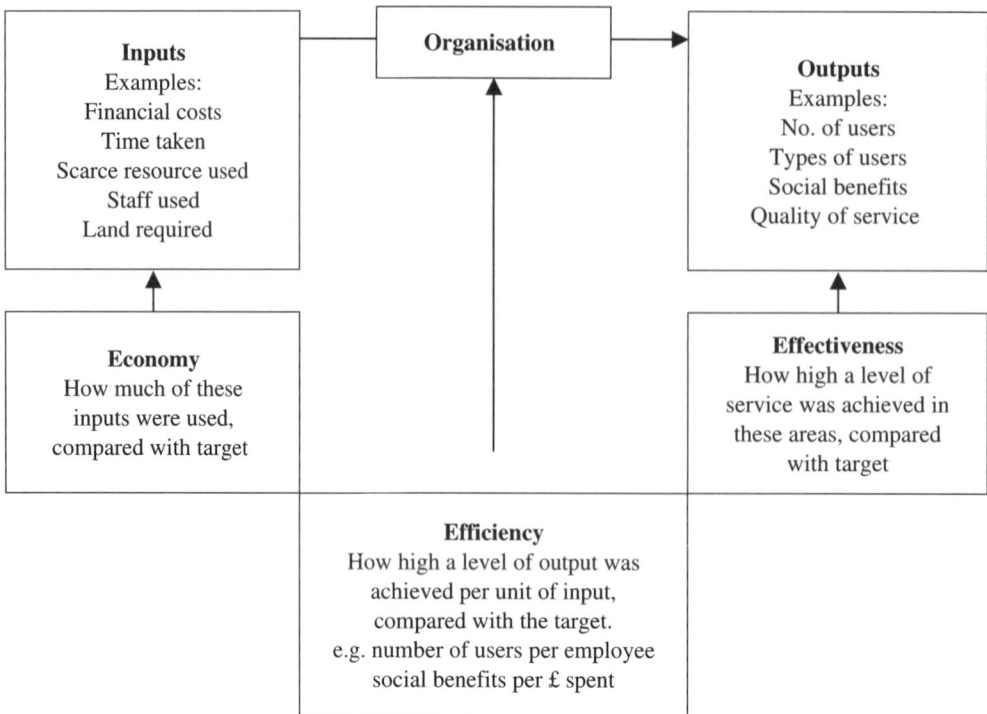

Questions

Question 1 Library missions (Practice question)

Consider these three mission statements from 3 UK-based libraries. Assess the quality of each:

Brent library service

We aim to be a focus of community access to knowledge, information, works of the imagination, culture and heritage.

To achieve this we will:

Provide opportunities for lifelong learning and education's development; Promote the positive enjoyment of reading and provide opportunities for participation in literature and cultural activities; Support the essential basic skills of literacy, numeracy and IT literacy; Provide access to information to enable people to participate actively in their communities; Record, interpret and make accessible the history of the people of Brent; Listen to and involve all communities in Brent.

This will help to improve the quality of local people's lives.

Northamptonshire public libraries

Our mission is to serve the people of Northamptonshire by delivering the vision of Northamptonshire Libraries and Information Service through the development and maintenance of a coherent range of policies and services, understood and valued by the community.

Bodleian library – Oxford university

The Library's mission is to maintain and develop collections and services in support of the present and future teaching and research needs of the University of Oxford, and of the national and international scholarly community. In order to carry out this mission, the Library will always aim to:

(a) develop and maintain an understanding of the needs of its users and potential users and respond to them;
(b) build the necessary collections and services and provide access to them;
(c) preserve the collections for future users;
(d) develop appropriate skills and motivation of staff at all levels;
(e) ensure its financial viability;
(f) foster good relationships with other University bodies, including the Colleges;
(g) co-operate with other libraries within Oxford and in the world at large;
(h) exploit in all areas the potential of technology in order to achieve these aims.

Question 2 Possible objectives (Practice question)

Consider the following objectives for the production manager of an organisation and assess whether they are SMART and what problems may arise from any deficiencies in them.

Objective 1

To have great quality products.

Objective 2

To be great.

Objective 3

To reduce our current level of defects from 69 per 1000 to 0 per 1000 by the end of the month.

Objective 4

To increase sales of products by 10% over the course of the next year.

Objective 5

To reduce the number of defective products from 2 per 1000 to 1 per 1000 over the course of the next year.

Question 3 Hospital stakeholders (Practice question)

Consider what groups of stakeholders there might be for a hospital. Identify what might be important to each and whether they are powerful stakeholders or not.

Question 4 BZ

BZ Ltd is a service company which was founded by L, its proprietor, investing his redundancy payment to establish the business. In addition to his own capital, L obtained a bank loan, and these were the only two sources of finance used to start the business. The company has achieved success by providing a very differentiated service. L has personally carried out the full range of planning and operational management activities required to develop the business ever since it began.

It has become apparent to L that in order to continue growing, further capital needs to be injected. Additionally, it is clear to L that he needs to appoint other senior managers to maintain the operational side of the business. He believes this will leave him free to pursue BZ Ltd's strategic development.

L's strategic objective has been to exploit market opportunities, and he has achieved a high level of return on his investment. However, L now considers that in order to continue growing, BZ Ltd needs to raise more capital than he personally is able to introduce.

L is actively considering raising the new capital by a public issue of shares.

Requirements

(a) Explain in what ways the strategic objectives of BZ Ltd may change if it obtains new capital from the public issue of shares.

(10 marks)

(b) Describe and comment on the appropriate strategic planning processes which BZ Ltd should adopt in order to satisfy its organisational objectives following the public issue of shares.

(10 marks)
(Total = 20 marks)

Question 5 Publicly funded

A publicly funded department within a local administrative authority provides a health advisory service to its local community. This is not a hospital. Its function is purely advisory in respect of preventative medicine and focuses on good health promotion and prevention of accidents and illness.

In recent years, the funding for this service has been reduced in real terms, requiring greater levels of efficiency to be provided. The manager of the service has recognised the need to make economies. Despite receiving criticisms and complaints from the local administrative authority's elected representatives, the manager has reduced the level of service provision in an attempt to remain within budget. However, there has been no reduction in the staffing level which accounts for about 80% of expenditure.

Last year, an independent public audit report criticised the management of the service. The report focused on the fact that the service overspent its budget, was considered to be inefficient in its methods of delivery, and wasted resources allocated to it. The report went on to state that according to annual performance indicator statistics, there is a decline in the numbers of people using the service. It concluded that the service was failing to operate economically, efficiently or effectively. The result of this was that the local administrative authority reduced the funding still further and gave the manager a warning that the whole service would be reviewed if there was not an improvement in this financial year. The manager has responded by making further cuts to the service, but has protected the staffing levels; it is projected that the service will remain just within its budget allocation this year.

Requirements

(a) Discuss the reasons why the service has received criticism.

(4 marks)

(b) Explain how the manager can improve the effectiveness and efficiency of the service while ensuring that it remains economic and within its allocated budget.

(16 marks)
(Total = 20 marks)

Question 6 Objectives

All organisations have objectives in some form or another. The methods of setting these objectives vary depending on the nature of the organisation. After they have been set and an appropriate period of time has elapsed, organisations should assess to what extent their objectives have been achieved.

Two organisations with very different characteristics set strategic objectives and evaluate their achievement. The two organisations are

1 A publicly funded local administrative authority which provides housing, education, social and road maintenance services for an area within a country, and
2 A multinational conglomerate company (MNC).

Requirements

(a) Explain the differences between how the local administrative authority and the MNC should set their strategic objectives.

(10 marks)

(b) Discuss how each organisation should assess how well it has performed in respect of the attainment of its strategic objectives.

(15 marks)
(Total = 25 marks)

Question 7 School stakeholders

A school operated by a local administrative authority provides educational opportunities for teenage pupils within an area in a city. The school has achieved varying levels of success in public examinations and, in terms of examination results, is performing neither better nor worse than other comparable schools serving the city. Its teaching and administrative staff are conscientious and committed to providing quality education to the pupils. The headteacher is required to improve the school's success in respect of examination performance, but the local administrative authority is unable to provide any resources beyond those which are already available.

The headteacher works within the following parameters:

- there is a maximum number of pupils that the school can admit each year;
- the budgets for the school's teaching activities are allocated in accordance with the subjects which are taught;
- the pupils admitted to the school study some core subjects and they may also choose to study some subjects from a range of options, which can be extended, or reduced.

The headteacher has an industrial background and has attempted to apply Boston Consulting Group analysis to the situation of the school. He has concluded that "market growth" could be regarded as relating to the numbers of pupils within certain segments such as socio-economic group and ethnicity. He thinks "market share" relates to how much of the local market for pupils the school obtains in comparison with other schools in the area.

Requirements

(a) (i) Identify the stakeholder groups that the school is seeking to serve within its "customer" portfolio and briefly outline their requirements.

(6 marks)

(ii) Discuss ways in which the headteacher and staff can determine the requirements of these stakeholders.

(6 marks)

(b) Discuss how far analysis of market growth and relative market share as defined by the headteacher can help him and his staff to determine the best way to meet the requirements of the school's stakeholders within its "customer" portfolio.

(13 marks)
(Total = 25 marks)

Question 8 Genetic code

Scientists from various countries in the world have researched into and achieved success in mapping the genetic code of human beings. It is considered that this research may identify how serious life-threatening diseases develop. It is believed that this will lead to improved treatments and in time removal of these diseases altogether. Eventually this may result in the directors of world-class pharmaceutical suppliers facing a conflict of interests. These conflicts may arise because of the need to satisfy the demands of their shareholders in terms of maximised long-term wealth and also the need to discharge social responsibilities by developing treatments which eventually may render its products redundant.

Requirement

Discuss the ethical implications of this research for major world-class pharmaceutical companies. In your discussion, comment on how the directors might reconcile conflicts between satisfying the demands of shareholders and discharging their social responsibilities.

(25 marks)

Question 9 Eastborough

Eastborough is a large region with a rugged, beautiful coastline where rare birds have recently settled on undisturbed cliffs. Since mining ceased 150 years ago, its main industries have been agriculture and fishing. However, today, many communities in Eastborough suffer high unemployment. Government initiatives for regeneration through tourism have met with little success as the area has poor road networks, unsightly derelict buildings and dirty beaches.

Digwell Explorations, a listed company, has a reputation for maximising shareholder returns and has discovered substantial tin reserves in Eastborough. With new technology, mining could be profitable, provide jobs and boost the economy. A number of interest and pressure groups have, however, been vocal in opposing the scheme.

Digwell Explorations, after much lobbying, has just received government permission to undertake mining. It could face difficulties in proceeding because of the likely activity of a group called the Eastborough Protection Alliance. This group includes wildlife protection representatives, villagers worried about the potential increase in traffic congestion and noise, environmentalists and anti capitalism groups.

Requirements

(a) (i) Discuss the ethical issues that should have been considered by the government when granting permission for mining to go ahead.

(6 marks)

(ii) Explain the conflicts between the main stakeholder groups.

(6 marks)

(b) (i) By use of some (mapping) framework, analyse how the interest and power of pressure and stakeholder groups can be understood.

(5 marks)

(ii) Based on this analysis, identify how Digwell Explorations might respond to these groups.

(8 marks)
(Total = 25 marks)

Question 10 Doctors with Wings

Doctors with Wings is a registered charity that raises funds to send volunteer doctors and nurses to medical emergencies around the world. Those emergencies can arise for any reason, ranging from famine to war or major outbreaks of disease. Funding primarily comes from Government agencies and corporate donations, although the charity seeks donations from the public, as well as medicines and other supplies from manufacturers. The majority of volunteers are recruited, often with the support of teaching hospitals, immediately after qualification. These new doctors are often persuaded to donate their time to the charity during presentations made by volunteer doctors who have just returned from a medical emergency.

Bryson, in his 1995 book, *Strategic Planning for Public and Non-profit Organisations*, makes the following statement:

I would argue that if an organisation has time to do only one thing when it comes to strategic planning, that one thing ought to be a stakeholder analysis.

Requirements

(a) Critically discuss the components and process of such an analysis and the benefits that *Doctors with Wings* would gain from the exercise.

(10 marks)

(b) Evaluate the principal stakeholders in the organisation and analyse the nature of the influence and importance that they hold in their relationship with the charity.

(15 marks)
(Total marks = 25)

✓ Answers

Question 1 Library missions

Brent library service
- Good broad overview of purpose in first line.
- Good statement of ultimate purpose, and who they are there for in last line.
- Good statement of how they aim to achieve this (including values "lifelong learning" and policies "listen and involve communities in Brent").
- Relatively brief, clear and focused.

Northamptonshire public libraries
- Unclear purpose – does not say what the libraries stand for, who they are working for.
- What are "coherent policies and services"?
- Unclear how this is going to be achieved.

Bodleian library – Oxford university
- Very clear purpose.
- Very clear how they aim to achieve this.
- Covers a broad range of key areas.

Question 2 Possible objectives

Objective 1

"To have great quality products"

Not measurable or time-bound. Hard for the manager to know what they're trying to achieve, and so they lack focus in their actions and are demotivated.

Objective 2

"To be great"

Not SMART in all five areas. (Great at what? How do you measure great? How do you achieve greatness? Is it relevant for the manager to be great? By when should they be great?) Hard for the manager to know what they're trying to achieve, and so they lack focus in their actions and are demotivated.

Objective 3

"To reduce our current level of defects from 69 per 1000 to 0 per 1000 by the end of the month"

Probably not achievable, but SMART in other respects. Demotivating as too difficult. The manager does not strive to achieve it.

Objective 4

"To increase sales of products by 10 per cent over the course of the next year"

Not relevant enough to what they do, but SMART in other respects. They can't control the target directly so it does not motivate them to improve what they do.

Objective 5

"To reduce the number of defective products from 2 per 1000 to 1 per 1000 over the course of the next year"

A SMART objective.

Question 3 Hospital stakeholders

Internal

Management	Pay, bonus, overall performance and job security
Healthcare employees	Pay, bonus, personal performance and job security
Other employees	Remuneration and job security
Specialists	Respect and status, remuneration

Connected

Patients	Health, standard of care
Suppliers	Assured custom, high prices for drugs and equipment

External

Government	Well-being of the nation, pay and conditions of workers
Local community	Standard of healthcare for the area
Wider community	Confidence in the health service

Powerful stakeholders

Government, specialists, management team, suppliers of key materials, for example, drug companies. The government derives its power from its ability to dictate standards and targets for the hospital and to control its funding, while the management and specialists derive theirs from their expertise and specialised knowledge. Suppliers of key materials have the power to withhold supplies.

Stakeholders with little power

Cleaners, foreign nationals on holiday in UK, suppliers of routine materials such as stationery.

Question 4 BZ

(a) Changes in strategic objectives

In order to assess the changes necessary, we need to examine the changes being proposed in the various stakeholders and how new stakeholders will introduce new requirements or existing stakeholders will change their demands.

The existing key stakeholders are L, who is the owner and the bank. They are likely to require a reasonable standard of living from the business and safe payment of interest and loan by relying on interest cover and security (the bank). While these stakeholders are likely to continue with the same demands, there will be additional stakeholders of new shareholders and the new managers.

The new shareholders will require a return on their investment, probably in the form of a dividend, but also partly through profitable ventures leading to an increase in the capital value of the business. They may ultimately require an exit route so that they can rely their investment. These requirements may conflict in some circumstances with Bank's requirements to maintain liquidity, or L's desires to expand the business may conflict with the need to pay dividends.

The new managers will need to be motivated and will expect remuneration and other incentives, such as profit sharing or bonuses and possibly even share options. Clearly, satisfying the needs excessively would impact on interest cover, profit and dividends, bringing them into conflict with other stakeholders.

L needs to realise that as the stakeholder groups increase, decisions will increasingly become compromises in satisfying the various competing needs.

(b) Strategic planning process

So far, it is likely that L has not followed a formal strategic planning process, but instead used an opportunistic approach, taking advantage of short-term opportunities as they arose. This makes a small firm very flexible and able to respond very quickly but tends to be short term in its view with no long-term plans. With more stakeholders to consider, L might consider a more formal approach to be a useful exercise, if nothing else, in identifying long-term targets and problems.

The rational planning model has a number of logical stages:

Objectives

Starting with the key stakeholders, long-term plans should be identified which set measurable and achievable targets within a realistic time frame.

External analysis

The firm then assesses the political, legal, economic, social and technological environment in which it operates, as well as the nature and source of the competition in its industry, in order to assess the potential threats and opportunities it faces.

Internal analysis

The organisation itself should then be assessed in a position audit, looking at its strengths and weaknesses in terms of its products, resources, financial performance and systems.

Corporate appraisal

This summarises the internal and external analysis to come up with the key strengths, weaknesses, opportunities and threats of the organisation.

Strategic choice

The next stage is to look at the possible strategies that could be implemented, using a number of different frameworks to generate them, and to assess their suitability, given the corporate appraisal, their acceptability given the objectives and desires of the stakeholders, and their feasibility given the likely access to resources.

Implementation and control

Finally, the chosen strategy is implemented and the results and progress towards objectives carefully monitored so that corrective action can be taken if any gap appears.

Although it may not be sensible for L to stick rigidly to such a process as it might impede the flexibility of a small organisation, it would be a useful exercise to review the long-term plans in the light of the new stakeholders and set targets for both the new managers and the level of profits and dividends for the new shareholders.

Question 5 Publicly funded

(a) The advisory service has been criticised for overspending its budget and being inefficient. The manager has been protecting the service levels but this may not be directly connected with the service provided, but more to do with maintaining good relationships with the staff. This would suggest that the manager is ineffective as the staff costs must be addressed if the service is to manage its budget properly, as 80% of costs relate to staff.

(b) It is important that the whole operation is reviewed in terms of its use of the resources which have been funded by the public and the level of service provided. These issues can be looked at under the 3 "E"s of Economy, Effectiveness and Efficiency.

Economy

Approximately 80% of the costs relate to staff, so the service needs to look carefully at the staffing levels to establish how many staff are actually required.

Other resources must also be considered to ensure that they are being put to the best possible use, and that the service provided does not use any more resources than it should.

The advisory service will need to have some idea of the resources which are regarded as reasonable for the level of service provided. To benchmark this, the service might look at similar services offered in other areas and the resources required by them. However, care must be taken to ensure that service offered is at a similar level, both in quantity and quality.

Effectiveness

To assess the service provided, it will probably be necessary to go back to the original aims and objectives of the organisation. This may mean identifying the stakeholders in the service and assessing the needs of the various competing interests before coming up with objectives which promote a reasonable compromise. The managers will need to set performance indicators so that progress towards the objectives can be measured.

In order to set realistic targets and performance indicators, it would again be useful to look at other similar services. However, these quantitative and qualitative measures can be very subjective and it is important to adjust any benchmarks for differences between the service and the comparative organisation. Some obvious measures, such as number of appointments, may not be appropriate as the resources needed for each appointment may vary enormously.

Efficiency

Having put in place measures and targets for input resources and the service provided, the advisory service needs to monitor the service in terms of the resources used, by looking at the service per unit of resource. This could look at the number of people helped per staff member or the average cost per appointment or the percentage of time spent by staff on front line, as opposed to support and services. Finally, demonstrating that the managers are looking to identify, set benchmarks and measure performance in these areas will help to answer some of their critics.

Question 6 Objectives

(a) Setting strategic objectives

In setting strategic objectives, an organisation should first consider its main stakeholders and formulate its mission statement to encapsulate their demands.

As the stakeholders are likely to be very different between a local administrative authority and the MNC, so too will be the mission statements and objectives.

Local Administrative Authority (LAA)

The main stakeholders are the local community, but it is likely to have some objectives set by central government. It must assess the needs of the community through wide-ranging consultation and an objective balancing of these needs.

The objectives are likely to be set in the context of the 3Es – that is effectiveness relating to the level of service provided, economy in terms of the cost and the annual budget and efficiency relating to the service provided per unit of resource.

MNC

The MNC can more clearly identify its main stakeholders as shareholders, and their objective will therefore focus on maximising their wealth and boosting the value of the business for the shareholders. The MNC may have other supporting objectives which will help to achieve this, such as customer satisfaction, employee motivation and ethical practices, which in the long term should also help to increase the value of the business.

(b) Assessment

Any assessment of performance against objectives needs to be measurable in some way, although not necessarily financial, and ideally a target should be SMART (Specific, Measurable, Achievable, Relevant and Time-bound).

LAA

The LAA is likely to have numerous targets relating particularly to its service level. Most of these will be non-financial such as the number of people waiting to be housed and the number of people visiting the leisure facilities. Some targets may relate to the cost in both monetary and manpower terms.

In assessing the LAA overall performance, it will have to adopt some kind of balanced scorecard approach which tries to balance the different areas of its operations, as well as comparing its performance to other authorities. Some targets, such as satisfaction, may not be easy to measure and may have to rely on community surveys.

MNC

The MNC can measure its performance more easily (at least in terms of its primary objective). This will be a result of the market view of the company which will then impact on its share price. For its supporting objectives, the MNC may also use the balanced scorecard to measure its overall performance, building in customer satisfaction and quality assessments as well as employee motivation, which can be more subjective in their measurement.

Question 7 School stakeholders

(a) (i) Stakeholders and customers

A commercial business can easily identify its customers, but a public sector organization like a school serves a number of different groups, who could be classed as direct or indirect customers of the school.

(ii) Requirement of stakeholders

These might include:

- *Pupils*. These receive the education and are clearly direct customers of the service.
- *Parents*. These choose the school their children will attend and will have a clear interest in the education they receive. Once the children are at the school, they will monitor the quality of the service carefully.
- *Local authority*. The local authority funds the school and therefore sets the resources available. In addition, many of the services offered by the school may have to be agreed with the authority.
- *Employers*. The employers of the children after they leave school are indirect customers as they are looking for a certain level of education in the different subject areas. A failure to meet these expectations would lead to dissatisfaction amongst the other stakeholder groups as school leavers would be unable to obtain jobs.
- *Further education institutions*. The same arguments apply to universities and other higher education bodies as for employers.
- *Community*. The local and national community could be regarded as indirect customers as ultimately they provide the funding through taxation. However, they will be more interested in achieving value for money and seeing general improvements than in the day-to-day running of the school.

The school needs to maintain close links with its direct, and to some extent its indirect, customers so that it can ensure its services are broadly in line with their needs. This will occasionally mean compromise as some of the requirements may conflict.

Looking at each group in turn, views might be determined as follows:

- *Pupils*: school council with a representative from each class.
- *Parents*: a formal annual parent meeting and annual parent survey, along with informal discussions between parents and staff.
- *Local authority*: to an extent the requirements will be imposed so it might be sensible to scrutinise ongoing discussions for likely future developments.
- *Employers*: follow up sample surveys of school leavers and of employer satisfaction.

- *Further education institutions*: again, a sample of leavers could be selected and feedback obtained.
- *Community*: open days at the school and local questionnaires could be used.

(b) Boston Consulting Group (BCG) matrix

The BCG plots the overall rate of market growth against market share and identifies four main product or service areas. Although only approximate, it helps to classify the success or otherwise in the various areas of the organisation and gives broad guidance on the strategy to follow.

The market growth analysis might give a useful idea of areas in which needs are developing, but this will require careful monitoring of the requirements in the local area through the stakeholder groups mentioned above. In addition, the indirect customers may have more of an influence in determining the longer-term trends, as may the central government if it has proposals for education. Although looking at the growth in different socio-economic or ethnic backgrounds may identify some needs, it will not pick up all the trends the school needs to plan the future. For example, changes in subject requirements by higher education institutions would not be identified.

The market share analysis compares the school to its competitors in order to assess its relevant strengths. The main problem here is that used in a commercial context, products with low market share and low growth (dogs) for example might be dropped and high market share and low growth (cash cows) allowed to produce cash with little additional investment. In a school, much of the overall content is dictated by the local authority and central government, so it is unlikely that anything other than peripheral subjects can be dropped.

The BCG Matrix can be useful in identifying areas of greatest growth and need, and in assessing in which areas the school falls behind its competitors. However, it is unlikely to have full application to a school as services cannot be dropped or changed extensively without agreement of external stakeholders such as the local authority.

In the light of this, a more appropriate model for a public sector organisation is the Maslin Multidimensional Matrix, which plots needs or wants of the client groups (high or low) against a number of different factors, such as level of concern or level of provision by other agencies. This involves some difficult judgements in assessing the wants (rather than the needs) of the different client groups, and in identifying the factors to be considered, but it is likely to be more useful to the school, reflecting as it does the complex nature of the stakeholder compromises required in the public sector.

Question 8 Genetic code

A pharmaceutical company will have the maximisation of shareholder wealth as its primary objective, but will also have subsidiary objectives relating to other stakeholders. Amongst these is likely to be its ethical responsibilities to society. The ethical question is whether the pursuit of shareholder wealth should take precedence over all other concerns, and in the case of a pharmaceutical company mean they should refuse to develop cures for diseases, if this becomes possible, and only produce drugs to ease the suffering of patients.

There is no absolute answer to this question. Some would say that the company operates in society and therefore needs to take the views and well-being of society into account, and so should develop cures where possible. Others would say that the views of society are reflected in the government who enact laws to provide for society's needs. In other words, the government sets down certain codes of behaviour for companies (testing of drugs, withdrawal if new evidence shows they are harmful, etc.) and imposes taxes. This money raised can be used to fund non-profit making social concerns (such as the genetic mapping partly being carried out by publicly funded universities).

However, it could be argued that the second argument is somewhat short sighted. Concentrating only on relief and not on cure will allow competitors to introduce cures (assuming no industry agreements which would be illegal) and so remove the market for relief drugs. Not only would this eventually lead to reduced revenues and profits, the company would not receive any revenues from the drugs designed to cure diseases (which could be considerable). Finally, a number of shareholders are becoming more ethically conscious in their investing and may disinvest if they became aware of the company policy. If this happened in sufficient numbers, it would have a detrimental effect on the share price, thus affecting the wealth of the remaining shareholders.

Question 9 Eastborough

(a) (i) Ethical issues and main stakeholders

Ethical issues and decisions relate to taking the "right" decision by reference to a certain moral code. This can be difficult as any course of action may require a balancing of advantages and disadvantages.

In the case of Eastborough, the government should have considered the costs and benefits of allowing mining in the area in the context of its own concerns and aims for the area. It might have weighed up, amongst other considerations:

- The impact on the local community in terms of regenerating employment and the knock-on impact on local businesses which might supply Digwell.
- The impact on the environment and in particular on the initiatives to promote tourism, although this has not been successful so far anyway.
- The impact on the beauty of the coastline (it may have protected status) and on the wildlife.
- The impact of any pollution, both in terms of the landscape and in waste disposal and water table impacts.
- The possible deterioration in roads due to heavy traffic or the need to improve the infrastructure.
- The need to promote a healthy national economy, producing profits and taxes.

(ii) The main stakeholders and the conflicts between them are probably:

- Digwell shareholders who expect to make a profit on any mining project. Where additional costs are incurred, such as in protecting wildlife and the environment, these would reduce the profit available.

- Local people hope to gain employment either with Digwell or associated companies in order to improve their quality of life. Very high wages however would conflict with the shareholders' aim of high profits. In addition, some local people may feel the mine and its associated impact on the environment is too high a price to pay for more employment.
- Those on the Eastborough Protection Alliance, with the exception of the anti-capitalists, are concerned to protect the quality of life in terms of traffic levels, landscape and wildlife and view the mine as unacceptable.
- The anti-capitalists will not want any profits to be made out of the mining as they do not agree with the capitalist system of investing capital for others to use in exchange for a profit as they feel this means the profit motive overrides all other concerns. As a result it would be difficult to reconcile this with the aims of Digwell shareholders.
- The government wants to promote employment and a healthy economy may, as stated above, be in conflict with some of these groups.

(b) (i) Stakeholder mapping

One way to assess the concerns that need addressing is to plot the level of interest against the power of the different stakeholders.

		Level of interest	
		Low	High
Power	Low	Minimal effort	Keep informed
	High	Satisfy	Key stakeholders

(ii) Those with low power or interest can have their views virtually ignored without causing any problems. In this case, it would include the general public.

Those with high interest but low power need to be kept informed so that dangerous rumours do not start and they can understand the decisions and plan their actions accordingly. In this situation, this might include the local unemployed, the local media and local businesses, the employees of Digwell, and some members of the Eastborough Protection Alliance.

Those with low interest but high power need to be managed so that they are not sufficiently annoyed by the decision that they exercise their power. Here this might include the shareholders of Digwell.

Lastly, the key stakeholders, whose aims will have to reach a compromise, have a high level of interest and high power. In this situation, they include the government, the board of Digwell, and possibly some of the key activists for the environment in the Alliance.

Question 10 Doctors with Wings

(a) Stakeholder Analysis

Stakeholders are groups of individuals or organisations that have an interest in how an organisation operates and therefore have some benefit in mind that they would like to see. Being a stakeholder does not necessarily confer any power over the organisation and those with little power may find their interests ignored.

The process of the analysis would be as follows:

- Identify the stakeholders
- Identify their interests
- Identify the source of any power they hold over the organisation
- Identify those groups with the most power over the organisation
- Identify relationships and conflicts between groups
- Identify the resulting impact on the organisation's strategy.

In identifying stakeholders it is probably best to ask a chosen group in the organisation to brainstorm as many stakeholder groups as they can think of, not forgetting that stakeholders can be both internal and external to the organisation.

Their interests may be financial, philanthropic, lifestyle-related or related to factors such as the quality or delivery of the goods or services.

The power can often be assessed by considering the action the group might take if it did not have its interests satisfied. For example, the workforce could leave or go on strike or produce lower quality goods while customers might buy their goods elsewhere. The group's power will, therefore, be affected to some extent by the level of competition for their interest (e.g. Are there other employment opportunities or competitors producing similar goods?).

Those groups that seem to exhibit a high level of power over the organisation need to be identified so that it can build in their expectations into future plans. All stakeholders will have some power so the organisation will need to produce a ranking in terms of relative power and concentrate on those at the top of the list.

Those with no power and little interest (such as casual labour) can safely be ignored, while those with high power but little direct interest in the organisation need to be monitored as there is a risk that actions by the organisation will displease them to such an extent that they exercise their power. Those with high interest but low power (such as major suppliers) can be kept informed of the results of any strategic review but do not need to be consulted as to their views, whereas those with high power and high interest will form the major stakeholders that the organisation must involve in its future plans.

The benefits to *Doctors with Wings* will be in setting out clearly the groups of powerful stakeholders and hence the strategic direction it must take to keep those stakeholders involved. Any new plans will require some changes and it will be far easier to introduce those changes if it has the support of its major stakeholders. In addition it will give the charity a clear idea of what all the different stakeholders are seeking and enable them to more closely match those needs in what it gives to them.

(b) Principal Stakeholders

There are a number of stakeholders involved in this organisation with different interests and levels of influence over its strategic plans. These include:

- *Volunteer doctors and nurses*. They will want to feel that they are giving their time and energy to a worthwhile cause, but will also gain from the post-qualification experience. In addition, they will probably get personal satisfaction from helping the charity. As the charity needs qualified medical staff, the power of this group is relatively high and the charity needs to ensure that it is satisfying their requirements to a large extent.

- *Returning medical staff*. This group advertises the benefits to new volunteers and will want to feel that they have contributed to a worthwhile operation. As they are the primary means of recruitment, this group is powerful and if they felt disappointed after their volunteer work, could easily put others off joining.

- *Government funding agencies*. This group will want to see that their funds are being put to good use, hence enhancing the reputation of the government, and that they are getting value for money. In addition they might be concerned to ensure that the charity does not encroach on areas the government views as its own political areas. As a major funding source, this group will carry substantial power and the charity needs to measure its performance in terms of value for money carefully as well as establish guidelines of how it will act if faced with any kind of conflict of interest.

- *Corporate donors*. These will have similar interest to those of the government; their power will depend on the money or resources donated by them.

- *Medical company donors*. This group will also want to see their reputation enhanced through their donations but may be concerned if the charity's activities seriously undermine the company's sales. Their power, particularly if branded drugs with no generic drugs yet available are given, may be quite high and the charity needs to be careful that it does not appear to be denigrating pharmaceutical companies in public while still accepting their donations of drugs.

- *Public donors*. This group will want to feel that they are supporting a worthy cause, and while their power is not great they could be useful unofficial ambassadors for the charity by recommending it to others. It is therefore important that the charity takes care over its public image.

- *Staff at the charity*. This group also needs to feel that it is doing something worthwhile as the wages in the charity sector are generally below those of the commercial sector. Although a demotivated administrative staff could disrupt the operations, as other staff could be recruited this group is relatively less powerful than some of the others.

- *Teaching hospitals*. As the hospitals support the charity, it would appear that the teaching hospitals recommend it to their newly qualified doctors as a worthwhile experience. They have an interest in helping a worthwhile cause and could have the power to dissuade its doctors from volunteering if the charity was found to be involved in something controversial.

- *Beneficiaries of the charity*. Given the nature of the charity, the beneficiaries are desperate for help and have no power whatsoever in how the charity operates.

- *Other charities*. This group will be interested in the charity as a collaborator in emergencies as well as a competitor for donor funds. They will have little direct power over the charity but might be able to suggest ways of working together more effectively.

External Analysis 3

✏️ Exam focus

External analysis is undertaken to enable an understanding of how the external environment has or will change so that the *opportunities* and *threats* which may arise by these external changes can be assessed and appropriate action taken. It is therefore crucial that you can apply this to scenarios in the exam.

🔑 Key points

PEST

Also known as SLEPT (Social, Legal, Economic, Political and Technological factors) and STEP (Social, Technological, Economic and Political factors), this examines the broad environment in which the organisation is operating. PEST is a mnemonic which stands for Political and Legal, Economic, Social and Technological factors. These are simply four key areas to be considered in deciding how current and future changes may affect the business (and by you in relation to the scenarios in the exam). Strategies can then be developed which address any potential opportunities and threats identified.

Political factors include government spending, policies of different political parties, new laws likely to be passed, regulation (such as trains, telecoms, electricity production).

Legal factors include areas such as health and safety, tax changes, tariffs and trade barriers, foreign laws when operating in different countries and employment law.

Economic factors include areas such as interest rates, exchange rates, position in economic cycle, inflation rates, strength of the stock market, and the strength of the global economy.

Social factors include areas such as demographic changes, cultural attitudes and social trends.

Technological factors include areas such as new products being developed, new purchasing mechanisms (intranet, extranet), new production technology, new distribution mechanisms (internet) and new methods of working (e.g. mobile telecommunications).

Porter's Five Forces model

This can be used to understand how profitable a target industry might be and to understand the forces impacting upon the current industry's profitability.

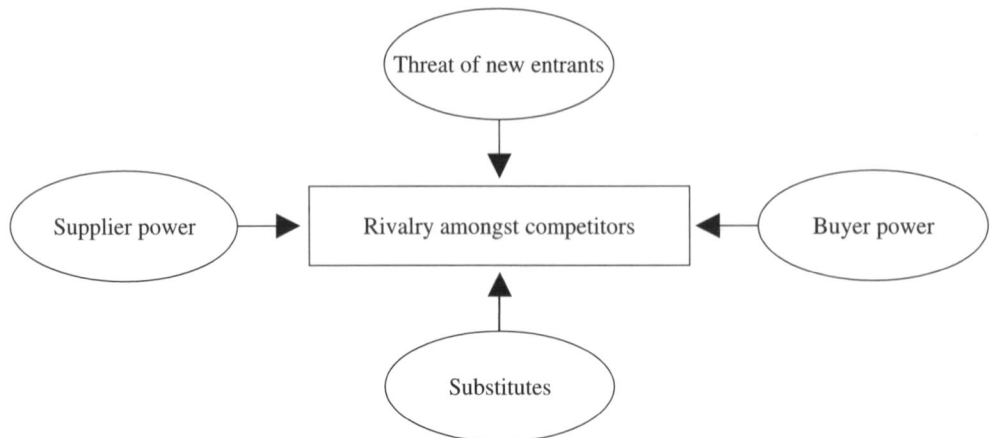

(Adapted from Porter 1980) © The Free Press/Macmillan

The threat of new entrants looks at how easy it is for newcomers to enter the market and will be heavily influenced by any barriers to entry, such as high investment, patents, legal restrictions or strong branding.

Buyer power looks at how easy it might be for customers to force their prices down.

Supplier power looks at how easy it might be for suppliers to put their prices up.

Substitutes consider whether customers could get what they require from a product or service from a different industry.

Competitive rivalry looks at the number and size of the competition, as well as the stage of life the market has reached and competitors' strategy. Clearly, competitor intelligence information is a vital way to remain profitable in a competitive environment.

Each of these forces threatens to either decrease prices or increase costs, and hence reduce profits, for the current players.

Scenario analysis

Whether analysing the broad environment (PEST analysis) or the industry environment (Porter's Five Forces) it is important to remember that we are trying to identify future opportunities and threats. Although we start with the current position, we must consider future possible scenarios.

So, for example, scenarios might consider:

- The economy goes into recession or exchange rates fall dramatically.
- A competitor enters or leaves the market.
- Competitors develop a new product or a major supplier goes into liquidation.

Analysis of the consequences might help the organisation to define a strategy to avoid the problem if one is identified, or plan its response.

Porter's Diamond

After having looked at the general factors which make an industry profitable, Michael Porter turned his attention to that factors which make one nation more profitable in a particular industry than another.

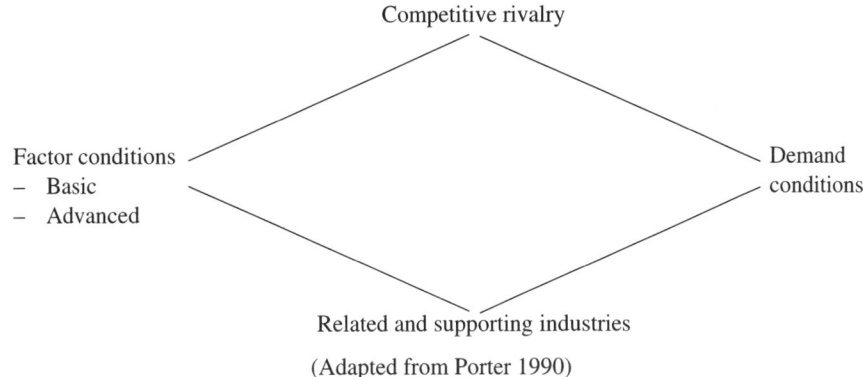

(Adapted from Porter 1990)

Factor conditions relate to the availability of inputs. Countries that have access to the factors necessary to produce the product will have an advantage over countries which do not. Basic factors require no investment, whereas advanced factors require investment.

Demand conditions (in the home market) are important as the greater the demand and more discerning the consumers in the home market the greater the need for innovation and cost reduction by companies in that market.

Related and supporting industries (in the home market) refer to the suppliers to the industry. If they are plentiful and competitive it will enable cheap and effective production of products.

Competitive rivalry in the local market will encourage innovation and cost reduction amongst competitors.

Using Porter's Diamond

Porter's Diamond can be used to assess the organisation's likely competitiveness in foreign markets. The company is likely to be competitive where the four factors are significant in the home market and are not present in the target market.

It can also be used to assess the likely threat from overseas competition. There is likely to be a significant threat when the four factors are not present in the home market but are present in the foreign competitor's market.

Questions

Question 1 Clothing company

A clothing company based in the United Kingdom believes that its domestic market is limited and is proposing to expand by the manufacture and sale of its products abroad. At this stage it has not identified where it will locate its manufacturing facility. The company believes that there are major advantages to be gained by setting up a factory in a country with a low wage economy.

The company recognises the need to understand the marketing environment of the country within which it establishes its manufacturing facility. It appreciates that besides labour, there are other local environmental issues which need to be fully considered before entering negotiations to build a factory.

Requirements

(a) Compare and contrast the environmental factors which apply in both the UK and the other country.

(15 marks)

(b) Explain the possible cultural influences on the effectiveness of the workforce in respect of local education and training, technology, working hours and domestic amenities.

(10 marks)
(Total = 25 marks)

Question 2 PD

PD has traded very successfully in its domestic country for many years. It has built up its reputation for quality and reliability as a result of supplying products which are specifically designed to meet the needs of its customers.

PD's directors are now considering launching the company's products in other parts of the world, but they have no experience of trading internationally. The Managing Director has heard of Porter's Diamond Theory of the competitive advantage of nations. He has turned to you as the management accountant to provide some advice on whether Porter's theory can be applied to assist PD in its international development, and the factors which should be considered before developing internationally.

Requirement

Advise PD's board of directors of the factors which it should consider before launching the company's products internationally.

Your advice should include an assessment of how Porter's Diamond Theory can be applied to assist the company in determining whether or not it should develop internationally.

(25 marks)

Question 3 E

E, a well known cosmetics manufacturer, obtains worldwide sales for its global branded products. The directors price themselves on having a clear understanding of E's consumer market which consists of both men and women. Its products mainly comprise deodorants, perfume, after-shave lotions, facial and body washes.

In carrying out an analysis of its competitive environment, the Marketing Director has applied Porter's Five Forces model and analysed the factors which affect E under each heading as follows:

- *Threat of entry.* Little threat as although major competitors exist, the size of E presents a large entry barrier.
- *Power of buyers.* Very important as the customers worldwide have much choice from different competitors products.
- *Power of suppliers.* Little threat as most suppliers of materials are small scale and E could easily source from other suppliers if necessary. Labour is relatively cheap in E's production facilities in developing world locations.
- *Substitute products.* There are many alternative products offered by competitors but there is little by way of a substitute for cosmetics, and therefore this poses little threat.
- *Rivalry among competitors.* There is strong competition in the cosmetics market with new products constantly being developed, and therefore this is a major threat.

The Marketing Director is reasonably confident that he has judged the impact of these competitive forces correctly as they apply to E. However, he would like some re-assurance of this. He has asked you, as Management Accountant, to provide some appropriate performance indicators by which the strength of the five competitive forces as they apply to E can be judged.

Requirement

Recommend to the Marketing Director suitable performance indicators which could be used to judge the strength of the five competitive forces as they apply to E. Include in your discussion consideration of whether or not you agree with his judgement regarding the impact of each force on E.

(25 marks)

Question 4 Five forces

Professor Michael Porter developed the "Five Forces" model in order that it may be used by profit-orientated organisations for the purposes of industry analysis.

Requirements

(a) Explain how the model can be used by profit-orientated organisations.

(12 marks)

(b) Assess the usefullness of the model when it is used in a period of uncertainty in the business environment.

(13 marks)
(Total = 25 marks)

Question 5 Competitor analysis

From the 1980s onwards, organisations have been increasingly conscious of the need to develop appropriate competitive strategies. More recently, competition has increased in many areas due to factors such as a more global dimension to trade and an opening of new markets. It follows that, in order to gain and maintain competitive advantage, it may be worthwhile for organisations to identify and carefully consider the present and likely future activities of its competitors.

Requirements

(a) Evaluate the importance of competitor analysis, with reference to the benefits and potential dangers of undertaking such an exercise.

(10 marks)

(b) Discuss the key issues to be addressed when conducting a competitor analysis, including potential data sources and tools that may be helpful.

(10 marks)

(c) Explain the relationship between the product life cycle and competitor analysis.

(5 marks)
(Total = 25 marks)

Question 6   Don Mac

Don Mac is the world's largest and best known foodservice retailing group with more than 30,000 "fast food" outlets in over 120 countries. Currently half of its restaurants are in the USA, where it first began 50 years ago, but up to 1,000 new restaurants are opened every year worldwide. Restaurants are wholly owned by the group (it has previously considered, but rejected, the idea of a franchising of operations and collaborative partnerships).

As market leader in a fiercely competitive industry, Don Mac has strategic strengths of instant global brand recognition, experienced management, site development expertise and advanced technological systems. Don Mac's basic approach works as well in Kandy or Kuala Lumpur as it does in Kansas; although the products are broadly similar, menus are modified to reflect local tastes. Analysts agree that it continues to be profitable because it is both efficient and innovative. The group's vision is to be "the world's favourite" through service, cleanliness and value, and it is following three main strategies:

1 To achieve profitable growth by building on key strengths.
2 To "delight" every customer in every restaurant.
3 To be a good employer in each community in which it has a restaurant. (Despite this, some critics claim staff are mainly unskilled and lowly paid.)

Don Mac's future plans are to maximise global opportunities and continue to expand markets. Don Mac has long recognised that the external environment can be very uncertain and consequently does not move into new locations or countries without first undertaking a full investigation.

You are part of a strategy steering team responsible for investigating the key factors concerning Don Mac's entry for the first time into the restaurant industry in the Republic of Borderland.

Requirements

(a) Justify the use of a PEST framework to assist your team's environmental analysis for the Republic of Borderland.

(8 marks)

(b) Discuss the main issues arising from applying this framework, and highlight what more information is needed by Don Mac on Borderland.

(17 marks)
(Total = 25 marks)

Question 7 Breakland

A political party has recently been elected to govern the island nation of Breakland after a long period of opposition. The new government wishes to bring about lasting change within an economy that suffers from high unemployment. It has established a "think tank" in which government advisers, specialists and experts explore implications of ideas and advise on various alternative courses of action.

Breakland is a multi-cultural country with free elections and a mixed economy. Its industrial base is relatively well established but it has no truly world-class industry or experience. Past government policies mean there is little in the way of product safety legislation. Spending on education and training for those aged over 16 years old is low. In addition, Breakland has traditionally discouraged foreign competition in home markets with threats of tariffs, quotas and other protectionist measures. As a consequence, a few American and Japanese companies have set up high technology manufacturing plants on the island.

The government is keen to consider ways in which they can make the country's industry more competitive internationally, specifically they wish to identify policies they should pursue over the next 10 years to make this happen.

Requirements

(a) Advise the members of the "think tank" on the components of Porter's Diamond framework and why it might assist their deliberations.

(12 marks)

(b) For each element of Porter's Diamond, discuss potential government policies that might help encourage Breakland's industries to compete more effectively abroad. Provide an explanation for the suggestion you make.

(13 marks)
(Total = 25 marks)

Question 8 Budget Airlines

Over the past few years the major airlines have suffered a decline in profitability and some have even filed for bankruptcy. At the same time, some budget airlines have shown considerable success offering a 'no frills service' to an increasing number of passengers at heavily discounted fares.

The traditional airlines have, in the main, a vertically integrated service with many activities such as baggage handling, ticketing and maintenance delivered by their own subsidiaries. Additionally, they have continued to offer a variety of classes ranging from luxury to economy thus catering for all segments of the travelling market from business to tourist. These airlines compete fiercely for landing rights at city centre airports and have formed into two main alliances to share routes giving them global coverage. The traditional airlines tend to purchase their aircraft directly from the manufacturers whereas budget airlines tend to use leasing to source their fleet.

By contrast, the budget airlines have concentrated on the short-haul market and have heavily promoted low-cost flights to secondary airports with no service other than the flight. These low costs have been partially supported by subsidies provided by the secondary airports. An additional advantage of these airports is the rapid turnaround of aircraft on the ground since they are handling fewer flights. Aircrew, at minimum permitted staffing levels, are responsible for aircraft cleaning. The budget price includes only the flight; passengers have no in-flight services and book their tickets directly via the Internet. The budget airlines spend heavily on advertising in all popular media.

Requirements

(a) Using an appropriate model of the competitive environment, discuss the difference in performance between the traditional airlines and the budget airlines and the business models they are operating.

(20 marks)

(b) Evaluate the business model operated by the budget airlines as a source of sustainable competitive advantage.

(5 marks)
(Total marks = 25)

 Answers

Question 1 Clothing company

(a) Environmental factors

The environment in which the company operates could be quite different in the other country from that in the UK. These can be looked at under the following factors:

Political and legal

The stability of the government, the current and prospective laws will have a significant impact on the company's operations. These could be very different from the UK and need to be researched, as does the extent of government interference in the markets.

Economic

The other country may be at a different stage of the economic cycle, and inflation and interest rates could be very different. This may well impact on the sales made as the target market may not have enough disposable income to purchase the clothes. Conversely, it may affect the number of unemployed and hence the ability to recruit a workforce.

Social, cultural and demographic

Clothing sales depends very much on fashion and social trends. These could be quite different from those in the UK. It may not be culturally acceptable to buy many clothes, and the clothing company will be targeting a certain age group which may be a much smaller group than the similar market in the UK. All of these require extensive research before committing the company. The impact on production is looked at in (b).

Technological

The technological factors may well be different from those in the UK. These would include the availability of supplies and infrastructure for distribution, methods of advertising and communications. All of these could make the business more difficult to operate.

Competition

It is also important for the company to research the competition carefully. The government may support, or even own, competing companies while the company will need to ensure that it is able to access local suppliers. Either impacts on the competitive nature of the market will be the ease with which competitors can set up; this may be affected by the existence or otherwise of patent rights which are enforceable.

(b) Cultural influences

Looking at the possible production overseas, there could be a number of differences from the UK, which will have to be taken account of when planning the operations.

Education and training

The level of literacy and numeracy, ability to understand English – particularly in technical documents – and the general attitude to work could have serious impacts on the style of production.

Technology

The level of knowledge with regards to the technology needed may not be the same as in the UK. This may mean a training programme will have to be instituted to ensure the workforce understands the technology, and possibly any health and safety regulations.

Working hours

Peoples' attitudes to work can vary between countries, and this can extend to the hours kept, the discipline at the work place or even the ethical perspective of business decisions.

Domestic amenities

In considering the cultural influences on the workplace, and hence on production, it may be sensible to consider the facilities available outside the workplace. A lack of healthcare or transport, for example, could impact on the reliability of the workforce. The company should investigate this carefully, and consider the provision of health and transport, and possibly even housing, education and food.

Question 2 PD

1 **International expansion**

   It would appear that PD wish to expand internationally to increase their overall profits, possibly as a result of declining growth in their home market. However, international expansion is always fairly high risk, and it might be worth considering new markets domestically or launching new products.

2 **Porter's Diamond**

   Porter identified four factors which he felt contributed to national success in international markets:

3

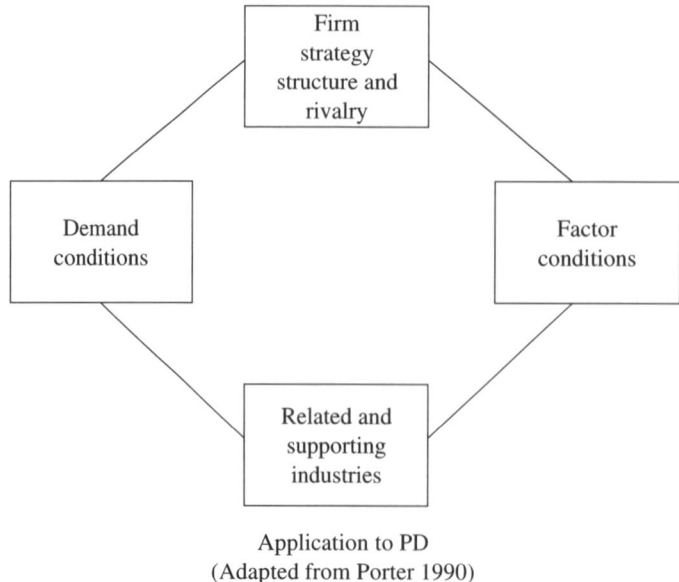

Application to PD
(Adapted from Porter 1990)

The four elements could be applied to PD's proposal as follows:

1 *Demand conditions.* This relates to the domestic demand. A high level of demand stimulates production and encourages innovation and quality which can then succeed internationally.

PD has already achieved a high level of quality so it must research international markets carefully to assess the best target in terms of customer requirements and size. Care needs to be taken in terms of any marketing undertaken (which could be very different from the home market) and in terms of any adverse impacts on the home market production quality and sales.

2 *Factor conditions.* Any infrastructure and specialist facilities need to be in place to support any production or sales overseas. The extent to which this is an issue will depend on how specialized PD's products are and whether they intend to produce overseas as well.

These conditions also include the financial factors such as exchange rate management, the ability to send funds back to the home country and the ability to raise finance.

PD's ability to deal with a different culture needs to be accessed as well as considering the different levels of education which will vary between countries.

3 *Related and supporting industries.* To succeed, a company needs reliable and high quality support from other industries. PD needs to consider whether its current suppliers will be able to support it internationally or whether it will need to find new sources overseas. These new sources will then need to be assessed very carefully to ensure that the quality of PD's product is not compromised.

4 *Firm strategy, structure and rivalry.* Strong domestic competition is likely to keep costs low and encourage innovations, which can then be used internationally.

PD has a good reputation in its domestic market but may face intense competition internationally. It needs to consider whether the differentiation built in its home market will be sufficient to beat the competition internationally. It also needs to assess whether the elements which have helped it capture its domestic market will appeal to the international market.

External Analysis **39**

Lastly, PD needs to consider the political risk in going overseas, particularly if production overseas is envisaged. Although not covered by Porter's Diamond, a change in political temperament in a country can have a severe impact on a foreign business operating there.

Question 3 E

Performance indicators for competitive forces

The Five Forces model was developed in order to assess the nature of competition within an industry and to identify the strongest influences on the level of competition. Where strong forces are identified a company can try to position itself to reduce its impact, where it identifies weak forces there may be opportunities to exploit its position and achieve higher profits. It can also help more generally in deciding whether or not to enter an industry, in deciding on appropriate strategy in the industry and in deciding on the level of its investment.

Performance indicators might include the following:

Threat of entry

Although the threat may be low, it is always possible for new smaller companies to enter the market. Many of E's products are not technically difficult to produce and a specialist producer could make inroads into E's market share.

Performance indicators might include the number of new entrants in a year and the particular product or market targeted as it might identify those which are more vulnerable.

Power of buyers

E will sell to retailers who buy in bulk and who track the requirements of their consumers very carefully. E's products are particularly sensitive to changes in fashion and they need to monitor such trends carefully.

Performance indicators might include demographic analysis to determine the age range attracted to the products with regular surveys of the appropriate group of their attitudes to the products.

Power of suppliers

Although the individual suppliers may have little power to exercise over E as they are much smaller, they still have the power, unwittingly, to affect E's market share. A poor-quality ingredient could lead to a major impact on E's sales if it causes consumers harm or has unpleasant smell or appearance. As a result, it would be important to establish performance indicators which look at quality, as well as flexibility to E's requests, price and volume provided.

Substitute products

There are possible substitutes to products like facial and body washes such as alternative methods of skin cleansing. It is important to identify these substitute products and analyse their effectiveness. This can be done by measuring their sales revenue, number of sales and, if possible, profits or at least gross profit, and comparing them with any consequent loss in sales by E. This analysis may lead E to launch other products to compete against these substitutes.

Rivalry among competitors

Competitor analysis is needed to continually assess the threat posed by competitors. This will include monitoring market share of major rivals compared with E, along with the pricing strategies employed, revenue and estimates of gross profits. From this, E can assess in which products it has a lead and in which it is starting to lose out to rivals.

Overall, the five forces is a very useful model and performance indicators should be established and monitored regularly in order to place the company in a strong competitive position.

Question 4 Five forces

(a) The five forces model gives five influences on the level of competition in the industry in which an organisation operates. The organisation can use the model to assess the areas with the greatest force or greatest possible threat and design its strategy to deal with these threats.

The five forces are:

The threat of new entrants

This is the danger of new organisations entering the market and increasing the competition. Some industries have high barriers to entry such as patents or licences or a very high investment needed which reduces the impact of this force.

The threat of powerful customers

In a similar way, customers may be able to negotiate lower prices if they are powerful. This can happen when one particular customer buys a large proportion of the organisations' output.

The threat of substitutes

When customers can acquire the same result from a different industry (e.g. take the train or fly), the price of the substitute compared with the price of the company's product can have a major impact on the demand.

The threat of competitive rivalry

When there is an unsegmented market in its mature stage (i.e. little growth) and a number of similar sized competitors, the level of competition will tend to be fierce.

(b) In an environment of uncertainty, the model is useful in suggesting areas to examine but it becomes more difficult to judge which might give concern and need to be addressed.

For example, it may be that current barriers to entry will be easily overcome in the future through new technology avoiding the need for a large capital investment. Alternatively, a pharmaceutical company's patent may offer little protection if a new drug is designed which is better.

Suppliers and customers can both change so an organisation would need to examine carefully its future needs (such as for some technical skill in short supply) and its likely future customer base.

To identify possible new substitutes means scanning the environment to assess which industries might offer customers a substitute. To assess competitive rivalry involves trying to assess which competitors might leave the market and how many might enter.

To summarise, the model is helpful in identifying the current sources of competition, but in an uncertain environment cannot help the organisation identify which forces will be powerful in the future. This will involve some educated guesswork, possibly working back to indirect factors which will ultimately affect the company. In a very uncertain environment, a company should undertake scenario planning to formulate its reaction if any of the forces became unexpectedly powerful due to unforeseen circumstances.

Question 5 Competitor analysis

(a) Competitor analysis

In a competitive market, it would be sensible to analyse the competitors in terms of their strategy and their likely reaction to any moves made by the company. However, this can sometimes be difficult when the competitors themselves change frequently; this therefore reduces its usefulness as a technique when there are low barriers to entry to or exit from the market. Similarly, when there is a very large number of competitors, the company needs to be careful in its selection of those to analyse.

The benefits will include:

- Being better able to design strategies which take into account the likely response of competitors.
- An insight into strategies tried by competitors and their results, which may help the company in its own strategic planning.
- A benchmarking process for various operations, so that the company can identify areas in which it falls short of or exceeds that achieved by the competition.

However, there are dangers in such an approach, including:

- Spending too much time and energy on the exercise and neglecting customers.
- Trying to copy strategies that may be inappropriate for the organisation.
- Relying on the analysis to predict reactions, when the competitors may not react in the way that the analysis would suggest.
- Not allowing for any change in key personnel to affect a competitors method of competing and strategic mentality.

(b) Key issues in competitor analysis

The key issues to be addressed in competitor analysis are:

(i) Who are our competitors?

We need to identify those who target the same customers, that is, those in the same market segment and probably those of a similar size. Useful information to help us would be market share trends, funding sources, range of products and capital structure.

(ii) What are the competitors' objectives?

If we can identify their objectives, it may give us some idea of their intentions in the market and how seriously they might react to any move on our part. For example, would they jealously guard every percentage point of market share or be less concerned if their overall profits were not affected? Information regarding this might be found in t1he annual reports and other press releases as well as in professional analysts' reports.

(iii) What strategies are the competitors following?

Both existing and past strategies are useful in trying to predict a competitor's future strategy. To establish a pattern, a company might look at its competitors' annual reports and by analysing their past actions, such as cutting prices to complete on a least cost basis or expanding into other markets.

(iv) What are the competitors' strengths and weaknesses?

As the competitor is in the same industry, the environmental analysis will be the same as for the company. The major difference will be in its internal analysis of strengths and weaknesses. It may be difficult, however, to ascertain cost structures and a complete assessment of a competitor's resources. Where information is available through observation, tools such as the nine Ms Resource Audit and the Value Chain could be used.

(v) How will competitors behave?

This links to the other issues but is making the connection between analysis of the past and present and their future actions. In some cases, such as when a competitor runs a pilot scheme or trials a product, the intentions are obvious. In other cases, management must assimilate all the information obtained and try to imagine themselves in their rivals' position. Models such as the generic strategy developed by Porter to examine competitive advantage, and Ansoff's product/market matrix can help here. However, as mentioned earlier, a change of key personnel, such as the Chief Executive, may mean that a study of that individual's past behaviour is more useful than studying that of the company.

(c) Product life cycle and competitor analysis

The number of competitors and their strategies will be influenced by the stage that has been reached in the product life cycle. At the introductory stage, there are unlikely to be many competitors as the product is new and unfamiliar. The growth stage will attract new entrants who will try to capture market share through differentiating their products and building their brand. In maturity, there are unlikely to be any new entrants and some of the weakest competitors will have left the market; overcapacity may lead to price-cutting strategies.

Finally, in the decline stage many of the remaining competitors will leave the market as it becomes unprofitable, possibly selling at less than cost to dispose of stock before doing so.

Question 6 Don Mac

(a) PEST framework

A PEST analysis looks at the main areas which can have a major external influence on any industry. They cover:

Political and legal factors

These look at current and projected legislation in all areas that might affect the industry, such as anti-monopoly laws, employment, health and safety, taxation, environmental laws and restrictions on remittance of profits or currency.

Economical factors

These look at the impact the economic cycle might have, including interest rates and unemployment, and the consumer's view of the product as being a necessity or a luxury.

Social, cultural and demographic factors

These examine the social traditions, habits and trends in the country to establish the likely trend in demand and the most appropriate marketing approach. Demographics looks at the population distribution in terms of age, income and geographical dispersion to help assess demand in different segments of society.

Technological factors

These look at the technology in areas such as production and telecoms both currently and expected that might influence the approach taken in Borderland in both its operations and its marketing.

Although a useful approach, other analyses such as the Five Forces Model to analyse the strength of competition and competitor analysis, as well as Porter's Diamond to assess such things as the availability of resources and supporting industries, should also be undertaken.

(b) Main issues

The main issues arising and the information needed is as follows:

Political and legal factors

We need to check whether there are legal restrictions on operating a company in Borderland, or on controlling it from America. It is important to also consider the political stability of the country and intentions of any likely future government. It would also be sensible to assess the political feelings with regards to American fast food outlets and the possible "Americanisation" of the local culture.

Economic factors

One major economic issue will be the likely level of disposable income of consumers, as a fast food outlet is unlikely to be viewed as a necessity. The level of sales will also be affected by the level of unemployment (although this will reduce wage costs). However, wage levels may impact on the number of expatriates from America used to run the operation, as opposed to local managers being employed (as Don Mac have ruled out franchising).

The economy will also impact on the exchange rate against the dollar, which will affect the remittance of funds to America. It is therefore important to assess the economic cycle and its likely trend over the next few years.

Social, cultural and demographic factors

The cultural attitude and social norms will be crucial to Don Mac's future plan. The lifestyle in Borderland may not lend itself to fast food outlets, and attitudes to education and health may have an impact. As well as researching these values, it will be important to forecast the demographic profile of the country, as the young are the most likely segment of the market to be attracted by a fast food outlet.

Other issues to be investigated include Borderland society's attitude to food safety and health awareness as well as the enthusiasm or otherwise for American products.

Lastly, there is a growing concern around the world about environmental issues such as packaging and energy efficiency; Don Mac needs to check the level of such concerns in Borderland so that it can design products and marketing accordingly.

Technological factors

It is important that Borderland has sufficient infrastructure to allow easy transportation of supplies, both physical and energy such as electricity. Main highways are likely to be prime locations for outlets and the demand may be heavily influenced by the state of the road network and hence the volume of users.

Technology in communication will have a direct impact on the methods used in promotion, whether in newspapers, television, internet or other mass media. The ability to have fast reliable contact with America is likely to be important to Don Mac.

Question 7 Breakland

(a) Porter's Diamond

Porter's Diamond looked at why some nations, and some industries within those countries, appear to have a competitive advantage internationally. He felt that the domestic conditions could be crucial in producing such world-beating companies and identified a number of factors which influenced their development.

Factor conditions relate to the ready supply locally of the basic resources required, such as a skilled labour force, raw materials, land and capital. More advanced factor conditions refer to the structure developed by the government in areas such as levels of education and training, infrastructure in terms of road and rail and communication links.

Domestic demand would ensure that companies can generate economics of scale in production locally before going overseas, as well as gaining valuable experience. The more similar the requirements globally are to those in the domestic market, the more useful this experience will be.

Related and support industries must be available locally who can produce any supplies needed at the appropriate quality level.

Firm strategy, structure and rivalry looks at the level of competition within the domestic market and how this is managed. A highly competitive environment can lead to innovation and the development of world-beating products.

By using Porter's Diamond, the think tank could consider various policies that would improve the employment levels in Breakland, by helping existing businesses and encouraging new ones. By considering various economic and political policies, the think tank may be able to identify actions that would encourage the development of the above four factors.

(b) Policy options

In looking to encourage national competitive advantage, it might be sensible to look at what Breakland already has. It currently has four American and Japanese companies in high technology which might provide the basis of a cluster of similar companies along with their support industries. Alternatively, it could use its island status to look at key industries in shipping and ports.

Looking at each factor in turn:

Factor conditions

The government clearly needs to concentrate on developing factor conditions. These will be influenced by the advanced factors which can be encouraged by the government. Training in key areas and enhancing skills, coupled with ensuring the transport infrastructure and communications are reliable, will help enormously. To encourage research and innovation, tax incentives could be offered to firms; this could be extended to incentives for taking on more staff, thus alleviating the unemployment, and for providing training.

Domestic demand

The government can introduce a number of measures to increase and stimulate domestic demand. In addition, the government could legislate to ensure that products produced will satisfy international requirements. This might mean introducing wide-ranging product safety legislation and advising companies on how to build these requirements into products.

Lastly, they could develop trade links with countries whose culture and society most closely match that of Breakland, so that products produced domestically can succeed internationally.

Related and support industries

It will be important for Breakland to encourage support industries for any clusters it identifies, and to encourage the quality levels needed by the main companies. This may mean initially reducing the protectionist measures so that companies can access the supplies they need.

Firm strategy, structure and rivalry

The government needs to encourage competition domestically so that firms can develop their competitive advantage. They should consider relaxing some of the restrictions on foreign competition in the home market as such competition could force the domestic companies to improve and strengthen.

46 Exam Practice Kit: Business Strategy

Question 8 Budget Airlines

(a) Traditional Airlines and Budget Airlines

An appropriate model to assess the competitive environment would be Porter's five forces model. The five forces are:

1. The bargaining power of suppliers
2. The bargaining power of buyers
3. The threat of new entrants
4. The threat of substitutes
5. The level of competitive rivalry within the industry.

Looking at the traditional airlines:

The barriers to entry have been relatively high because of the high cost of the aircraft, the regulation of routes and landing slots, the restrictions on airport services and government concern for national flag carriers.

The power of suppliers has been medium as they depend on supplies of aircraft and fuel as well as on the labour force and other non-core services such as catering. Although there are few suppliers of both aircraft and fuel, the aircraft suppliers have few customers and rely on volume which reduces their power while the fuel suppliers are subject to the world oil price and intense price competition. Non-core services have often been outsourced which increases the power of the sub-contractors and the labour force, being skilled and well-paid has high power.

The threat of substitutes has risen as rail becomes a viable alternative for short-haul flights and conferences and meetings can be conducted without all the participants being in the same place using sophisticated technology

The power of buyers is not high for individual customers but large corporate customers might exercise some buying power. However, in the context of the airline's total revenue, this is minor.

Competitive rivalry is increasing as customers become more cost conscious and the industry has a high level of fixed costs and high exit barriers. This has been partly offset by forming alliances between airlines.

The budget airlines have managed to manipulate the five forces to their advantage as follows:

- Barriers to entry have been overcome by using secondary airports, remote from city centres, at which landing slots are available, leasing rather than buying aircraft and focusing on short-haul flights.
- Supplier power has been reduced by leasing aircraft through intermediaries, dispensing with many non-core activities and hard negotiations with staff.
- Buyer power has been kept low by concentrating on the consumer market and selling direct, often over the Internet, to reduce costs.

Although the threat of substitutes has been reduced by competing simply on price, the competitive rivalry remains intense.

(b) Sustainable Competitive Advantage

Competitive advantage is usually achieved through either differentiating the service and charging extra, or offering lower than normal prices. The budget airlines have clearly gone for the second of these, but it will only be sustainable if they can continue to make profits at these low prices. This depends on their ability to maintain large volumes (to compensate for their small margins) and to keep their costs at the lowest possible level so that they still make a margin on such low prices.

Having recognised the potential of this market, the companies concerned have enjoyed the advantage of being first into this market over the traditional airlines. However, the low cost approach is highly susceptible to any fall in volumes and threats of terrorism, or a downturn in the economy could have an impact on the number of flights taken by consumers.

As more budget airlines are set up and look for secondary airports, the balance of power is shifting to these airports so that the price of landing slots and other services may rise; at the same time the first of these airlines often received regional subsidies for bringing employment to the local economy but these have now declined as the local authorities have achieved their objectives.

The traditional airlines have responded to the budget airlines by becoming more cost conscious and in some cases have set up their own budget airlines which use slots at more centrally located airports, which are far more convenient to customers.

As a result, although budget airlines have developed a business model that has been successful in the short term, it is unlikely that all of these companies will continue to achieve this level of success in the future.

Position Analysis 4

✎ Exam focus

Internal analysis is undertaken to understand the *strengths* and *weaknesses* of the organisation in comparison with its competitors. This enables the organisation to capitalise on its strengths and overcome its weaknesses and is an important skill for you to master in scenario questions.

🔑 Key points

The resource audit – the nine M's

This model is used much like the PEST analysis for external analysis. It is simply a reminder of the nine key areas to consider when examining the organisation's strengths and weaknesses. The nine areas are:

1 **Money** includes areas such as profit, cashflow and financing.
   In the exam, case study financial performance is usually analysed over a number of years. It is important to consider trends from year to year, in gross profits (sales – cost of sales) and net profits (sales – all costs), gross and net profit margins (profit/sales), costs in a number of different categories and sales. This will often highlight how effective the organisation has been overall, and areas where specific improvement is required.
2 **Men** includes all matters connected with human resources, such as skills, numbers, costs, training and recruitment processes and motivation.
3 **Management** includes those areas relating to directors and managers.
4 **Materials** include matters connected with supply and purchasing, such as the reliability, flexibility, exclusivity and cost of suppliers.
5 **Markets** looks at areas connected with marketing and sales, such as market share, image, brand, reputation, sales outlets and sales teams.
6 **Machines** relates to all matters connected with production, such as productivity, flexibility, quality and R&D.
7 **Make-up** looks at all matters connected with the organisational structure.
8 **Methods** includes all matters connected with business processes, such as the use of modern technology (e.g. internet, extranets, expert systems) and the efficiency of the processes.
9 **Management information** includes an assessment of the strategic, tactical and operational information provided.

Porter's value chain

The company receives inputs to the left of the value chain and converts these into outputs on the right of the value chain. In doing so it adds value to the inputs so that it can sell the outputs for more than the sum of the input costs, hence creating a margin. By examining the activities between inputs and outputs the organisation can understand what is adding value to the customer and increase the margin and profits.

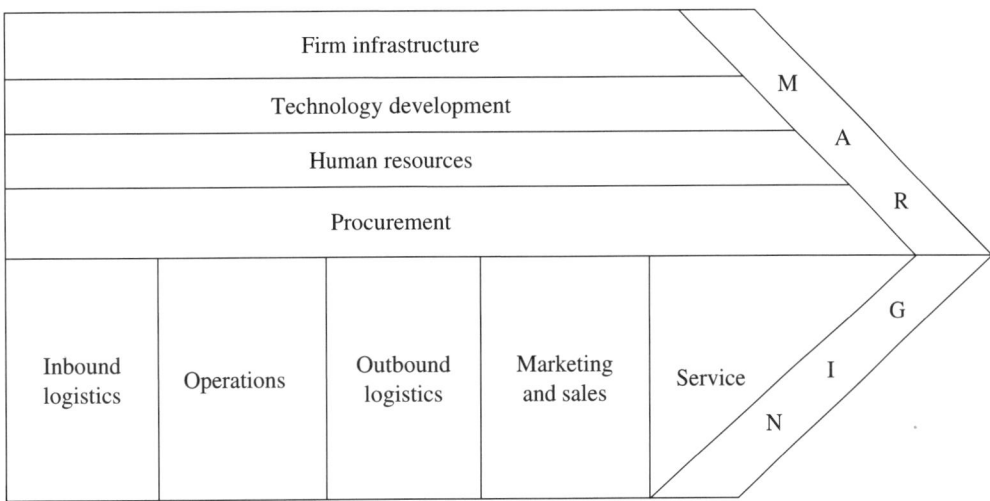

Value chain (adapted from Porter 1985) © The Free Press

Most organisations engage in hundreds, even thousands, of activities in the process of converting inputs to outputs. These activities can be classified as either primary or support activities that all businesses must undertake in some form.

Primary activities
(a) Inbound logistics looks at the relationships with suppliers including all the activities required to receive, store and disseminate inputs.
(b) Operations looks at activities which transform inputs into outputs (products and services).
(c) Outbound logistics looks at activities required to collect, store and distribute the output.
(d) Marketing and sales looks at activities which inform buyers about products and services, induce buyers to purchase them and facilitate their purchase.
(e) Service looks at activities required to keep the product or service working effectively for the buyer after it is sold and delivered.

Support activities
(a) Procurement includes the acquisition of inputs, or resources, for the firm.
(b) Human resource management consists of all activities involved in recruiting, hiring, training, developing, compensating and (if necessary) dismissing or laying off personnel.
(c) Technological development relates to the equipment, hardware, software, procedures and technical knowledge brought to bear in the firm's transformation of inputs into outputs.
(d) Infrastructure serves the company's needs and ties its various parts together; it consists of functions or departments such as accounting, legal, finance, planning, public affairs, government relations, quality assurance and general management.

The value chain can be used:

(a) To examine the firm in terms of the processes it uses to serve customers, and the value added.
(b) As a basis to drive a competitive strategy of cost leadership or differentiation (see Chapter 6).
(c) To understand the linkages between processes (e.g. how technology supports each of the primary activities, or how production quality affects after-sales service).
(d) As a way to analyse competitors for their strengths and weaknesses.

The firm's value chain links to the value chains of upstream suppliers and downstream buyers. The result is a larger stream of activities known as the value system. The development of a competitive advantage depends not only on the firm-specific value chain, but also on the value system of which the firm is a part.

For example if our basis of competition is to sell at the lowest prices, it is important that we buy from low cost suppliers, and distribute through low cost distributors, so that the product the customer receives is at the minimum cost.

Questions

Question 1 R

R is a large high-class hotel situated in a thriving city. It is part of a worldwide hotel group owned by a large number of shareholders. The majority of the shares are held by individuals, each holding a small number, and the rest are owned by financial institutions. The hotel provides full amenities, including a heated swimming pool, as well as the normal facilities of bars, restaurants and good-quality accommodation. There are many other hotels in the city which all compete with R. The city in which R is situated is old and attracts many foreign visitors, particularly in its summer season.

Requirements

(a) (i) State the main stakeholders with whom relationships need to be established and maintained by the management of R.

(2 marks)

(ii) Explain why it is important that relationships are developed and maintained with each of these stakeholders.

(8 marks)

(b) Explain how the management of R should carry out a benchmarking exercise on its services, and recommend ways in which the outcomes should be evaluated.

(15 marks)

Note: Do NOT describe different methods of benchmarking in answering this question.

(Total = 25 marks)

Question 2 University

A university which derives most of its funds from the government provides undergraduate courses (leading to bachelors degrees) and post-graduate courses (leading to masters degrees). Some of its funds come from contributions from student fees, consultancy work and research. In recent years, the university has placed emphasis on recruiting lecturers who have achieved success in delivering good academic research. This has led to the university improving its reputation within its national academic community, and applications from prospective students for its courses have increased.

The university has good student support facilities in respect of a library which is well stocked with books and journals and up-to-date IT equipment. It also has a gymnasium and comprehensive sports facilities. Courses at the university are administered by well-qualified and trained non-teaching staff who provide non-academic (i.e. not learning-related) support to the lecturers and students.

The university has had no difficulty in filling its courses to the level permitted by the government, but has experienced an increase in the numbers of students who have withdrawn from the first year of their courses after only a few months. An increasing number of students are also transferring from their three-year undergraduate courses to other courses within the university but many have left and gone to different universities. This increasing trend of student withdrawal is having a detrimental effect on the university's income as the government pays only for students who complete a full year of their study.

You are the university's Management Accountant and have been asked by the Vice Chancellor (who is the Chief Executive of the university) to review the withdrawal rate of students from the university's courses.

(Candidates do not require any knowledge of university admission and withdrawal processes to answer this question.)

Requirements

(a) Apply value chain analysis to the university's activities.

(20 marks)

(b) Advise the Vice Chancellor how this analysis will help to determine why the rate of student withdrawal is increasing.

(5 marks)
(Total = 25 marks)

Question 3 PA

The PA company supplies professional homecare support services to elderly people. The company has been in business for 20 years and has expanded from its local base to become a national organisation. The services undertaken in the home include provision of meals, domestic cleaning and linen washing.

The services provided by PA were initially undertaken by local administrative public authorities but over the years such activities have been privatised and PA now has numerous contracts with authorities throughout the country.

Two years after PA was formed, it began to enjoy rapid growth. The market then began to mature after 6 years of growth and remained static for a further 10 years. Over the last 2 years, PA has lost some contracts from local administrative authorities, causing its turnover and profitability to decline.

The Managing Director of PA has turned to you to provide advice as to how to carry out what she calls "an examination of the state of the entity". The purpose of this is to determine what action should be taken to halt the decline in turnover and profit. In carrying out this review, the Managing Director instructs you to look at the firm's resources, markets, service, operating systems, internal organisation, results and returns to shareholders.

You have carried out some preliminary research and established that there exists the Ms model. This indicates that a position audit can be carried out using headings beginning with the letter M, as follows:

Men, Money, Management, Make-up, Machinery, Methods, Markets, Materials and Management information.

Requirements

(a) Recommend to the Managing Director how a position audit should be carried out for the PA company.

(7 marks)

(b) Discuss, with reasons, the issues that need to be addressed under each heading using the Ms model.

(18 marks)
(Total = 25 marks)

Question 4 Supermarket

A supermarket company employs you as management accountant. The organisation is undertaking a comprehensive analysis and evaluation of its product and customer portfolio. You have been asked to help because of your knowledge (through study) of value chain analysis.

Requirements

(a) (i) Using the example of a supermarket (or similar large mainly food-retailing organisation), discuss the main components of the value chain.

(12 marks)

(ii) Discuss the particular skills that you as management accountant can bring to an analysis of the value chain.

(5 marks)

(b) Discuss the contribution of value chain analysis in the effective implementation of generic strategies.

(8 marks)
(Total = 25 marks)

Question 5 Competitor benchmarking

Organisations are reporting a growth in the sophistication, volume and nature of data that is regularly collected and interpreted for strategic purposes. This data collection supports a number of strategic approaches. Some firms regularly monitor customer expectation and market conditions for instance, while others prefer to attempt to stay in touch with their competitor's methods of doing business, strategies and future intentions.

Requirements

(a) Compare and contrast competitor analysis and competitor benchmarking.

(17 marks)

(b) Discuss how benchmarking might be successfully applied in the public sector. You may use examples drawn from any area of the public sector to illustrate your answer.

(8 marks)
(Total = 25 marks)

✓ Answers

Question 1 R

(a) (i) Stakeholders

The main stakeholders with whom R needs to maintain relationships include customers, shareholders, staff, suppliers, the local authority and the local tourist board.

(ii) Importance of relationships

Customers

A good relationship with customers is essential to ensure that they both return themselves and recommend the hotel to others. Customers provide the income that allows the hotel to continue in business. It is important that R analyses its customer base to decide what different services each customer requires in order to maintain this relationship.

Shareholders

R needs to give a reasonable return to its shareholders. This can only be achieved by continuing to attract customers. R might also look at the shareholder base and special relationships maintained with the larger investors.

Staff

The quality of service provided by the staff is paramount, so they must be competent and efficient to ensure a customer's satisfaction with the hotel. R must ensure the staff have commitment and training, and by as far as possible to keep staff turnover low so that they are familiar with the hotel and its procedures.

Suppliers

R needs good quality supplies and services to maintain its reputation. It therefore needs to select them very carefully, based on quality, and try to maintain long-term relationships with those suppliers that understand its needs well.

Local authority

The local authority and its regulators could impose conditions on the hotel's operations or close it down. It is therefore important that R maintains good relations with the local authority and abides by all its regulations.

Local tourist board

The city attracts many foreign visitors in the summer, many of whom will ask the tourist board for advice and recommendations on where to stay. A good relationship with the board could therefore pay dividends in having its hotel recommended to visitors. In turn, the tourist board will only recommend the hotel if it is confident that visitors will receive a good service.

(b) Benchmarking exercise

Benchmarking compares performance against other organisations in a variety of areas so that we can identify areas for improvement. The different areas of the hotel processes could be examined, such as reception, bars, restaurants, housekeeping, room service and laundry. These can be examined in other organisations, once management have decided on a number of performance measures for each area. However, it may be difficult to obtain this information from hotels against which R is competing. Alternative sources might be hotels in other cities or completely different organisations which nevertheless undertake cleaning, with restaurants, and with any organisation dealing with a large number of bookings and admissions.

It may well be difficult to obtain such confidential information from these other organisations. Once acquired, R needs to identify the differences in the other organisations processes from those at R and establish if this difference accounts for the difference in the performance measure.

Benchmarking can be a very large and time-consuming task, so it is probably sensible to consider the most important aspects of the service, or those over which there is most concern, rather than trying to look at all areas at once.

Once, established the management of R should continue to measure performance in these areas to see if improvements are made upon the introduction of new systems and processes.

Question 2 University

(a) Value Chain Analysis (VCA) looks at how value is added for customers of an organisation. It reviews all the activities undertaken by the organisation and tries to assess how they, and the linkages between them, add value.

VCA divides activities into primary and support activities, and each of these is subdivided further.

Primary activities

These deal with the provision of courses for students and taking new students and turning them into graduates.

Inbound logistics looks at the "raw materials", the students, the courses on offer, the staff and the facilities. It is possible that students are coming from less academic backgrounds or that good research staff do not make good lecturers.

Operations looks at the running of the degree course and may use feedback forms to assess the effectiveness of the various lecturers, and attendance registers for the students. It would be interesting to see why a disproportionate number leave in the first year – is it different from that advertised or do they not want to take the courses outlined for the next 2 years?

Outbound logistics would look at the graduates produced to see how many are employed, and what the perception was of the course by both graduates and employers.

Marketing would look at the key elements which attract students and whether these are unrealistic compared with reality.

Service looks at any service provided after graduation and any additional services given to undergraduates, such as a sense of community. These may compare unfavourably to other universities but would not explain the move to other courses within the university.

Support activities

These relate to the policies in place which support the primary activities, and they may need to change depending upon the results of our investigation.

Procurement looks at the efficiency and adequacy of the supplies required.

Human resource management looks at recruitment, development and retention of staff in all areas.

Technology development may help to deliver courses more effectively.

Infrastructure looks at the general facilities available and the overall culture within the university.

(b) Each of these areas needs examining to assess the extent to which it helps the students complete their course or impedes progress. The analysis might help by giving a clearer structure to the problem and allowing a detailed consideration of each of the components of the possible competitive advantage that the university may have.

Once the area to which a problem relates has been highlighted, we need to examine the linkages with all the other primary and support activities to establish the likely cause or causes, and then consider the changes needed to rectify it. This may mean changes of staff or work practices, so needs to be handled sensitively and be seen to have the backing of the senior management.

Question 3 PA

(a) **Position audit**

PA appears to be following the product life cycle in that it experienced rapid growth for 6 years, matured with a static period of 10 years, followed by a decline period which has lasted for 2 years so far.

The position audit looks at all aspects of an organisation which can impact on its success, including, as mentioned in the scenario, resources, markets, operating systems, the internal organisation, current results and returns to shareholders. This means that it would be sensible to have a team with the expertise to look at all of these areas, and thus include specialists from marketing, finance, human resource management, systems and possibly legal, given that PA provides services through a contractual arrangement. The management accountant's role would be to provide information on costs and revenues to date and forecasts as well as non-financial indicators.

As with any project, the objectives and terms of reference should be clearly stated and a deadline of the report agreed. The team will also need sufficient resources for its review, including staff under secondment and possibly some external expertise. In order to get sufficient co-operation from staff, it would also be sensible to have a strong chairperson who has the clear backing of the board and the Managing Director.

(b) Issues under Ms model

Looking at each of the nine Ms in turn would include the following issues for PA:

Men

This relates to the workforce and their skills, training, attitude and cost. As a service organisation it is essential that PA employs people who are not only qualified for their role but also provide a positive impression on the elderly it services.

Money

This obviously relates to the financial position and would consider the overall trends over a number of years of both turnover and profits. Forecasts of cash flow and profits would also be useful information.

Management

This considers the senior management of PA and tries to consider if the company is getting value for money. This is clearly a sensitive issue and will, to some extent, be subjective as it will consider the attitude and strategic skills of the management. As this is part of the reason for the position audit, it becomes rather pointless if the senior management are not prepared to reconsider their approach.

Make-up

This looks at the structure and culture of PA, considering how it developed and why, and how it might develop in the future. It needs to consider whether these represent the best structure and culture to meet the needs of the elderly in the future.

Machinery

This looks at the physical assets of the company such as vehicles and any other equipment needed. It will therefore not take long to undertake a review of their condition and their appropriateness to the service provided.

Methods

This considers the processes adopted by PA in both winning clients and providing its services. In particular for a service company the checks and controls on the amount, the length and the quality of any service provided. Speed may be improved by the provision of more equipment but PA needs to be careful it does not impinge on quality.

Markets

It is important the PA understands its markets. It may be possible to segment the market into these with different needs, such as those who are able bodied and those who are infirm. This also needs to consider any other markets which could be serviced, such as schools or hospitals and whether there is likely to be a move politically to offer these to the private sector. Alternatively, some of its existing services to the elderly may be taken back into public authority control. It may be that PA need to examine their pricing policy carefully.

Materials

This looks at the relationship with its suppliers, such as the latest labour force. It would include reviews of contractual arrangements with agencies, as well as the purchase of materials needed in the services.

Management information

This looks at the quality and timeliness of the information provided to managers. It is important that the information is reliable as a base for making decisions and for comparing actual results to those forecast.

It is important that the review is started immediately as it is likely to take some time and the board of PA would undoubtedly want to halt the decline in profits and revenues as soon as possible.

Question 4 Supermarket

(a) (i) Value chain

The value chain looks at an organisation as a series of connected activities and tries to identify those individual activities which add value for the customer.

It divides the activities between those involved in the direct production of the product or service (primary activities) and those that support these activities (support activities). It can be represented in the following diagram:

Firm infrastructure				
Technology development				
Human resource management				
Procurement				
Inbound logistics	Operations	Outbound logistics	Marketing and sales	Service

The primary activities would relate to the supermarket as follows:

Inbound logistics involves the receipt and storage of goods required and in this case would include the bulk warehousing, storage and delivery to the individual supermarkets.

Operations convert the materials received into the final product. In this case, it involves placing the items on the shelves in the supermarket and preparing displays.

Outbound logistics covers the distribution to customers. In this case, the customer often takes the purchases to the checkout themselves and takes them home. However, online purchases are often delivered by the supermarket.

Marketing and sales covers the promotional aspects in which the customer is made aware of the service or product, and in this case would include newspaper and television advertisements, inserts in the local press and posters in the supermarket windows.

Service covers any other service offered to the customer in addition to its usual products, such as training or insurance. In this situation, it might include a returns and complaints department and an enquiry service.

The support activities would be:

Procurement which covers purchasing of all items, including the products for resale and such things as advertising space.

Technology development which covers all the systems in the operation. In a supermarket, this would include the electronic point of sale system (EPOS) that monitors stocks, reorder levels, sales data and pricing results.

Human resource management which looks at the recruitment, training, retention and remuneration of the staff throughout the organisation.

Infrastructure which covers the structure and systems in place in the organisation. This would include the corporate policies which influence management decisions at an operational level.

(ii) The management accountant

The management accountants' role is to help in collecting and presenting information which will allow management to identify value-adding and non-value adding activities. This will involve looking at each of the nine activity areas and considering what they do which helps to increase the value of the service to the customer. The management accountant can then consider ways to reduce the cost of the service without affecting the quality and use techniques such as activity-based costing to identify the drivers of costs.

The management accountant will also be involved in interpreting the analysis generated and considering its impact on the organisation's business strategy.

(b) Value chain analysis and generic strategy

Successful strategies concentrate either on overall cost leadership or on differentiation and either apply these across the entire market or focus on a smaller strategic target.

Cost leadership involves reducing costs to a minimum while producing a product or service of similar quality to competitors. The value chain can help by identifying activities which incur unnecessary costs and which could be reduced or eliminated without affecting the service. It is crucial that any such action does not impact on the quality and hence on the price the customer is willing to pay.

Differentiation involves producing a service regarded as unique by the customers and adds value in the sense that the customer is prepared to pay more for the service. This can be very difficult to maintain as competitors can copy many of the differentiating factors over time. The company therefore needs to be continually innovating as well as building up its brand name (which cannot be copied). The value chain can help identify areas of value-adding activity which can be enhanced or extended to other areas, either to lock in the customer more securely in that they prefer our service, or to enable us to maintain or increase our prices.

Question 5 Competitor benchmarking

(a) Competitor analysis and competitor benchmarking

Competitor analysis consists of a systematic review of the organisation's competitors, while competitor benchmarking examines the organisation's own performance against its competitors. In more detail, they encompass the following:

Competitor analysis

In order to maintain competitive advantage, it is crucial for an organisation to understand its competitors. This will include information on pricing and costs, customers and market share, but will also look at how competitors are likely to react to any strategic moves by the organisation. A study of competitors' actions and any public information such as annual reports may give a guide to the strategies being employed by competitors. Continuous monitoring of competitors will be necessary to ensure that the organisation can take appropriate action.

Generally, competitor analysis allows us to identify our competitors and their likely objectives, strategies and strengths and weaknesses. This will give the organisation an informed basis for developing its strategy.

Competitor benchmarking

It is important for managers to monitor progress towards objectives by setting targets and measuring performance. However, it can be difficult to establish reasonable, challenging and yet achievable targets. It can therefore be useful to use as a benchmark the performance of a competitor or an industry average. Benchmarking can be applied to a number of areas, such as products, service, qualify and pricing.

However, the more internal the process, the less easy it will be to obtain information about such private areas. In some industries, the trade press or association will accumulate data from companies on a host of key areas and publish them without identifying companies or produce reports for companies showing their position relative to the "best in class".

Benchmarking should lead to improvements in performance as the organisation tries to alter its practices. This may only be possible if the organisation is able to discover the methods used by the competitor that has set the benchmark standard. When this is very difficult to discover, the company will have to rely on innovation, efficiency and service improvements identified by managers and staff.

(b) Benchmarking in the public sector

Benchmarking is wider than competitor benchmarking, as it involves setting standards for performance in a number of areas. These standards can be set by reference to internal or external information about performance.

In the context of public sector organisations, they are mostly trying to provide social services and their success will be measured by the services they deliver and the costs of those services. In deciding what is reasonable in these areas, benchmarking is often used to establish a standard. Thus in a hospital, waiting times, size of waiting list, bed utilisation or number of re-admissions might be used. A school may be judged in a number of ways, including test results of its leaving pupils.

In contrast to the private section, in which the company itself instigates the benchmarking process, it is likely in the public sector that the government or regulatory authority instigates the proves in its role as guardian of the public's finances and to ensure that a reasonable standard of service is provided for the public. However, in deciding on appropriate measures of performance and on benchmark standards in those areas, there is a significant degree of subjectivity. Whereas a private company will clearly be interested in prices, revenues and costs and the quality of the product as it relates directly to its primary objective of maximising shareholder wealth, the numerous stakeholders in the public sector makes this less straightforward. A school judged simply on exam results may feel that other aspects of its service have been overlooked and publication of league tables which only look at one or two measures can exacerbate this. In addition, the service provided has to be relevant to the users, so that school assessments should take account of the academic ability and background of the children who attend the school.

It is therefore important, when introducing benchmarking to a public sector organisation, that the areas of performance to be measured are appropriate and that benchmarks set are reasonable, given the organisation's particular circumstances. It would be sensible to start with four key areas agreed with the managers before slowly increasing the breadth of the benchmarking exercise. Benchmark targets which are not agreed by managers in the organisations, will only lead to resistance to these externally imposed standards and de-motivation. This is almost the exact opposite of the intention in setting such targets.

Lastly, unlike in competitor benchmarking in the private sector, there should be no great difficulty in obtaining information on other schools or hospitals and how they manage to produce such good results. For this reason, any system of benchmarking should be accompanied by reports of best practice around the country, along with the processes used and standards achieved.

Corporate Appraisal 5

✏️ Exam focus

A corporate appraisal, or SWOT, is an overview of the organisation's current position and leads directly on from the analysis undertaken to date. Questions often require the results of a corporate appraisal.

🔑 Key points

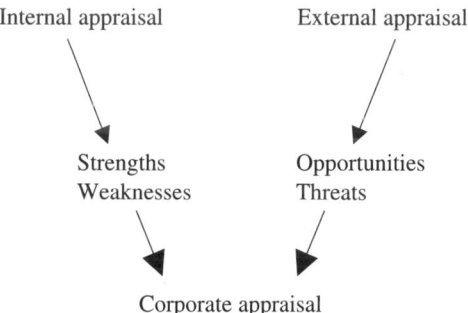

As the company works towards achieving its objectives, the corporate appraisal is a summary of the company's:

- Strengths
- Weaknesses
- Opportunities
- Threats.

The company must then develop a strategy which:

- capitalises on and continues to build the strengths
- overcomes or mitigates the impact of weaknesses
- takes suitable opportunities
- overcomes or mitigates the threats.

Gap analysis

Gap analysis looks at the expected shortfall between the forecast results and the objective relating to that area. It then considers possibilities put forward in the light of their ability to close this gap.

Questions

Question 1   T plc

Introduction

T plc is a well-established company providing telecommunications services both nationally and internationally. Its business has been concerned with telephone calls, the provision of telephone lines and equipment, and private telecommunications networks. T plc has supplemented these services recently by offering mobile phones, which is an expanding market worldwide.

The company maintains a diverse customer base, including residential users, multinational companies, government agencies and public sector organisations. The company handles approximately 100 million calls each working day, and employs nearly 140,000 personnel.

Strategic development

The Chairman of T plc stated within the latest Annual Report that there are three main areas in which the company aims to develop in order to remain a world leader in the telecommunications market. He believes that the three main growth areas reflect the evolving nature of the telecommunications market, and will provide scope for development.

The areas in which development is planned are:

1. Expansion of the telecommunications business in the national and overseas markets, both by the company acting on its own and through partnership arrangements with other suppliers.
2. Diversification into television and multi-media services, providing the hardware to permit telephone shopping from home and broadcasting services.
3. Extension of the joint ventures and strategic alliances which have already been established with companies in North America, Europe, India and the Far East.

The Chairman explained that the company is intent on becoming a world leader in communications. This will be achieved through maintaining its focus on long-term development by improving its services to customers, developing high quality up-to-date products and being innovative, flexible and market driven. His aim is to deliver a world-class service at competitive cost.

Financial information

Comparative statistics showing extracts from the company's financial performance in its national telecommunications market over the last 2 years are as follows:

	Last year (£m)	Previous year (£m)
Turnover	16,613	15,977
Profit before interest and tax	3,323	2,876
Capital employed	22,150	21,300

The company estimates its cost of capital to be approximately 11 per cent.

The Chairman expressed satisfaction with the increase in turnover and stated that cost efficiencies were now being generated following completion of a staff reduction programme. This would assist the company in achieving a target return on capital employed (ROCE) in this market of 20 per cent over the next 3 years.

Business opportunities

The Chief Executive of T plc has stated that the major opportunities for the company lie in the following areas:

- Encouraging greater use of the telephone.
- Provision of advanced services, and research and development into new technology, including the Internet and systems integration.
- The increasing freedom from government control of worldwide telecommunication services.

An extensive television and poster advertising campaign has been used by the company. This was in order to penetrate further the residential market by encouraging greater use of the telephone with varying charging incentives being offered to residential customers.

To further the objective of increasing long-term shareholder value, the company is actively considering investment of £200 million in each of the next 3 years in new technology and quality improvements in its national market. Because of its specialist technical nature, the investment is not expected to have any residual value at the end of the three year period.

Following the investment, the directors of T plc believe that its rate of profit before interest and tax to turnover in its national telecommunications market will remain constant. This rate will be at the same level as last year for each of the 3 years of the investment.

Markets and competition

The company is currently experiencing an erosion of its market share and faces increasingly strong competition in the mobile phone market. While T plc is the leader in its national market, with an 85 per cent share of the telecommunications business, it has experienced a reduced demand for the supply of residential lines in the last 5 years as competition has increased.

The market for the supply of equipment in the national telecommunications market is perceived to be static. The investment of £200 million in each of the next 3 years is estimated to increase T plc's share of this market to a level of 95 per cent. The full improvement of 10 per cent is expected to be received by T plc next year, and its market share will then remain at this level for the full three year period. It is anticipated that unless further investment is made after the three year period, T plc's market share will revert to its current level as a consequence of the expected competitive response.

Industry regulation

The government has established an industry regulatory organisation to promote competition and deter anti-competitive behaviour.

As a result of the activities of the regulator and aggressive pricing strategies, it is anticipated that charges to customers will remain constant for the full three-year period of the new investment.

All cash flows can be assumed to occur at the end of the year to which they relate. The cash flows and discount rate are in real terms.

Requirements

(a) Explain the nature of the political, economic, social and technical forces which influence T plc in developing its business and increasing its market share.

(10 marks)

(b) (i) Apply Ansoff's Product/Market Growth Vector matrix to assess the extent of the potential market development opportunities available to T plc.

(15 marks)

(ii) Explain how this matrix may be incorporated into the strategic planning process to determine the extent of the planning gap.

(5 marks)

(c) Evaluate and comment on T plc's proposed investment in new technology and quality improvements in its national telecommunications market.

Assume that variable costs are 80 per cent of the incremental revenue, and that fixed costs will not increase. Ignore working capital.

(15 marks)

(d) (i) Assess to what extent the investment in new technology and quality improvements in T plc's national telecommunications market contributes towards the closure of the company's planning gap in respect of its target ROCE.

(5 marks)

(ii) Recommend a strategy which T plc could employ to close the planning gap and achieve the strategic development aims identified by the Chairman. Ignore taxation.

(10 marks)
(Total = 60 marks)

Question 2   SWOTs

Many private and public sector organisations undertake a corporate appraisal of themselves by producing an analysis of their strengths, weaknesses, opportunities and threats (SWOT).

Requirements

Evaluate the usefulness of SWOT analysis as a tool for carrying out organisational position appraisals.

(25 marks)

Question 3 Gap analysis

Most organisations recognise that continuing as at present, sometimes referred to as the "do nothing" option, is rarely advisable as it is likely to lead to a performance shortfall against objectives. Even new policies may not guarantee meeting organisational objectives.

The planning technique "gap analysis" is a means by which an organisation can assess whether proposed policies are likely to achieve their objectives or the degree to which they might fall short.

Requirements

(a) Typically, an organisation might construct and then respond to a gap analysis as part of an overall (rational) approach to strategic management. Evaluate the usefulness of the "gap analysis" technique as part of such a system and the main criticisms of this rational approach.

(10 marks)

(b) Some people feel that gap analysis has declined in popularity particularly within the private sector.

   (i) Discuss why this should be the case.

(7 marks)

   (ii) Using examples, explain how gap analysis could be particularly helpful to public sector organisations.

(8 marks)
(Total = 25 marks)

Answers

Question 1 T plc

(a) PEST analysis

Political

T faces a concerted political effort to develop competition in the market, and regulation to reduce its market share. It is unlikely, given these factors, that T will be able to expand or even keep its market share in the long term.

Economic

A phone is now generally viewed as a necessity and so is less influenced by people's economic situation. As different countries develop and grow their economies there will be a growing need for telecoms. Without a fixed line system already in place, T can introduce new technology overseas to compete more effectively.

Social

The use of telecoms seems set to continue to grow. This is particularly true in the area of mobile phones, which have been targeted at all ages. The increase in Internet use, and other needs such as telephone banking, has increased the use of fixed lines.

Technology

Telecoms benefit from major changes in technology, but these can happen rapidly, superseding previous technology and making it risky to invest in technology with a long payback. Recent changes include fibre optic cables, the Internet and improvements in mobile phone technology.

Overall, the particular problems T faces are that it is very expensive to make a major investment but rapidly changing technology means they must try to be as flexible as possible.

(b) (i) Ansoff

Ansoff's matrix divides potential strategies into four categories:

Existing products, existing market

T already has 85 per cent of the fixed line telecoms business, so it is unlikely, despite the proposed investment, that this can grow in the long term. The most T can hope for is to maintain its market share. The mobile phone market, and T's sales within it, are growing although it is a highly competitive market. T needs to continue to compete aggressively in this area.

New products, existing market

This involves introducing new products to those who are already customers. This might include selling mobiles to residential customers, selling equipment, or accessing the television and internet market in the homes by designing new packages and products to appeal to their residential customers.

Existing products, new markets

This would suggest using T's expertise in telecoms in other markets, the most obvious being overseas. Coming into a country without any equipment in place, T will be able to leapfrog the technology installed some time ago by any domestic player.

New products, new markets

This involves selling new products to those not currently customers. In T's case this might include designing TV and internet products and access packages and marketing them to a wider audience than its current customers.

(ii) Planning gap

The planning gap is the difference between the objectives of the organisation and the expected results. Ansoff's matrix helps by identifying general strategies for closing this gap, in that it formulates the most viable direction and focuses the thinking of management for idea generation.

However, Ansoff's matrix does not specifically look at risk, although as a general rule the further away a strategy is from the existing market and existing product, the more risky it will be. Before deciding on a strategy to close the planning gap, it would be sensible to compare the anticipated return against the risk involved.

(c) Proposed investment

	t_0	t_1	t_2	t_3
Profit (20% × 10/85 × 16,613)		391	391	391
Investment		(200)	(200)	(200)
		191	191	191

NPV = 191 × 3 yr AF at 11%

= 191 × 2.44 = 467m

The NPV would indicate that the proposal is viable.

The company uses ROCE as its target:

As the investment has no residual value and £200 m is spent each year, £200 m will have to be depreciated each year, which means that at the end of each year there is no net increase in the net assets and hence capital employed. Thus the annual ROCE for the project is 191/0 = infinite.

This obviously exceeds the current 3,323/22,150 = 15% and will help to close the gap but will only take it to 3,514/22,150 = 15.9%

Other comments:

- There is such uncertainty in the industry that the predictions can only be rough estimates and the company needs to undertake sensitivity analysis.
- No account has been taken of how the competitors may react to an attempt to increase the market share from 85 per cent to 95 per cent (or the regulator).
- There may be other opportunity costs or benefits involved; for example, not undertaking this investment may mean T loses market share rather than staying at 85 per cent.

(d) (i) Current ROCE = 3,323/22,150 = 15%

To achieve 20 per cent we need profit of 22,150 × 20% = 4,430m

This is an increase of 1,107m over last year

The project provides 191m per annum which is approximately 1/6

T therefore needs to find other ways to help bridge the gap

(ii) Strategies

The planning gap relates to the objective, which is expressed in terms of ROCE

$$\text{ROCE} = \frac{\text{Revenue} - \text{Costs}}{\text{Investment}}$$

So increasing revenues or decreasing costs or investments would help.

To increase revenues, T could enter overseas markets (new markets), develop the television and internet services (new markets) or form alliances with other companies.

Reducing costs or investment does not seem to be in line with the Chairman's aims, but could be achieved through cost cutting after an in-depth review of operations or by outsourcing various services to reduce the investment base.

To close the planning gap in the short term, major expansion plans are not going to be effective as they will take some time to implement. T has more chance of achieving its target if it concentrates on its current customers in their home market, cuts costs where possible, and develops new enhanced products to sell to their existing customer base.

Question 2 SWOTs

A SWOT analysis looks at the strengths, weaknesses, opportunities and threats of an organisation and is equally useful to a private or public sector organisation before deciding on its future strategy.

Strengths and weaknesses relate to the current position of the organisation and suggest areas at which the organisation excels, possibly outperforming any competitors, and those at which it is not so good, leaving it open for competitors to exploit their advantage.

Opportunities and threats mostly relate to future possibilities and are areas that could possibly be exploited to the organisation's benefit or dangers that the organisation will be disadvantaged in the future due to some external influence (such as a competitor).

Generally, strengths and weaknesses will emerge from an internal analysis, while opportunities and threats come from an examination of the external environment including competitors. An issue may be both a strength and a weakness, such as a high production capacity which can mean a company can take advantage of a large volume with economics of scale but may have high fixed costs at low levels. In a similar way, a change in tastes and fashion may be view as an opportunity or a threat.

The benefits of conducting a SWOT include:

- It helps assess the progress of an organisation towards its targets and helps managers to assess the organisation in a clear way before going on to set strategies.
- It is straightforward to apply and understand and encourages managers to benchmark performance against competitors.
- It can help to identify the gap between current performance and its stated aims, and starts to identify areas which could be targeted for improvement to help close the gap.
- Once a number of issues have been listed, the SWOT format can easily be used to rank individual strengths, for example, in order of critical importance to the organisation.
- The SWOT itself helps to suggest some possible courses of action. Some weaknesses may be turned into strengths, such as being only able to supply small quantities could be used as a selling point as the product may be portrayed as rare and valuable. In the same way, threats might be turned into opportunities with some thought. Those weaknesses and threats that are left can then be addressed.

Problems with a SWOT analysis include:

- As the rational planning model concentrates on the longer term, using a SWOT may miss short-term opportunities that a more flexible, possibly smaller, organisation might take advantage of.
- Trying to prioritise the weaknesses, in particular, can be difficult and subjective, as managers have a tendency to list all the short-term problems as well.
- Deciding whether an issue is an opportunity or threat, a strength or a weakness can be problematic as discussed above.

Overall, the SWOT analysis is a useful tool, but one that has to be used carefully when interpreting the information gathered and deciding on future plans. It fits into the rational planning approach which can prove inflexible in the short term and is therefore more suitable for strategy design in those companies which face less volatile environments in the short term.

Question 3 Gap analysis

(a) Usefulness of gap analysis on rationals approach

Gap analysis involves comparing an organisation's objective with the expected performance in this area; the shortfall highlights the gap which needs to be addressed. Various strategies can then be developed and their impact on closing the gap addressed.

As a theoretical approach, gap analysis can be useful in regularly assessing progress towards objectives and taking action to correct this where necessary.

However, there are likely to be some practical problems in its application:

- Objectives of an organisation may conflict to some extent, and closing the gap for one objective may widen it elsewhere.
- Some objectives may not have been put in measurable terms, or at least are capable of being measured in other ways.
- It may be acceptable not to achieve the objective in absolute terms if there are longer-term benefits (such as accepting government work at a low profit with the expectation of further contracts).
- It assumes that the expected performance can be accurately predicted, but in an uncertain environment this will depend on externals factors such as competitor, customer and government actions.
- It also assumes that any new initiatives taken on to close the gap are predictable in terms of costs and revenues.

This tends to mean that most organisations find their strategy emerges as a combination of planned strategy and day-to-day opportunities that present themselves.

(b) (i) Gap analysis

Gap analysis has become less popular in the private sector because of the rapidly changing environment in which companies operate, as discussed above. Companies will find it difficult to judge accurately, for example, the reaction of customers and competitors, or to predict the future changes in the economy and its impact on the market in which the company operates. As a result, forecasts can never be totally relied upon and while the concept of gap analysis may be useful to highlight major areas of concern, it is less popular as a means of driving strategy planning.

(ii) In the public sector

In the public sector, although the environment in which it operates can change, this tends to happen much more slowly. This means that outcomes are relatively predictable in the medium term, particularly where it relates to predictable factors, such as demographic influences on the health service and education needs. In this situation, the gap in objectives can be more easily measured and the impact of strategies in closing the gap assessed.

Strategic Options and Evaluation 6

✏️ Exam focus

Strategic choice is the process of generating strategic options and deciding which option the organisation will take to enable it to meet its objectives, given the strengths, weakness, opportunities and threats identified.

To generate a strategic choice an organisation can follow three stages:

(a) Develop the generic strategy.
(b) Decide on the strategic direction.
(c) Decide on the method for achieving the strategy.

🔑 Key points

Porter's generic strategies

Competitive advantage
Firms that are more profitable than the average in the industry have a competitive advantage over the other companies in the industry.

Michael Porter identified two basic types of competitive advantage, cost advantage and differentiation advantage.

Cost advantage
This means being the lowest cost producer in the market. For similar products selling at the market price the cost leader will generate higher profits. They can alternatively sell at lower prices and generate market share. In times of falling prices, the cost leader is able to sustain profitability for longer and survive where other companies may fail.

Cost advantages can be achieved by minimising costs throughout the value chain. For example, through:

- making a significant investment in efficient production machinery
- designing products for efficient manufacturing
- using efficient distribution channels, minimising sales and distribution costs
- sourcing low cost supplies
- generating economies of scale through mass production.

Differentiation advantage

A differentiation strategy calls for the development of a product or service that offers unique attributes that are valued by customers and that customers perceive to be better than or different from the products of the competition. The value added by the uniqueness of the product may allow the firm to charge a premium price for it. The firm hopes that the higher price will more than cover the extra costs incurred in offering the unique product.

Ways in which differentiation can be achieved include:

- offering better quality product
- offering better customer service
- having better brand image
- including different features from the competition
- providing a better after-sales service.

Porter also noted that both cost leadership and differentiation strategies could be followed with narrow market focus. In this instance an organisation focuses effort and resources on a narrow, defined segment of a market. Competitive advantage is generated specifically for this niche. This strategy is often used by smaller firms who cannot afford to target the market as a whole.

Michael Porter argued that to be successful over the long term, a firm must select only one of these generic strategies. Otherwise, with more than one single generic strategy the firm will be "stuck in the middle" and will not achieve a competitive advantage.

Strategic direction – Ansoff's matrix

To portray alternative approaches to the growth of the organisation, Ansoff developed a matrix that focused on the firm's present and potential products and markets (customers). Different strategies can be followed depending on the product and market in which the organisation develops.

In the exam, this provides a useful selection of possible strategic options that the organisation can take, and can be used to help generate ideas for strategic choices.

PRODUCT

	Current	New
MARKET Current	Market penetration	Product development
MARKET New	Market development	Diversification – Related – Unrelated

(Adapted from Ansoff 1965)

Market penetration

The firm seeks to achieve growth with existing products in their current market segments, aiming to increase its market share, perhaps though reducing prices, increasing advertising or further differentiating the product.

This is the least risky strategy since it builds upon many of the firm's existing resources and capabilities. In a growing market, simply maintaining market share will result in growth. However, market penetration has limits, and once the market approaches saturation another strategy must be pursued if the firm is to continue to grow. One approach to penetrate the market is through *horizontal integration*, the buying of a competitor. This achieves a very quick increase in market share and instantly removes a competitor.

Market development

The firm seeks growth by targeting its existing products to new customers:

- selling the same products to new market segments (e.g. selling DVD's to pensioners)
- new geographical regions (e.g. overseas expansion)
- finding different uses for the same product (e.g. Lucazade used as a sports drink).

Product development

The firm develops new products targeted to its existing market segments. This may be appropriate if the firm's strengths are related to its specific customers rather than to the specific product itself. In this situation, it can leverage its strengths by developing a new product targeted to its existing customers.

Diversification

The firm grows by diversifying into new businesses by developing new products for new markets.

Diversification is the most risky of the four growth strategies since it requires both product and market development and may be outside the core competencies of the firm. However, diversification may be a reasonable choice if the high risk is compensated by the chance of a high rate of return.

Other advantages of diversification include the potential to gain a foothold in an attractive industry and the reduction of overall business risk through not being dependent on just one industry.

Related diversification is the diversification into product and markets which are new, but related in some way to the existing products and markets in which the organisation operates. The most common way this is done is through *vertical integration* which is the degree to which a firm owns its upstream suppliers and its downstream buyers. Expansion of activities downstream is referred to as forward integration, and expansion upstream is referred to as backward integration.

Methods of strategic development

There are a number of different methods by which strategy can be achieved. Deciding how to develop the chosen strategy is the next step in strategic choice:

- An acquisition of an established business is quick, less risky, eliminates a competitor, buys expertise and might overcome legal/regulatory barriers.

- Internal (organic) development means the firm developing the strategy themselves. This gives control, allows time to learn, allows a gradual investment and avoids cultural clashes and the high costs associated with an acquisition.
- Joint development is a strategy undertaken in conjunction with other parties. Types of joint development include joint ventures, strategic alliances, franchising and licensing.

Strategy evaluation

An organisation must evaluate possible strategies; three criteria commonly used to assess strategies are suitability, acceptability and feasibility:

Suitability	*Acceptability*	*Feasibility*
Given our SWOT analysis and identification of major problems	Will it meet the objectives? Is it an acceptable risk?	Have we the resources required (finance, skills, time and assets)?

Questions

Question 1 S and L

S is a company which has traded very successfully within its domestic market for many years. It has achieved high levels of profitability in providing ground and soil sampling and testing services for a large range of clients in both the public and private sectors. This sampling is mainly undertaken to assess the suitability of former industrial land for building and public use.

In recent years, S has experienced strong competition and its Managing Director (L) has recognised that it is becoming more difficult to obtain new business from within its domestic market. Increasingly, it has been found necessary to offer more than the original basic ground and soil sampling and testing services in order to retain the loyalty of existing clients. This has necessitated a whole range of other services being offered such as testing for the presence of polluted substances in buildings, chemical analysis of water sources, geological surveys and providing for unfit land to be cleaned prior to becoming available for public use.

While these other services have been relatively successful, L is increasingly concerned about the prospects for sustaining the company's profitability because of increasing competition and saturation of the domestic market. With this in mind, L has asked you, as Management Accountant, to advise on the rationale for an overseas expansion strategy and the issues to be considered in its implementation.

Requirements

Produce a report to L which

(a) explains the business case for expansion overseas;

(10 marks)

(b) discusses the strategic and operational issues which the directors of S should consider before making a decision on whether to implement an overseas expansion strategy. There are 2 marks available for the formal required.

(15 marks)
(Total = 25 marks)

Question 2 Qualispecs

Qualispecs has a reputation for quality, traditional products. It has a group of optician shops, both rented and owned, from which it sells its spectacles. Recently, it has suffered intense competition and eroding customer loyalty, but a new Chief Executive has joined from one of its major rivals Fastglass.

Fastglass is capturing Qualispecs' market through partnership with a high-street shopping group. These shops install mini-labs in which prescriptions for spectacles are dispensed within an hour. Some competitors have successfully experimented with designer frames and sunglasses. Others have reduced costs through new computer-aided production methods.

Qualispecs has continued to operate as it always has, letting the product "speak for itself" and failing to utilise advances in technology. Although production costs remain high, Qualispecs is financially secure and has large cash reserves. Fortunately, the country's most popular sports star recently received a prestigious international award wearing a pair of Qualispecs' spectacles.

The new Chief Executive has established as a priority the need for improved financial performance. Following a review she discovers that:

1 targets are set centrally and shops report monthly. Site profitability varies enormously, and fixed costs are high in shopping malls;
2 shops exercise no control over job roles, working conditions, and pay rates;
3 individual staff pay is increased annually according to a pre-determined pay scale. Everyone also receives a small one-off payment based on group financial performance.

Market analysts predict a slowdown in the national economy but feel that consumer spending will continue to increase, particularly among 18–30 year olds.

Requirements

(a) Produce a corporate appraisal of Qualispecs, taking account of internal and external factors, and discuss the key strategic challenges facing the company.

(16 marks)

(b) Corporate appraisal offers a "snapshot" of the present. In order to focus on the future, there is a need to develop realistic policies and programmes. Recommend, with reasons, strategies from your appraisal that would enable Qualispecs to build on its past success.

(9 marks)
(Total = 25 marks)

Answers

Question 1 S and L

REPORT

To: Managing Director

From: Management Accountant

Date: xx of xx 20xx

(a) Business case for expansion overseas

Expansion overseas is one way of entering new markets. S has already expanded its range of services and is having difficulty expanding sales any further in its domestic market. An expansion overseas would therefore seem worth considering.

However, going overseas entails risks not usually encountered on the domestic market and the risks and opportunities must be carefully assessed. The risks relate to the environment in which S will operate and are concentrated on the political and legal environment and the social and cultural attributes. These may be different from S's home market.

(b) Strategic and operational issues

As S has no experience overseas, it will need to research the market carefully and make some strategic decisions:

Method of expansion

S could set up an operation overseas, acquire a business already there, or service the market from its own base. The organic approach of servicing the market from home and gradually expanding its base there is the least risky and least costly option.

Market research

S must assess the nature of the demand, which could vary in its requirements from the home market. It would be sensible to target the market which has a high demand for S's services, but at the same time assessing the difference in requirements from its usual service. There may well be legislation dealing with the area of ground, soil and water testing which needs to be taken into account.

S also needs to assess the level of competition in each potential market and the difficulty of attracting a profitable market share.

Resource availability

S needs to consider the reliability or existence of any sub-contractors or work force it might need. Different cultures, language problems in technical areas, and the level of education may all impact on the company's ability to deliver a high quality service.

Finance

S needs to consider how it will finance the expansion and whether it has sufficient internal funds or will need to raise new external finance. The amount that can be raised may provide an effective limit on the scale of any expansion programme.

There may also be the need to assess foreign currency exchange rate risk on contract pricing and to consider hedging if necessary.

Structure and Performance Reporting

The exact structure will depend on the method of entry into the market. Servicing it from the home office might involve a separate department within a functional structure or simply an additional area in the budget of the relevant department. Setting up an overseas operation or acquiring one is likely to see the creation of a divisional structure. Later, if clients use S in a number of countries, it might be appropriate to move to a matrix structure.

Senior management will want to study the results of the new venture carefully to assess whether it is likely to be successful strategically.

Before embarking on this expansion, we need to consider our rationale for expanding internationally and carefully assess each overseas market in the light of the above areas.

Question 2 Qualispecs

(a) Corporate appraisal

A corporate appraisal looks at the major strengths, weaknesses, opportunities and threats for an organisation. Strengths and weaknesses are usually associated with its current position, while opportunities and threats try to identify issues which may arise in the near future. These are then used, along with the objectives, to outline a plan of action, or strategy for the organisation.

In the case of Qualispecs, this might include:

Strengths

- A new Chief Executive with motivation, knowledge of the industry and in-depth knowledge of a direct competitor.
- Financial security and cash reserves.
- Reputation for quality.
- Well established and a number of shop sites.

Weaknesses

- Possibly inappropriate targets set centrally.
- Little evidence of cost control being applied to individual shops.
- No remuneration control at local level.
- High production costs.
- Little incentive for staff.

Opportunities

- Improve and speed up production using new technology.
- Design new products to appeal to the fashion-conscious in the 18–30 age range.
- Operate within other larger shops.
- Attract celebrity endorsements or sponsor people or events, particularly those which are attractive to the 18–30 year olds.

Threats

- Competitors take away Qualispecs' market share through cost-lowering technology or better differentiated products.
- An expansion of general chemists and other shops with well-known brands into optician services.
- Revenue reduces to such an extent that it fails to cover the high fixed costs.
- It is not clear if Qualispecs is a listed company, but if it is, then a decreasing market share along with its cash may make it a take-over target for a competitor.

The key strategic challenges are therefore to maintain and increase its market share by being responsive to the 18–30 year olds' requirements with new innovative products, incentivise and motivate staff, and reduce costs both on production and in the individual shops as long as it does not impact on the quality.

(b) Qualispec strategies

Strategies can be developed in a number of ways, one of which is to address the weaknesses and threats by utilising the strengths and opportunities. In the case of Qualispec, this might lead to:

- Reviewing shops and closing those which are loss making, while setting more appropriate targets and realistic incentives for staff in the remaining stores.
- Using the reputation of quality to negotiate space in the higher quality department stores.
- Develop innovative appealing new products for the 18–30 age range but emphasise the quality compared with others.
- Use the latest technology to "leapfrog" competitors and reduce production costs whilst safeguarding quality. This would be a productive use of the cash reserves.

Strategy in Marketing 7

✏️ Exam focus

Marketing is one of the key areas in which the company can put its strategy into action. You may be asked to comment on, or suggest, a strategic marketing approach.

🔑 Key points

The marketing concept

The marketing concept is the idea that to be successful the organisation should focus on meeting customer needs – "The customer is king".

In a sales orientated business, sales are the main focus of the organisation; the product and customer are secondary. However, while short-term sales may be achieved, if the product does not meet customer needs, long-term customer loyalty will not be gained and profits will be low in the long term.

The marketing mix outlines the controllable elements of product, price, promotion and place in a marketing strategy.

Boston consulting group matrix

The BCG matrix divides an organisation's products or services into four categories:

1. *Stars*   High market share and high market growth
2. *Problem children*   Low market share and high market growth
3. *Cash cows*   High market share and low market growth
4. *Dogs*   Low market share and low market growth

The likely strategies for each would be:

Stars   Hold market share by matching the investment of rivals
Problem children   Decide which to invest in and build market share and which to close down

Cash cows   Maximise cash flows by limiting investment and harvesting the product
Dogs   Divestment once its contribution becomes negative or there is a better use of the resources

This can be a useful technique but it can be difficult to define the market in order to decide whether the organisation has a high or low market share. It also ignores links between products and assumes that competitive advantage is gained in the market through economies of scale as it emphasises volume of sales. This is following a least cost approach, but a small player in a low growth market may differentiate its products and still make profits despite being classified as a dog.

Strategies to achieve a competitive position

Different strategies can be adopted depending on the company's relative position in a market.

Market leader
They have the largest market share, and so are likely to have the strongest brand in the market, good existing customer relationships and large economies of scale.

Market challenger
These have a lower market share than the leader but are aiming to be the market leader.

Market follower
These are competitors with a lower market share than the leader, who aim to follow the leader while remaining profitable. They do not have aspirations of market leadership.

Market niche strategy
Some competitors do not aim to compete with the other players in the broad market but to focus on specific niches.

Product life cycle

As products are developed, taken to market and sold, they are seen to go through discrete stages. Different marketing strategies are appropriate in each of these stages.

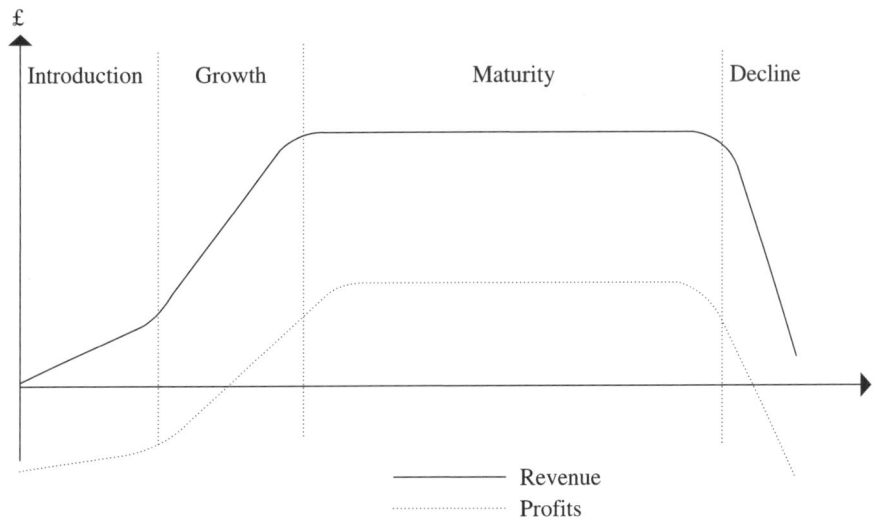

Performance measures for stages of the product life-cycle (adapted from Ward 1992)

Possible strategies for stages of product life cycle

Introduction	Charge a high price to cover high production costs and significant promotion to create awareness
Growth	Set a low price to win market share in an increasingly competitive marketplace, high advertising spending and an increased number of outlets
Maturity	Attempt to differentiate products by building brands to avoid price wars and intense competition
Decline	Either withdraw from market or retreat to a niche area

In reality very few products follow such a prescriptive cycle. The length of each stage varies enormously and stages can be affected by decisions made; so for example the maturity phase can be lengthened by price-cutting. Not all products go through each stage; some go from introduction to decline, others straight into the growth stage.

Brand strategy

A brand consists of a name and logo, packaging and associations made by consumers, such as attributes, benefits, values, culture, personality and the kind of person the user should be. Brands often have longer lives than products, which may decline due to obsolescence, and allow the company to launch new products or enter new markets more easily.

Brand strategies can be classified as:

Line extension	Apply the brand name to new sizes or flavours of the product
Brand extension	Launch a product in a new area using the brand name
Multibranding	Having numerous product brand names in the same product area
New branding	A new product is launched with a new brand name
Cobranding	Two brand names are combined in an area

Customer account profitability

CAP attempts to analyse which customers give the highest profits and the highest profit margins by identifying all the costs that can be traced to a particular customer. This includes not only the cost of goods sold, but also costs such as discounts given, special payment terms, commissions, dedicated staff time, special delivery arrangements, method of ordering, training and assistance and similar costs.

This enables a company to identify those customers who are valuable to the business and the expenditure it might be worth incurring in order to keep them. Those that do not appear to be valuable can be renegotiated or certain features or other costs reduced. However, care needs to be taken in drawing conclusions without investigating the impact it might have on consumer buying patterns.

It can also be misleading to only look at the results over one period and some writers feel that the present value of all revenues and costs over the entire lifetime of the relationship should be considered.

Questions

Question 1 Sports centre

A local administrative authority allowed a supermarket development to go ahead providing that the company concerned built an extension to the authority's sports centre on an adjoining site.

In recent years the sports centre has encountered a growth in competition from local commercial recreational organisations. Simultaneously, the authority has experienced a reduction in its central funding, and has steadily increased its charges for the use of its sports centre facilities.

In reviewing its services at the sports centre, the authority has applied the product life cycle (PLC) model. It has identified the stage within the life cycle at which each of its sports centre services is positioned, as follows:

Introductory stage	Martial arts, with little take up as yet
Growth stage	Squash playing facilities, which have required capital investment from the authority and on-going maintenance costs of the courts and equipment
	Demand for the facilities is increasing rapidly
Maturity stage	Gymnasium facilities, which require little maintenance expense and experience steady demand which generates surplus cash
	Swimming, which incurs a continual increase in maintenance and water purification costs
Decline stage	Badminton, with a continual reduction in demand

Requirements

(a) Recommend how the local authority could market its sports centre services.

(8 marks)

(b) Comment on the strategic resource allocation implications of each stage of the product life cycle when applied to the sports centre facility. You are NOT required to describe or draw the PLC model.

(12 marks)

(c) In the light of your answer to parts (a) and (b), and paying particular attention to the increasing competitive threat, recommend what services the authority should offer in the future within its sports centre.

(5 marks)
(Total = 25 marks)

Question 2 Marketing orientation

Marketing has been defined as identifying customer needs and wants and finding ways to satisfy them profitably. Selling has been described as supplying existing products or services to customers paying little regard to their particular needs and requirements. Whilst the marketing-oriented organisation recognises the value of satisfied customers, the sales-oriented organisation tends to have little understanding of the importance of customer satisfaction. As a consequence, the organisation which focuses on sales rather than on marketing is likely to have difficulty in analysing profitability derived from its different customer groups.

Requirements

(a) Discuss the benefits which an organisation may obtain from carrying out customer account profitability analysis.

(10 marks)

(b) Compare the management accounting information required to assess customer account profitability in a sales-oriented organisation with one which has a marketing orientation.

(15 marks)
(Total = 25 marks)

Question 3 Brand strategy

H plc is a leading manufacturer of food products and has for many years successfully developed a corporate brand name. The company has achieved high profitability following its success in creating the image that its brand name stands for good quality. The company has successfully established a corporate brand, in which all its products are clearly recognised under one corporate identity.

Until now the company has concentrated its efforts in manufacturing food products which are packaged in cans and distributed through supermarket chains worldwide. The company is increasingly being exposed to strong competition, with other manufacturers developing their own rival brands. H plc's directors are concerned to ensure that it at least retains its current market share and have determined the need to review its brand strategy. In carrying out this review, the directors are considering pursuing one or a combination of the brand strategy approaches of line extension; brand extension, multi-branding; new branding.

Requirement

To discuss the benefits and disadvantages to H plc of applying each of the brand strategy approaches, and recommend which of these the company should develop.

(20 marks)

Question 4 GC conglomerate

GC is a conglomerate which comprises five strategic business units (SBU's), all operating as subsidiary companies. Information relating to each SBU (and the market leader or nearest competitor) is given in the following table:

	Current market share			
	GC (%)	Market leader (%)	Nearest competitor (%)	Market growth expected by GC
Building brick manufacturer *(Declining profitability)*	3	25		Small
Parcel carriage service *(Long established, faces strong competition. Turnover and profitability over last 3 years have been stable but are expected to decline as competition strengthens.)*	1	6		Nil
Food manufacturer producing exclusively for household consumption *(Long established with little new investment. High levels of turnover and profitability which are being sustained.)*	25		5	Slowing declining
Painting and decorating contracting company *(Established 3 years ago. Continuous capital injections from Group over that period. Currently not making any profit.)*	0.025	0.5		Historically high but now forecast to slow down
Software development and supply company *(Acquired 2 years ago. Market share expected to increase over next 2 years. Sustained investment from Group but profitability so far is low.)*	10		8	Rapid

Requirements

(a) Comment on GC's overall competitive position by applying the Boston Consulting Group Growth/Share Matrix analysis to its portfolio of SBUs.

(8 marks)

(b) Discuss how GC should pursue the strategic development of its SBUs in order to add value to the overall conglomerate group.

(12 marks)
(Total = 20 marks)

84 Exam Practice Kit: Business Strategy

✓ Answers

Question 1 Sports centre

(a) Marketing

In order to market the sports and services offered by the centre, the local authority needs to undertake market research, segment the market according to people's different requirements, and design a marketing mix which will appeal to each group.

In researching the market the authority could:

- Study the local competition. It would be important to examine the number of uses, the facilities offered and their quality, the prices charged, the type of visitors and any perceived competitive advantage they might have.
- Interview the users of the different facilities at the sports centre, as well as users of competing centres and local people who do not use the centre at all.

Segmenting the market involves grouping users by similar needs, and might be by age (which will affect the facilities used and the time of day) or background or more simply by the use of the different facilities available.

A marketing mix for each segment will focus on the price, the product, promotion and the place. In considering the price, the authority will have to bear in mind not only the price of competing facilities, but also its social objectives in wanting the local population to be healthier (and it will not want the price to put people off). The product is the particular activity being offered; some such as the martial arts can be easily expanded if demand increases, whereas the squash courts have an obvious capacity ceiling in the short term. Place is where the activities are held; this is currently at the centre but there is the possibility of holding activities such as the martial arts classes at other convenient locations. Lastly, promotion could take the form of council advertisements and leaflets within the local community. Its association with and close proximity to, the supermarket may also be useful and the supermarket might be persuaded to help promote the sports centre.

(b) Product life cycle

The product life cycle (PLC) divides the life of a product or service into a number of stages – development, if appropriate, introduction, growth, maturity and decline. In the context of the sports centre, we may be able to estimate the stage of life of each of the facilities, and from that assess the approach needed in each area.

Martial arts would appear to be in the early stages of growth. Although this would normally mean significant investment of resources, it is unlikely that this is the case here; a few mats and some space in the hall is all that is required apart from the instructor.

The squash is also in the growth stage but has much higher cost implications, both in terms of maintenance of the courts and considering expanding the number of courts to keep pace with growing demand. The authority will need to balance the demand and revenue projections against the cost of any new build.

The gym would appear to be at the mature stage and producing a steady stream of revenue without having to spend much on it. A continuing maintenance programme and managing it to achieve optimal usage would be sensible.

The swimming pool would also appear to be at the mature stage but is a little more problematic. The running costs, including maintenance, cleaning and lifeguards are likely to be higher and there will be the decision at some point as to whether the pool should be refurbished. This will be a major investment decision which will need to be balanced against likely revenues and the authority's social objectives.

The badminton is possibly at the decline stage as demand reduces, suggesting that the authority should carefully consider if another activity could use the resources more effectively. Given that this is likely to consist of the space used, we need to ask what other activities could be run in that space and at what time.

(c) Services

Without further research, we can only make tentative suggestions. Looking at each activity in turn, we would recommend:

Martial arts

Conduct research to assess the level of demand and study the numbers at competing classes. If high, promote the classes and cater for expansion; otherwise continue to run the current classes.

Squash

Again, research the demand to assess whether the demand will continue to increase. A major expansion in the facilities would require considerable investment and the expected benefits should be carefully weighed against the cost. Before contemplating such an investment, every effort should be made to maximise the utilisation of the courts, by, for example, promoting day-time playing.

Gym

It seems reasonable to continue with this, while monitoring the demand carefully.

Swimming

It would be sensible to evaluate the income streams and identify any underutilisation of this expensive resource. It may be that the authority could promote more daytime use and consider potential users such as schools in order to halt any decline. The authority might also consider its social objectives with regard to the health of the community and to the extent to which a local swimming pool is an essential resource.

Badminton

The authority should carefully research demand, particularly at competitor's premises in order to ascertain if there is a general decline in badminton or whether it is only their own sports centre which is affected. If it is a general trend, then it would seem sensible to reduce the amount offered, possibly stopping it altogether if there are other uses for the space.

Question 2 Marketing orientation

(a) Customer Account Profitability (CAP) analysis

CAP analysis allows a company to examine each customer account and assess its profitability, allowing not only for the cost of goods sold but also any other traceable costs.

The main benefits are:

- It will encourage the company to consider all its costs and to ascertain which costs apart from the cost of goods sold actually relate to a particular customers. These might include discounts given, costs of tailoring standard products, shorter delivery times, longer payment terms, dedicated staff time and other similar costs.
- It will allow the company to identify those customers which generate the greatest profit for the company and those that have the highest profit margin.
- It will also show the company where low profits, or even losses, are being made, prompting them to reduce the discounts given or the other services provided or to put up the price.
- The company can then concentrate its resources on the more profitable clients and try to expand the amount of business conducted with those with the best margin.
- The importance of customers may change as one viewed as a major customer may incur so much in the way of extra costs that it is identified as less important and hence less powerful in any negotiations.
- In some cases, it may not be worthwhile continuing with some customers if the price cannot be increased.

(b) Management Accounting Information (MIS)

A sales-oriented organisation pays little attention to the particular needs of a customer, and therefore will have no systems in place to record the additional costs incurred by a particular order, apart from the standard cost of goods sold. Its emphasis will be on selling and the sales force and will therefore only be able to identify any discounts given off the price and any direct expenses of the sales force.

A marketing-oriented company will also be able to record and identify additional customer specific costs, such as the cost of adapting standard products, design and distribution costs, payment terms and the costs of customer liaison and monitoring customer satisfaction.

Question 3 Brand strategy

H has established a single corporate brand which represents good quality. In re-assessing this strategy, in the light of the strong competition, it can be useful to look at the possible branding strategies as follows:

	Existing products	*New products*
Existing brand name	Line extension	Brand extension
New brand name	Multi-branding	New branding

Considering each in turn:

Line extension

Here, H would extend the range of the existing products, with new flavours and different sizes, under the same brand name. This would be relatively easy to do and would take advantage of the reputation for quality associated with the brand name with only a limited amount of marketing. H needs to be careful that new products introduced do not reduce the sales of original products.

Brand extension

New products, such as other foods, could be launched under the same corporate brand. This relies on its customers buying the new products because they assume the quality in the original products will be found in these new ones. There is a risk that if the quality is not as high in the new products, that it will rebound on the original products as customers begin to question the quality behind the brand.

Multi-branding

The various products would be marketed under different brand names with multi-branding. This might be to appeal to different market segments, such as with soap powders or breakfast cereals, or to limit the damage to other products if one product has a problem. However, this will not use the goodwill built up by the current brand name and will be an expensive strategy as each of the individual brands will need its own marketing.

New branding

This is where new products are launched under different brands. Again, this will limit the damage if one of the new products receives bad publicity, but it will be expensive to market the different brands.

In H's situation, it would seem sensible to use the goodwill and reputation for quality that has been built up in its existing products. Multi-branding and new branding would be very expensive in terms of the marketing needed for the various products. Instead, H should concentrate on expanding its range within the same brand name, using line extension and brand extension. The only danger is that poor-quality products will impact on the brand name and hence on all other products, so H must monitor and control the quality of production very carefully.

Finally, the brand strategy must be consistent with the company's strategic objectives and the general business strategy to maintain competitive advantage in the market place.

Question 4   GC conglomerate

(a) Competitive position

Applying the Boston Consulting Group (BCG) Matrix to GC's portfolio of interests:

Market growth		Stars	Problem children
	High	Software	Painting
		Cash cows	Dogs
	Low	Food	Brick and parcels
		High	Low

Market share

Two of the operations, bricks and parcel carriage, are low shares in a static market. There seems little prospect of increasing market share and in the face of increasing competition and declining margins, they are likely to see profits fall further.

The painting and decorating market has enjoyed some growth but GC predict that this will now slow down. Even in a growing market with continual cash injections for 3 years, GC are not making any profits, so it is unlikely that, as the growth in the market slows and the competition gets stronger, they will in the future.

The software development and supply company offers the brightest hope as it is the market leader in a growing market. Both the total market and the market share are expected to grow in the future, but it is likely to need further cash injections in order to take advantage of, and hold its position.

The food manufacturer is the only cash cow, providing cash to help sustain the other operations. Although it is the market leader with high turnover and profitability, the market is forecast to slowly decline. This could cause problems for the group in terms of cashflow, particularly in terms of the funding for the software company.

In conclusion, the success of GC is currently dependent on the computer software development company for future profits and in the continuing ability of the food manufacturer to generate the cash required for investment.

(b) Strategic development

Initially GC should investigate the existence of any synergy between its business units. It is described as a conglomerate and the five businesses described would appear to be completely unrelated, so the possibility of operational synergy seems unlikely.

GC then needs to consider removing some of the poorly performing subsidiaries so that it can concentrate its resources on those areas which are likely to produce results. Looking at each in turn:

Parcel carriage

As the business is well established, and has presumably built a reputation, the subsidiary may be able to increase its market share and maintain its profitability even though the market will flatten and competition increases. Management should look to their customers through differentiating their service, and possibly use the skills of the software company to design tracking systems which competitors may not have.

Brick manufacturer

This has a very small share, compared with the market leader, in a market with very low growth forecast. It does not seem likely that management would be able to differentiate unless they specialised in unusual products. They will therefore, find it difficult to compete against the market leader who will be able to offer bricks at a lower price due to economies of scale. Unless the market increases in size dramatically, in response to a major demand for new houses (as in the South East of the UK), it does not look to be a good continuing investment. The market leader may be interested in purchasing the company to take its share to 28 per cent.

Painting and decorating

The continual cash injections over the past 3 years have not managed to sustain profits and the market growth is now forecast to slow down. This will make it even more difficult to increase market share. The market seems to be very fragmented with the market leader only holding 0.5 per cent. It might be possible to build a reputation for quality and reliability by consolidating a share through acquisitions of other operators. However, painting and decorating has traditionally been carried out by sole traders or very small companies, who have both lower overheads, being often based from home, and a local reputation which homeowners trust. Not only would it therefore be expensive to acquire others, but it might not succeed as a strategy. Overall, GC is probably better disposing of this business unless it can win some more lucrative commercial (as opposed to domestic) contracts.

Food manufacturing

GC enjoys a dominant position in this industry and needs to sustain its cashflow as long as possible. The management might look at expanding into food manufacturing for other markets besides the domestic household consumption in order to keep its current economics of scale. Organisations such as large schools, hospitals and hotels could be approached given its current market share and reputation in the domestic market.

Software development and supply

This is the only business in a market forecast to grow, but the software industry is notoriously volatile and fast changing due to the rapid developments in technology. It is therefore likely to need continual cash injections in order to maintain its position as market leader, given that its closest rival has 8 per cent of the market (compared to GC's 10 per cent). GC needs to study the market and the probable life cycle carefully to ensure that it will eventually make good profits in the near future as the market grows.

Strategy in IT

8

✎ Exam focus

Information systems can play a key role in the strategic direction of a company. Systems can be developed which provide high quality information to make better decisions, improve the quality of service offered, reduce costs, improve and measure performance, produce better products, facilitate distribution and enable better management of key areas such as human resources and marketing.

⚷ Key points

Where do we want to be?

Business strategy
↓
Critical success factors (CSF)
↓
Key business information

How are we going to get there?

Information systems (IS) strategy
↓
Information technology (IT) strategy
↓
Information management (IM) strategy

The Information Systems (IS) strategy sets out to provide a long-term direction for the development of information systems throughout the organisation. Having a formal, documented, planned IS strategy is important for the following reasons:

– Opportunity to gain competitive advantage
– Focused IT expenditure (which can be very high)
– IS are critical to some organisations, so it must be planned and organised

- Opportunity to reduce costs and gain efficiencies
- Many stakeholders are affected
- New systems take a long time to develop so need long-term planning
- Rapid changes in IT lead to constant opportunities and threats
- Compatibility of systems throughout the organisation.

The IT strategy is concerned with the development and maintenance of hardware and software to facilitate the overall IS strategy (e.g. to provide the required information).

The IM strategy outlines how the organisation will control and manage information in the organisation. It includes the IT function, financial control, technology development and planning.

Critical success factors

These are the key areas in which the organisation has to do well if they are to remain competitive and profitable. They should flow directly from the organisation's strategy; so, for example, an organisation growing through a strategy of buying lots of other companies will need to excel at effectively merging the joint operations. No more than 4–5 CSFs are usually defined for each organisation so that they are focused on the key points.

For each CSF the key business information required by the organisation to ensure the success in each of these areas can be defined. This can be identified by key performance indicators or by key decisions.

Data warehousing and data mining

A data warehouse is a database with a reporting and query tool, that stores current and historical data extracted from various transaction processing systems and consolidated for management reporting and analysis. They can store very large quantities of data.

Data mining is a technique which analyses large amounts of data (e.g. in a data warehouse) to find patterns and rules that can be used by an organisation to guide decision-making and predict future behaviour.

Real-life examples of use of data mining include:

Retail/Marketing	Finding buying patterns
	Predicting customer responses to advertising
Banking	Identifying patterns of fraud
	Identifying loyal customers
	Predicting customers likely to change credit card companies
	Learning associations amongst customer demographics
	Identifying stock trading rules from historical market data
Insurance and health care	Performing claims analysis (what claims are filed together)
	Learning patterns of behaviours of risky customers
Internet marketing	Targeting of advertisements
	Personalisation of web pages
	Association of items viewed or purchased together
	Segmentation of groups sharing common characteristics
	Prediction of future behaviour

Questions

Question 1 A and B strategies

A and B are complementary companies in the engineering industry. Each manufactures a range of components which are sold to the following types of customer.

- Large assembly companies which take big quantities and constitute around 60 per cent of each company's turnover.
- Wholesalers and agents who constitute around 30 per cent of each company's turnover.
- Direct sales to the general public who take the remainder.

As A and B have such similar markets and customers and they also employ identical technologies, they have decided to merge. As part of the process, they have conducted a review of their information systems. They each employ the following systems: CAD/CAM, stock control, financial and management accounting (including sales analysis, profit forecasting, budgetary control and annual and five year planning).

In each company these systems are computer-based. However, the organisation of computing within the companies is very different.

Company A has the following arrangements for its computing. It utilises a mainframe computer which uses "off the shelf" software packages to perform batch processing. User departments are charged a standard cost per hour for all the tasks performed for them and are not allowed to use external computing resources. The company's budget for hardware and software acquisition and for operational requirements is controlled by the computing manager, who is directly responsible to the Chief Executive.

Company B's computer strategy is "to empower the user". The company's early experience was with a system very similar to A's. However, 5 years ago it was decided to devolve the computing budget to functional managers. These managers were given the freedom to spend their computer budgets wherever and however they liked. This has led to most computing now being down on Personal Computers using "bespoke" or "user written" packages. A small amount of work, mainly of a developmental nature, is carried out on B's behalf by external agencies. There are no longer any centralised computing facilities, but there is a small number of computer staff who can be hired to give advice on users' requirements.

Requirements

(a) Discuss the advantages and disadvantages of the two computer strategies in A and B.

(8 marks)

(b) State which of these strategies you would recommend for monthly Management Accounting procedures. Justify your recommendation.

(7 marks)

(c) Suggest a computing strategy for the new company, if A and B were to merge. Explain your suggestion.

(10 marks)
(Total = 25 marks)

Question 2 RR university

The RR University provides tuition to degree level to 12,000 students, both on campus and by distance learning courses. The University has 34 different departments, each specialises in one specific area, such as economics, geography or astronomy.

Over the past 10 years, information systems have been developed in each department to meet the specific needs of that department. However, the systems are incompatible with each other and use a wide range of software applications.

The information systems are becoming expensive to operate, as well as requiring duplication of input where students study in more than one department. Additional duplication occurs when student details have to be entered into the central University database, which is used for monitoring total student numbers.

The Board of Management of the University has decided that the University should develop and implement an integrated database for future information requirements and place all existing data into a single data warehouse.

Moreover, any new system must meet the information requirements of the central database as well as those of the individual departments.

Requirements

(a) (i) Evaluate the use of data within the University.

(7 marks)

(ii) Explain how the Board of Management should use Critical Success Factors (CSFs) in revising the current information system.

(8 marks)

(b) Discuss the disadvantages of data warehousing with specific reference to the situation at the RR University.

(10 marks)
(Total = 25 marks)

Question 3 SI organisation

Background
The SI organisation builds and sells computers in 35 different countries. A customer can order a computer by telephone, mail order or the Internet. The computer is then built to the customer's specification using parts manufactured by SI or supplied from one of 86 different suppliers. The completed computer is then shipped to the customer and installed by SI technicians. The whole process takes between five and seven days.

Following installation, the customer is given access to the country-specific support system of SI. This comprises a country-specific Internet site containing detailed information on installation, errors with SI computers and answers to Frequently Asked Questions. The errors database is the same as that used by SI staff, so customers are effectively being given access to SI own systems. Technical staff are also available to provide human assistance if customers cannot find the answer to a query within the other support systems.

Databases are maintained in each country and contain information on the different customers, types of computer sold, queries raised and solutions to those queries, along with standard accounting and financial data.

No other computer manufacturer provides this type of service. Most other manufacturers prefer to sell computers via retail stores on the assumption that customers wish to "try out" the computers prior to purchase. This strategy of differentiation from competitors has provided SI with a substantial market share, along with significant profits. Customers are prepared to pay for the enhanced service. SI's distribution costs are slightly less than those of its competitors although selling prices are the same, providing additional contribution for SI.

SI organisation structure

Within each country, the SI organisation is run as a separate company. Each company has its own unique information system, resulting in a range of hardware, software and database formats being used. Although this is unusual, the philosophy of SI has been to allow each country to establish systems to meet its own individual requirements. This has resulted in an extremely successful SI company in each country, at the expense of worldwide compatibility.

Similarly, local suppliers supply parts for SI computers, so the SI company in that country can form good working relationships with the suppliers. Again, this has worked to the benefit of SI, as the quality of parts supplied has consistently exceeded expectations and resulted in fewer hardware failures in SI computers compared to other brands.

Each SI company is therefore run as a separate business unit. The head office of SI is located on a small island close to Western Europe. Budgets for each SI company are set after discussions with head office. Apart from this, as long as each company meets budget, no other intervention by SI's head office is considered necessary.

There is a centralised R&D unit, which provides model specifications for new SI computers to all locations. This unit employs 75 research and developmental specialists. Their main activities include:

- Research into existing SI products in order to make them more reliable and economical to run;
- Amending existing SI products incorporating minor design changes such as larger hard disks or additional RAM;
- Reviewing current developments in computing;
- Building and testing new products;
- Providing specifications for new SI computers to the individual SI companies in each country.

Information is provided by the R&D unit on a regular basis to sales and other departments in SI. However, the information flow is one way. The R&D unit does not have access to the sales staff of databases within each SI company.

Recent developments

In the last few years, the sales pattern of SI has shifted significantly away from individual customers purchasing one or two computers, to larger organisations purchasing up to 1,000 computers at a time. These requirements cannot always be met by the production capacity in one SI company, so orders are transferred to other SI companies in other countries.

Many customers also request additional support, including 24 hour telephone hotlines and access to worldwide databases of errors and information, which SI currently cannot provide. The Chief Executive of SI recently made a decision to provide this support, effectively authorising a worldwide network to be put in place to link all SI companies. All accounting, customer, financial, support and similar databases are to be linked within one year. Failure to meet this target may result in significant loss of sales if the larger corporate customers move to other suppliers.

Requirements

(a) Explain Porter's concepts of differentiation and cost leadership

(6 marks)

(b) Using Porter's differentiation and cost leadership concepts as a framework for your answer, discuss whether the recent decision of the Chief Executive of SI will detract from the overall customer-focus strategy of SI.

(14 marks)
(Total = 20 marks)

Question 4 SDW

The SDW Company has been trading for one year. It provides rail travel services between three major cities in the country in which it operates.

Mr M, the majority shareholder and Managing Director, is keen to expand its operations and, in particular, to use the Internet as the major selling medium. He has discovered, for example, that doubling sales on the Internet usually results in no additional costs. However, doubling sales using a call centre normally results in a doubling of staff and an increase in costs.

All tickets are currently sold via the company's call centre. The company has an Internet site although this is used for publicity only, not for sales or marketing. Competitors currently use a mixture of selling media, although detailed information on the success of each medium is not available to the SDW Company.

Mr M has asked you, as a qualified management accountant, to assist him in upgrading the company's Internet site and, in particular, showing how this will help to reduce operating costs.

Requirements

(a) Advise Mr M on how to establish and implement an appropriate Internet strategy for the SDW Company.

(13 marks)

(b) Discuss the key customer-orientated features of an Internet site, showing how these can be used to meet the objective of cost reduction required by Mr M.

(12 marks)
(Total marks = 25)

✓ Answers

Question 1 A and B strategies

(a) Comparison of systems

The main difference between the two computer strategies is that one has a centralised system and the other has a decentralised system. In more detail, the advantages of each system are as follows:

A centralised system (A's system)

- This gives consistency in actions in the data processing.
- This will lead to a standardisation of systems, hardware, software and communication, which should reduce costs of purchase due to economies of scale.
- The company could employ a select number of specialists who will have more expertise than the general employees.
- These experts could act as trouble-shooters for the rest of the organisation when they have computer problems.
- As the systems are centralised, there is likely to be more security and control over the processing.
- Company A also uses batch processing which enables the company to build in even stronger controls.

A decentralised system (B's system)

- Any problems in the software of processing in a centralised system would affect the entire business, whereas a problem in a decentralised system would be in an isolated area, and possibly would leave the rest of the business unaffected.
- The system would involve the end-users, who have a better understanding of what is required from that system.
- As the system probably uses personal computers, which are popular and user-friendly, it enables the operational managers to design their own data requirements.
- As the operational areas input the data, real time processing will be possible which means the information accessed will be more up-to-date.
- It will enable managers to have a shared database which can be accessed by the entire company.
- It will help users and operational managers to improve their IT skills, which may be motivating.

(b) Management Accounting Information System (MAIS)

Any MAIS has to support the managers in planning, decision-making and control. Its design therefore needs to take into account the exact information requirements of the managers. In particular, the level of detail, the speed, the level of accuracy and the cost of the information need to be considered.

The system also needs to be flexible enough to change in line with the changing needs of the business, which will be operating in a changing business environment.

More senior management will be making decisions based on a number of factors; the MAIS needs to accumulate and synthesise the data from a variety of sources within the business. At the strategic level, this data needs to include information on the external business environment, such as the actions of competitors and changes in the demand level. This might mean a connection to external business databases.

Without more detailed information about the business, it is difficult to say whether these needs would be better served by a centralised or decentralised system. The points raised above on the data requirements, the cost and the accuracy would tend to suggest a centralised system.

(c) Alternative computer strategies

There are three possible courses of action – adopt one of the systems, continue with both systems in the individual companies, or combine the two into one overall system. Taking each in turn:

1 *Adopt one of the systems.* This would mean choosing between the systems, both of which have advantages and disadvantages as discussed in (a). In addition, it would possibly be demotivating for those staff who were used to the system that was abandoned, as well as introducing the need for training.
2 *Run separate systems.* It is likely that this will happen in the short-term, as it will take time and resources to draw up an information system strategy. This will mean that staff are accustomed to their own systems, but in the long-term may mean duplication and certainly will contribute to a lack of integration of the two businesses.
3 *Combined systems.* A compromise system could try to use the advantages of both systems. A centralised mainframe, with the associated security and controls over processing, could be combined with a decentralised system of personal computers linked to the mainframe. Information could be processed in real time so that databases are up-to-date, while end-users can also use their terminals as stand alone computers for particular software applications.

The centralised mainframe could produce the routine reports for managers, while IT specialists would be available to help individual departments with their particular IT projects.

Finally, economics of scale in purchasing software and hardware could still be enjoyed if purchase requests are accumulated and placed by the central IT department. However, it may be very difficult to integrate the two systems and a careful study should be undertaken of the likely cost and feasibility before starting on such a project.

Question 2 RR university

(a) (i) Data use at university

There are serious problems with the use of data at RR University. These include:

- The various different systems in use are not compatible so that data cannot be transferred between them. Although the transfer of some data may be restricted, this will also stop the useful transfer of administrative information.
- The maintenance of a number of different systems will be more expensive, involving more staff and more expensive purchase costs for the different hardware and software.

- There will be duplication of data in the different department systems which mean that there has been an inefficient use of time in inputting the data twice into different systems.

However, the systems would appear to be providing the information that each department needs, so staff may not see the need for a major change. More senior university managers are likely to need information from a variety of systems, so that an integrated system would be more useful.

(ii) In order to redesign the systems, it would be sensible for the Board of Management to consider the Critical Success Factors (CSFs) which give the areas on which the Board require monitoring information. At the moment the systems appear to satisfy the needs of the individual departments but not those of the university as a whole.

Any new system must build in the CSFs of each department and the university so that appropriate performance indicators can be identified. A comparison can be made between the information produced by the current systems and that which is required. The systems can then be adjusted or new systems developed to close this information group.

(b) Data warehousing

A data warehouse would combine and store data from all the different departments. This can then be accessed by a variety of departments and by the Board. This will mean that data only has to be input once and is clearly more efficient.

There are however, disadvantages for the university in trying to introduce a data warehouse. These include:

- Writing the different reports required by the different departments will take some time and resources.
- It may involve buying new hardware and software for the new system and training for the users of the new system.
- The data is currently stored in different formats in the different departments, so that amendments will be necessary before it can be stored in a common format in the warehouse.
- The warehouse will contain valuable data for the university, so that backup systems will be needed to ensure that the system can be recreated if necessary.
- The warehouse needs to be capable of expansion as new reports and new data is required in the future.

Question 3   SI organisation

Competitive advantage

Competitive advantage can be maintained or enhanced in the long term by differentiation or by cost leadership.

Differentiation involves providing a product or service that is sufficiently different from that of the competitors, either in itself or in the manner it is delivered, that customers are prepared to pay extra. Examples might include a personalised product or service, the quality of the product, or a brand name.

Cost leadership concentrates on driving the costs down without impacting on the quality of the good or service, so that the price to the customer can be reduced. This is likely to mean an increase in volume in order to enjoy economies of scale in purchasing, production and distribution and marketing, so that the cost structure is lower than that of competitors.

SI's current strategy

SI currently concentrates on differentiation as a means of maintaining its competitive advantage. It does this by selling computers direct to the public which are built to individual customer requirements.

The Chief Executive is suggesting that customer support is centralised. This will help larger corporate customers as they will then be able to access information on all SI's computers. As this is not currently available, it will enhance the service and possibly further differentiate the service if SI's competitors do not provide such a service. Smaller businesses may find it more awkward that locally based information and expertise is no longer available, which may reduce the differentiation of SI in their eyes. SI will need to be careful that, for these smaller businesses, local information can still be accessed easily within the system.

It could be argued that this is starting to change the focus of SI's strategy to a cost leadership one as a centralised support system may be viewed as an attempt to reduce costs. However, it is unlikely that costs will be substantially lower given that a system will have to be developed. It is more likely to be differentiating SI's service from those of its competitors, or matching the service of its competitors in this area. The decision therefore does not appear to change the differentiation strategy of SI.

Question 4 SDW

(a) Establishing and Implementing an Internet Strategy

Before Mr M establishes an internet strategy, he should consider his overall business strategy as any IT strategy must support the overall business strategy rather than driving it. In the case of SDW this does not appear to be the case as developing e-commerce on the Web site is likely to complement the existing strategy; however, it is important that the implementation does not cause problems in other areas of the business.

Establishing the Strategy

There are a number of issues that need to be considered before starting the implementation:

Is the booking system going to be an addition to the current site or will it involve designing a new site? This may require expert advice, with an eye to possible future developments, and will probably need expertise from outside the company in web design.

Mr M should try to obtain as much information as possible about the sites of competitors and any other sites which are related to the travel industry. He needs to look closely at what features are useful and which are not and at how user-friendly the site is.

The introduction of e-commerce may have an impact on the rest of the business and SDW needs to anticipate this and have plans in place for dealing with the changes necessary. For example, it is hoped that it will lead to less use made of the call centre so staff must be kept informed of the plans and how the surplus staff in the call centre will be retrained and redeployed into other areas of the business.

Implementing the Strategy

A budget for the implementation and the operation of the new system needs to be prepared, including envisaged cost savings in other parts of the business. A cost-benefit exercise could be undertaken and this could form the basis of monitoring performance and costs.

In looking at other sites, Mr M should try to identify what areas give the competitors any advantage over SDW and think what features would be needed in SDW's own site.

Decisions will have to be made on the pricing structure for bookings made on the website. To encourage bookings it is likely that some kind of discount will be given, which can be a proportion of the envisaged saved costs through using this method of booking.

In order to attract customers to the website, the company will need to advertise its existence and promote the new pricing structure. Thought needs to be given as to where to advertise the service and how much should be spent on such a campaign. Possibilities might include e-mail, writing to existing customers, information given out at the call centre, details printed on tickets or other Web sites.

(b) Key Customer-orientated Features

The following features would be customer-orientated, while focusing on cost reduction:

The site should be easy to understand and quick to load. This will probably mean fewer graphics to provide a cleaner look, which will also cut down on the programming costs.

Providing a list of frequently asked questions (FAQs) with answers will often cut down on the number of calls to the company with questions. In the same way a good help system which guides users through their transaction will cut down the cost of expensive help-desk staff.

Other incentives to book on the Web site, such as cheaper prices or the ability to book earlier than by any other means would all encourage sales to flow via the website, which in turn will save costs in the call centre of staffing and equipment.

Other services, such as suggesting short stay destinations on a limited budget might encourage customers to browse the Web site for ideas and produce additional sales.

Impact on the Organisation 9

✏️ Exam focus

You need to be able to advise organisations on the advantages and disadvantages of reorganising in terms of the impact on their strategy and hence whether it will help them achieve their objectives.

🔑 Key points

Types of organisational structure

Functional structure

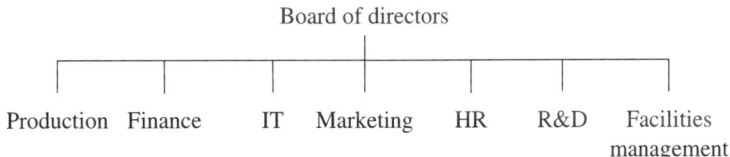

Advantages	Disadvantages
Functional expertise enables specific tasks to be done well	Poor communication between functions
Control is gained over key activities through clear responsibilities being assigned	Lack of goal congruence. People start acting for the benefit of their function not the organisation as a whole

Divisional structure

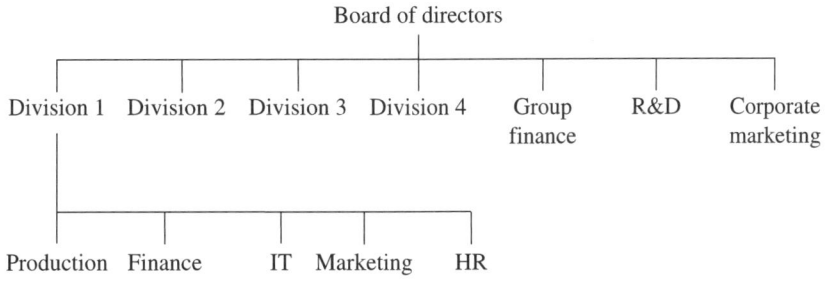

101

Each division has its own functional areas. Some functions may be managed centrally for the whole organisation (e.g. R&D in the structure above) while others have a function in both the division and for the group as a whole (e.g. finance and marketing).

Advantages	Disadvantages
Product/area/customer specialism	Poor communication between divisions
Performance management is easier and clear responsibilities for different sections	Lack of goal congruence. People act for the benefit of their division not the organisation as a whole
Develops managers	Repetition of work in each division

Matrix structure

In a matrix structure each employee has two areas of responsibility. In the example below each employee has responsibility to their functional area and customer team.

This allows the individual to retain their functional expertise, while concentrating on the needs of their customer, and working in a team with people from other functions also serving that customer.

These axes could also be swapped for area, product, or project expertise in any combination. In a consulting firm for instance people from different divisions (say IT, strategy and risk management) may join a project team to ensure the right expertise for the needs of the project. In a multinational firm with several distinct products you might have both an area and product responsibility.

```
                    Marketing    Finance    Production    Design
Customer A  ────────────┼───────────┼───────────┼───────────┼────────

Customer B  ────────────┼───────────┼───────────┼───────────┼────────

Customer C  ────────────┼───────────┼───────────┼───────────┼────────

Customer D  ────────────┼───────────┼───────────┼───────────┼────────
```

Advantages	Disadvantages
Retains expertise in two areas (e.g. functional and customer focus in the diagram above)	Higher administrative costs
Good teamwork and communication between people from different divisions/functions now in the same team	Each employee has two bosses and two areas of responsibility causing confusion and conflict

Centralisation

Centralisation is where the majority of decisions are made by senior management or by a centralised function, rather than by divisional or lower level managers. For example, if IT decision-making were centralised a single IT function would make all IT related decisions. The divisional or lower level managers act to carry out the wishes of the senior management or centralised function.

Advantages:

- Co-ordination between divisions.
- Decisions will be consistent with overall organisational objectives.
- Costs can be reduced by avoiding duplication of tasks (e.g. each divisional manager researching and negotiating their own deals on IT).
- Standardised processes ensure consistency of approach throughout the organisation.

Advantages of decentralised operations:

- Divisional expertise applied to make decisions appropriate to product/customer/local area
- Motivating for lower level managers
- Quick decisions
- Develops staff
- Senior management are free to concentrate on strategic issues.

Organisations can use a mixture of both a centralised and decentralised approach for different decisions. For example, IT might be centralised to create a consistent approach and save costs, while marketing might be decentralised, as it needs to be targeted at local customers.

Business process re-engineering

BPR starts with the desired outcomes, as stated in our objectives, and looks at the entire business process, particularly those areas in which an activity is repeated continuously. It then may completely redesign the operations to improve quality, cost and speed and may change organisational structures, job designs and control systems by considering those activities, which add value, and those that do not.

The seven principles of re-engineering are:

- Organise around outcomes not tasks.
- Those who use the output should perform the process.
- Information processing should be part of the real work and not a separate function.
- Access geographically dispersed resources as centrally held databases.
- Link parallel activities instead of integrating them into larger departments.
- Decisions should be made where the work is performed but build controls into the process.
- Only input information once at source.

Questions

Question 1 X restructuring

X plc has in recent years been forced to restructure. It has considerably reduced its size, as its former main business in electrical engineering has largely become obsolete because of technological advance. There remains a sound but much smaller business in specialist electronic equipment.

This electronics business, like the former electrical one, is a global business, with manufacturing, service and sales in a large number of countries. Operations in different countries vary in size. Some undertake sales and servicing and may have fewer than 10 employees, others manufacture and may employ up to 200 people.

Head office structures, procedures and control systems still reflect a much larger, stable, prosperous past. The detailed systems of planning, budgeting and reporting, with a requirement for head office approval for a wide range of actions, reflect a "financial control" style of management. The current requirement is for a control system to match a smaller, fast-changing business.

Requirements

To explain and justify the minimum central control system required to ensure that effective control is maintained in the global business. Your explanation should:

(a) Specify the decisions which will be retained for head office

(6 marks)

(b) Describe the minimum reporting system required for control

(4 marks)

(c) State the criteria for the performance evaluation of individual country operations and their managers

(5 marks)

(d) Discuss the main problems anticipated in evaluating the performance of individual country operations and those of their managers.

(5 marks)
(Total = 20 marks)

Question 2 Outsourcing

(a) Explain why an organisation may outsource some of its primary or support activities.

(7 marks)

(b) The directors of AB plc are facing increasing pressure from shareholders to increase earnings per share. The overhead costs of the company have increased as a proportion of total cost over the last 3 years and the directors are considering outsourcing the financial accounting, payroll, creditor payments and debtors functions in order to reduce the levels of operational gearing. However, the directors are concerned that AB plc will not receive the same level of service from these functions after they have been outsourced.

Impact on the Organisation

Requirements

(i) Summarise how AB should proceed to outsource the financial accounting, payroll, creditor payments and debtor functions.

(8 marks)

(ii) Discuss how the directors may be assured of the quality of the service which is subsequently received for these activities.

(5 marks)
(Total = 20 marks)

Question 3 J organisation

The J Company is engaged in providing management services to a wide variety of customers. Services provided include accountancy, payroll, resource planning, recruitment, information management and financial planning. While the J Company has achieved profitability overall, its directors are concerned that they do not have adequate control over all of the management services it provides. The J Company is structured along formal functional lines with a director responsible for each service provided. Increasingly, customers require a more comprehensive service in which the functional boundaries which the J Company has established in its structure are crossed. The directors now consider that the functional structure which is currently employed no longer enables the J Company to service its customers' needs effectively.

Requirements

(a) Discuss the problems of the current structure.

(10 marks)

(b) Recommend an organisational structure for the J Company which enables it to meet its customer needs more effectively and allows the directors to evaluate managerial performance.

(15 marks)
(Total = 25 marks)

Answers

Question 1 X restructuring

The restructured organisation will need to change the way in which it is managed, both in terms of devolving control and reporting.

(a) Devolving control

The organisation will want to have a more participative approach to management and to delegate both day-to-day operational and strategic planning and control.

Overseas businesses could form strategic business units (SBUs) which would then formulate their own strategic plans. This is likely to produce more appropriate strategies, given that they will be facing different business environments in the different countries. There may be still some global objectives set by head office, which could be adapted to the local situation.

It is likely that head office would continue to manage those services and policies which either benefit from economies of scale or could not be managed by the individual SBUs because international consistency is required. This might include treasury management, international data systems and management, environmental and social policies (given multinationals' sensitivities to accusations of unethical behaviour) and intellectual property management. This last one is particularly important in the electronics business, which depends on innovation to maintain a competitive advantage.

(b) **Reporting**

Head office will need regular reports detailing the SBUs' actions. Initially, the SBUs will need to report and agree the objectives and strategic plans for their regions as well as the performance indicators to monitor progress towards these objectives.

Once these have been agreed, the SBU will need to report regularly, probably monthly, on a variety of performance targets which relate to the strategic objectives. These need to look at both financial and non-financial, short- and long-term indicators, and can be combined in a balanced i.e. scorecard.

(c) **Criteria**

Such a balanced scorecard might include financial, customer, internal and innovation considerations. Typical financial measures would include ROCE or Residual Income along with profit margins and cost control elements; internal issues might look at the quality of production and the efficiency of the operations; customer considerations would consider the level of customer satisfaction, market share and level of sales. Innovation encompasses the number of new products introduced and improvements in the manufacturing process.

(d) **Main Problems**

A multinational company may have problems in evaluating SBUs as:

- Taxation can vary dramatically between jurisdictions, which can distort the profits reported.
- Governments may interfere in the markets so that the prices are controlled.
- Exchange rates may affect the profits reported.
- Cultural differences may make some of the more qualitative measures more difficult to compare across SBUs.

Question 2 Outsourcing

(a) Reasons for outsourcing

An organisation may feel that some support activities distract attention from its core activities. It may be worthwhile paying others to carry out these services, and benefiting from their economies of scale via the price charged, and devoting more resources to the main business.

In addition, it may free up other resources such as space, as well as avoiding long-term employment contracts.

The organisation which undertakes the work will have expertise in the area, and is likely to carry out the work more efficiently and effectively.

(b) AB outsourcing procedures

 (i) The directors first need to establish their objectives with regard to the outsourcing Once these have been established, the likely costs and benefits, both financial and non-financial, of outsourcing the different functions need to be assessed against these objectives.

 The main aim appears to be driving down costs to increase earnings per share, but the directors need to consider more than just the short-term cost saving that may be achieved through outsourcing. There will need to be some monitoring of the service provided, and the cheapest provider may have longer-term costs to the business, such as deteriorating relations with customers due to insensitive handling of debtors.

 When assessing the outsourcing bids, the directors should therefore balance a range of measures, such as:

 - Cost
 - Evidence of quality work and reputation
 - Ethical behaviour (given the sensitive nature of the financial information)
 - Competence.

 (ii) To be assured of the quality of the service, the directors need to specify measures that would indicate the quality and set targets in these areas within the contract. These will then need to be monitored, possibly by internal audit, to ensure that AB is getting the service promised. A wider review would encompass the economy, effectiveness and efficiency of the operations to ensure they are getting value for money.

Question 3 J organisation

(a) Current structure and problems

J Company is currently structured along functional lines. Although this can take various forms, it appears that J divide the services provided into separate areas, each of which is run by a director.

This structure has a number of benefits, in that it allows specialisation within an area, leading to less mistakes and higher quality. It also allows for easy delegation of duties and responsibilities within a closely defined sphere of operation, making evaluation of managerial performance relatively straightforward. The gradual change in client requirements means that this structure now has some weaknesses. As clients require a service which crosses functional lines, the specialisation of staff and managers, who only know one service well, becomes a problem, as they are unable to discuss all the requirements with a client. In addition, assessing performance on a functional basis becomes a problem as client revenues and associated costs are spread across a range of functional areas.

(b) Possible new structure

There is no one structure which will solve all the problems for J, but one possibility is a matrix structure. In this type of organisation, although staff stay broadly within specialised functions, the company forms client orientated cross-discipline teams headed by client managers. The client manager can then assess the overall requirements of a client and access the different functions, via the designated member of the client team, as appropriate. This will give the client a more comprehensive service and allow the team members and the client manager more of an overview of the operations and hence be more flexible and responsive to client needs.

Managerial performance assessment could be much more closely linked to how well the client manager has managed to meet the customer requirements, as all revenues and costs could be accumulated for the managers' client portfolio and compared to a budget.

An administrative problem would be assessing the cost of the various functions. If the managers in charge of the service areas are also to be assessed, there will need to be some kind of recharging of costs between the functional areas and the client teams. This can sometimes lead to a complex recharging system.

The other main problem is the confusion that can be caused by giving staff a number of different managers – both functional and client-based. This can be overcome by careful planning and clear instructions on priorities for the individual's own time management, as there will be no one manager that has a complete picture of an individual's workload. Training might, therefore, be necessary.

Control and Performance Measurement

10

✏️ Exam focus

You need to be able to calculate and talk sensibly about possible performance measures for an organisation.

🔑 Key points

Shareholder value analysis

In practice the information shareholders have is limited, and many of the estimates will be very rough approximations. Traditionally, managers were rewarded for producing strong profits, but this often led to short-term behaviour and did not necessarily result in a high share price.

Shareholder Value Analysis (SVA) tried to reward managers for improving the share price by identifying seven factors under the control of the management which influenced the share price:

- Sales growth
- Profit margin
- Marginal cash tax-rate
- Investment needed in fixed assets
- Investment needed in working capital
- Cost of capital (to reflect risk)
- The competitive advantage period.

Various performance models have been developed to set objectives and reward managers accordingly.

Economic Value Added (EVA) takes the profit before interest and takes off tax and then the return required by shareholders (the cost of capital applied to long-term debt and equity). This gives the excess over the shareholders' expectations and should lead to an increase in the share price. Expenses such as R&D, advertising and goodwill are often capitalised and amortised over a number of years to reflect the longer-term benefits derived from them.

Financial assessment of divisions

The two most common financial measures both use the profit generated in the period and the value of the investment in the division.

$$\text{Return on Investment (ROI)} = \frac{\text{Profit}}{\text{Investment}}$$

Residual Income (RI) = Profit − Notional interest on investment

ROI gives a percentage while RI is an absolute figure in £.

Investment will be net assets, either at the beginning or end of the period in question, depending on how the value being compared has been calculated.

RI builds in the target return as an interest charge so any positive RI is welcome; the ROI has to be compared to some target return.

If RI has interest equal to the cost of capital, the PV of the Residual Incomes = NPV of the project.

Problems

- ROI, in particular, can cause divisional managers to take decisions that may not be in the best interests of the company, as they are likely to compare any new investments returns to the return currently being achieved rather than with an absolute company standard.
- Both ROI and RI suffer from being annual short-term measures. Many investments, when the calculations are based on an investment base including depreciated assets, show a poor return in early years and a higher return later.
- No one financial measure (either ROI or RI) can summarise successfully a division's performance. We need a collection of financial and non-financial measures, both short and long term, to assess this.

There needs to be a balance between having enough measures to control the most important aspects of the business without having too many to be sensibly managed. It is important to form a rounded impression of the performance of the organisation, which encompasses past and future, short and long term, and financial and non-financial areas.

Kaplan and Norton designed the balanced scorecard, which emphasises four distinct "perspectives" of the business.

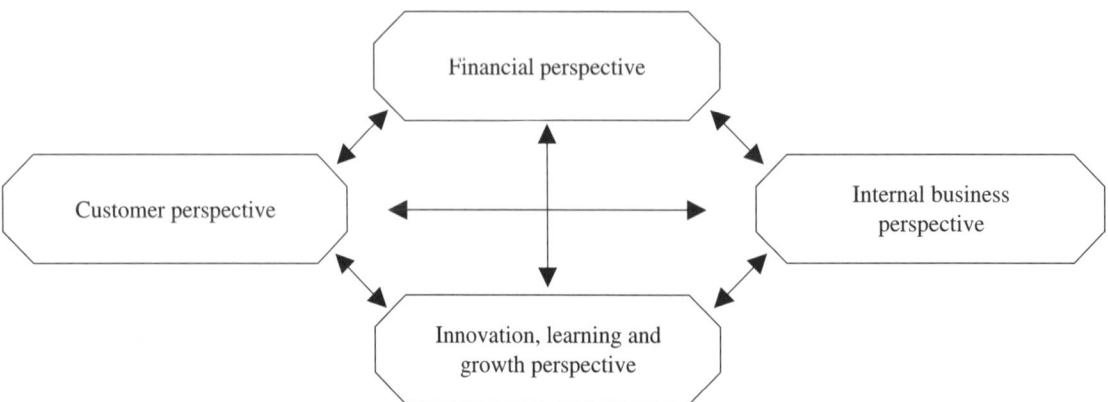

Typical goals and measures in each perspective might be:

Perspective	Goals	Possible measures
Financial	Success Wealth Survival	Sales and profit growth Returns on equity, share price Cash and profits
Customer	Flexibility Quality Expansion	On time deliveries Customer views Percentage of new product sales
Internal business	Product development Efficiency	Introduction timescales Costs and time taken
Innovation, learning and growth	Product range focus Innovation	Spread of sales across products Number of new products

The dimensions of a service business

Fitzgerald and Moon realised that a service business cannot store services for later sale and delivers a slightly different service every time. They therefore felt that the key areas or "dimensions" for a service business were:

- Financial performance
- Competitiveness (performance against the competition)
- Quality
- Flexibility (in delivering what customers require)
- Resource utilisation
- Innovation (to attract and keep customers).

Performance pyramid

Lynch and Cross looked at how to set targets in order to ensure consistency throughout the organisation and to help organisations improve their information systems. They therefore start with the corporate vision, and translate that into targets for both market action and financial results for business units. Market action in turn depends on the systems in place for customer satisfaction and flexibility; these can be measured in departments by looking at quality, delivery and cycle time.

In other words, the balance of performance indicators for departments is given by the four areas at the bottom of the pyramid, but the measures used and the targets set are consistent with the overall corporate vision.

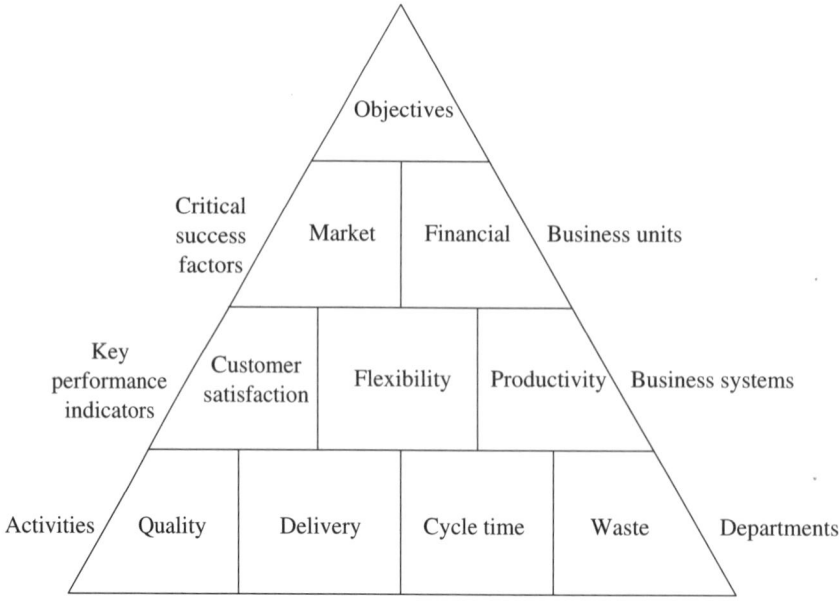

The performance pyramid (adapted from McNair, Lynch and Cross, 1990)

Questions

Question 1 Division X

Division X is in a stable market. The first draft of its plan for the next 3 years is regarded as unacceptable to group management because it shows a slow decline in profit and return on investment.

	Year 1 £m	Year 2 £m	Year 3 £m
Profit before interest and tax (PBIT)	3.0	2.7	2.4
Asset base (at beginning of year)	24.0	25.0	26.0

Proposals which may improve the situation in the next 3 years are being discussed; only one can be accepted because of cash limitations. Projects are evaluated with a 10 per cent requirement on investment. These proposed projects are shown below:

(i) *Special purpose machine*

   Capital expenditure in years 1 and 2, followed by operating cash flow in year 3:

Year 1 £m	Year 2 £m	Year 3 £m	NPV £m
−0.5	−0.5	2.0	0.634

(ii) *R&D project*

   Revenue expenditure in years 1 and 2, followed by operating cash flow in year 3:

Year 1 £m	Year 2 £m	Year 3 £m	NPV £m
−1.0	−1.0	4.0	1.269

(iii) *Advertising*

This can be done in each year if required. Each annual campaign costs £1m, but produces additional contributions of £0.4m in the year of the campaign and £1.1m in the subsequent year. A decision has been made to run annual campaigns in years 1 and 2 only. The combined cash flows are

Year 1 £m	Year 2 £m	Year 3 £m	NPV £m
−0.6	+0.5	+1.1	0.694

Managers are currently evaluated on return on investment (ROI) and are paid bonuses when this reaches or exceeds 10 per cent. At 10 per cent ROI the manager of division X will receive 25 per cent of his salary of £50,000 per annum. For each 1 per cent increase in ROI above 10 per cent, and pro rata, he will receive an additional 2.5 per cent of basic salary with an upper bonus limit of 50 per cent of salary for that year.

Thus, for the first draft of the plan, the bonus based on the ROI has been correctly calculated as

	Year 1 £m	Year 2 £m	Year 3 £m
Bonus	£15,625	£13,500	zero

Calculations ignore tax and depreciation. The asset base represents the assets employed in the division at the beginning of each year, and excludes cash balances which are transferred to the group, and is used for the calculation of residual income (RI) and ROI.

Requirements

(a) Calculate the ROI, and the manager's bonus each year for the three alternative proposals. Comment on the effects of the bonus system on the manager's choice of project.

(14 marks)

(b) A proposal is under consideration to change the bonus scheme to 2 per cent of residual income (RI) with a limit of 50 per cent of salary. A 10 per cent rate of interest would be used in the calculation of RI.

For the plan including the special purpose machine, the bonus, based on the RI, has been correctly calculated as:

	Year 1 £m	Year 2 £m	Year 3 £m
Bonus	£12,000	£3,000	£25,000

Requirements

(i) Calculate the RI and bonuses each year, both for the first draft of the plan and for the R&D and advertising alternatives.

(ii) Comment on whether the proposed revised bonus system would influence the manager's choice of project in a different way from that based on the ROI.

(10 marks)

(c) Explain whether the manager's project choices are beneficial to the company, under the current bonus scheme and under the proposed bonus scheme. If not, what would be the requirements for a bonus scheme which would produce better decision-making?

(6 marks)

(d) It has been argued that the debate on the use of ROI and RI is irrelevant, first because Boards, not divisional managers, take the major investment decisions, and secondly because managerial performance should be measured purely on controllable profit. Discuss this statement.

(10 marks)
(Total = 40 marks)

Question 2 Destroying value

The most recent published results for V plc are shown below:

	£m
Profit before tax	13.6
Summary consolidated balance sheet at 31 December	
Fixed assets	137.2
Current assets	137.2
Less: Current liabilities	(95.7)
Net current assets	41.5
Total assets less current liabilities	77.4
Borrowings	(15.0)
Deferred tax provisions	(7.6)
Net assets	54.8
Capital and reserves	54.8

An analyst working for a stockbroker has taken these published results, made the adjustments shown below, and has reported his conclusion that "the management of V plc is destroying value".

Analyst's adjustments to profit before tax:

	£m
Profit before tax	13.6
Add: Interest paid (net)	1.6
R&D (Research and Development)	2.1
Advertising	2.3
Amortisation and goodwill	1.3
Less: Taxation paid	(4.8)
Adjusted profit	16.1

Analyst's adjustments to summary consolidated balance sheet at 31 December:

	£m
Capital and reserves	54.8
Add: Borrowings	15.0
Deferred tax provisions	7.6
R&D	17.4
Advertising	10.5
Goodwill	40.7
Adjusted capital employed	146.0
Required return	17.5
Adjusted profit	16.1
Value destroyed	1.4

The chairman of V plc has obtained a copy of the analyst's report.

Requirements

(a) Explain, as managerial accountant of V plc, in a report to your Chairman, the principles of the approach taken by the analyst. Comment on the treatment of the specific adjustments to R&D, advertising, interest and borrowings and goodwill.

(12 marks)

(b) Having read your report, the Chairman wishes to know which division or divisions are "destroying value", when the current internal statements show satisfactory returns on investment (ROIs). The following summary statement is available:

	Division A (Retail)	Division B (Manufacturing)	Division C (Services)	Head office	Total
Turnover	81.7	63.2	231.8	–	376.7
Profit before interest and tax	5.7	5.6	5.8	(1.9)	15.2
Total assets Less: Current liabilities	27.1	23.9	23.2	3.2	77.4
ROI	21.0%	23.4%	25.0%		

Some of the adjustments made by the analyst can be related to specific divisions:

(i) Advertising relates entirely to Division A (Retail)
(ii) R&D relates entirely to Division B (Manufacturing)
(iii) Goodwill write-offs relate to:
  Division B (Manufacturing) £10.3m
  Division C (Services) £30.4m
(iv) The deferred tax relates to:
  Division B (Manufacturing) £1.4m
  Division C (Services) £6.2m

(v) Borrowings and interest, per division accounts, are

	Division A (Retail) £m	Division B (Manufacturing) £m	Division C (Services) £m	Head office £m	Total £m
Borrowings	–	6.6	6.9	1.5	15.0
Interest paid (received)	(0.4)	0.7	0.9	0.4	1.6

Requirements

To explain, with appropriate comment, in a report to the Chairman, where "value is being destroyed". Your report should include:

- a statement of divisional performance,
- an explanation of any adjustments you make,
- a statement and explanation of the assumptions made, and
- comment on the limitations of the answers reached.

There are 2 marks available for the formats required.

(20 marks)
(Total = 32 marks)

Question 3   M-HK

M-HK provides a passenger ferry service between two large cities separated by the mouth of a major river. The ferries are frequent, well-supported by passengers and cover the distance between the cities in one hour. M-HK also transports passengers and goods by water ferry to other cities located on the river mouth. There are other ferry operators providing services between each of these locations besides M-HK.

Requirements

(a) Explain what strategic information is required by M-HK's management in respect of customer demand, competition, competitiveness and finance in order to plan its future ferry services.

(10 marks)

(b) Using the information in your answer to part (a), discuss the nature of the reports that M-HK's Chartered Management Accountant should provide to M-HK's senior management for operational and strategic planning purposes.

(15 marks)
(Total = 25 marks)

Question 4   Scorecard

It has been said that "the Balanced Scorecard translates mission and strategy into objectives and measures, organised into four perspectives: financial, customer, internal business process and finally learning and growth". Kaplan and Norton developed the balanced scorecard as a means of combining financial control measures with non-financial measures.

Requirement

Critically evaluate the usefulness of the balanced scorecard in assisting organisations, both profit-motivated and not-for-profit, to achieve improvements in their operational performance.

(25 marks)

Question 5 PAL

PAL is a banking group specialising in loans for home purchase. It has a network of shops, cash machines and other outlets in and around the capital city (where it has its headquarters) with all outlets within 70 miles. It monitors interest rates offered by competitors and strives to match or better the lowest rates. This strategy has been successful, but in order to compete more fully, it has introduced a range of additional customer services, including home insurance.

A dedicated unit was established to extend existing benchmarking of price to other aspects of customer requirements. Following a survey, the following factors in addition to price have emerged as being relevant to customers:

- delivery;
- technical content of literature;
- customer service and correspondence.

Requirements

(a) Discuss the use of appropriate performance measures which home insurance could use as part of the proposed competitor benchmarking exercise.

(12 marks)

(b) (i) Analyse the strategies followed by PAL so far.

(8 marks)

(ii) Evaluate the possible effects of actions arising from benchmarking in supporting these strategies.

(5 marks)
(Total = 25 marks)

Question 6 RP manufacturing

Three months ago, the RP Manufacturing Company's Board of Directors surprised the workforce when they announced a radical new strategy. The new "approach" was announced as being "a shared journey to be more responsive to an ever-demanding and fast-moving market while becoming more cost-conscious and thereby profitable". The agenda for the current year was outlined as being:

- To scrutinise all core and other activities and identify potential for cost reduction. Outsourcing should be progressed as a realistic alternative.

- To develop a range of "partner relationships" with customers and suppliers.
- To develop a more flexible, fluid workforce (including multi-skilled, part-time and temporary employees) leading to an organisational restructure.

More recently, the company announced a "comprehensive supply chain management solution" in partnership with a logistics company starting initially with a transport solution.

The Head of Finance has been asked to provide a briefing paper on the implications of these changes for management reporting systems within the RP Manufacturing Company. He has asked for your advice in this matter.

Requirements

(a) Discuss the major callenges posed by the new strategy.

(8 marks)

(b) Given the major changes within the RP Manufacturing Company, explain why traditional management accounting approaches may **not** be appropriate.

(8 marks)

(c) Discuss the likely information demands upon the management accounting function given the changes within the organisation.

(9 marks)
(Total = 25 marks)

Question 7 Financial scandals

Over the past few years, there have been a number of high-profile financial scandals surrounding the reporting of company performance, and the associated role of accountants. As a consequence, organisations have been urged to consider future practice carefully. Some feel that an overemphasis by a company on market expectations and profitability may be detrimental to its long-term well-being. Such thinking has implications for the objectives of a company and the range of performance measures used both externally and internally.

Requirements

(a) Discuss the functions that organisational objectives should fulfil strategically and the main disadvantages of using only profit-related performance measures.

(12 marks)

(b) The balanced scorecard approach has been described as relating an assessment of performance to choice of strategy through four categories of measurement. It is used by many organisations in monitoring performance. Evaluate the use of the balanced scorecard in meeting stakeholder needs and determining objectives.

(13 marks)
(Total = 25 marks)

Question 8 Royal Botanical Gardens

The Royal Botanical Gardens has been established for more than 120 years and has the following mission statement:

The Royal Botanical Gardens belongs to the Nation. Our mission is to increase knowledge and appreciation of plants, their importance and their conservation, by managing and displaying living and preserved collections and through botanical and horticultural research.

Located towards the edge of the city, the Gardens are regularly visited throughout the year by many local families and are an internationally well-known tourist attraction. Despite charging admission it is one the top five visitor attractions in the country. Every year it answers many thousands of enquiries from Universities and research establishments, including pharmaceutical companies from all over the world and charges for advice and access to its collection. Enquiries can range from access to the plant collection for horticultural work, seeds for propagation or samples for chemical analysis to seek novel pharmaceutical compounds for commercial exploitation. It receives an annual grant in aid from Central Government, which is fixed once every five years. The grant in aid is due for review in three years' time.

The Finance Director has decided that, to strengthen its case when meeting the Government representatives to negotiate the grant, the Management Board should be able to present a balanced scorecard demonstrating the performance of the Gardens. He has asked you, the Senior Management Accountant, to assist him in taking this idea forward.

Many members of the board, which consists of eminent scientists, are unfamiliar with the concept of a balanced scorecard.

Requirements

(a) For the benefit of the Management Board, prepare a briefing on the concept of a balanced scorecard, which also analyses its usefulness for The Royal Botanical Gardens.

(10 marks)

(b) Discuss the process you would employ to develop a suitable balanced scorecard for The Royal Botanical Gardens and give examples of measures that would be incorporated within it.

(15 marks)
(Total marks = 25)

✓ Answers

Question 1 Division X

(a) Bonuses on ROI

Project 1	Y1	Y2	Y3
EBIT	£3m	£2.7m	£4.4m
Assets	£24m	£25.5m	£27m
ROI	12.5%	10.6%	16.3%
Basic bonus	£12,500	£12,500	£12,500
Additional	£3,125	£750	£7,875
Total bonus	£15,625	£13,250	£20,375

Project 2	Y1	Y2	Y3
EBIT	£2m	£1.7m	£6.4m
Assets	£24m	£25m	£26m
ROI	8.3%	6.8%	24.6%
Basic bonus	£–	£–	£12,500
Additional	£–	£–	£12,500
Total bonus	£–	£–	£25,000

Project 3	Y1	Y2	Y3
EBIT	£2.4m	£3.2m	£3.5m
Assets	£24m	£25m	£26m
ROI	10%	12.8%	13.5%
Basic bonus	£12,500	£12,500	£12,500
Additional	–	£3,500	£4,375
Total bonus	£12,500	£16,000	£16,875

Summary of bonuses	Y1	Y2	Y3	Total
Original	15,625	13,500	–	29,125
Project 1	15,625	13,250	20,375	49,250
Project 2	–	–	25,000	25,000
Project 3	12,500	16,000	16,875	45,375

It is likely that the manager will be influenced in his choice by the amount of bonus he will receive. Project 1 would therefore be the favourite, closely followed by Project 3, with Project 2 being viewed very unfavourably. This is contrary to the benefit to the company as demonstrated by the net present values, which ranks Project 2 first followed by Project 3 and then Project 1. In other words, the bonus system based on ROI means the manager is undertaking a dysfunctional decision by choosing the project with the lowest NPV.

(b) Bonuses on RI

Original draft	Y1	Y2	Y3
EBIT	£3m	£2.7m	£2.4m
Interest at 10%	£2.4m	£2.5m	£2.6m
RI	£0.6m	£0.2m	–
Bonus at 2%	£12,000	£4,000	–

Project 2	Y1	Y2	Y3
EBIT	£2m	£1.7m	£6.4m
Interest (10%)	£2.4m	£2.5m	£2.6m
RI	–	–	£3.8m
Bonus (limited)	£–	£–	£25,000

Project 3	Y1	Y2	Y3
EBIT	£2.4m	£3.2m	£3.5m
Interest (10%)	£2.4m	£2.5m	£2.6m
RI	–	£0.7m	£0.9m
Bonus	£–	£14,000	£18,000

Summary of bonuses	Y1	Y2	Y3	Total
Original	12,000	4,000	–	16,000
Project 1	12,000	3,000	25,000	40,000
Project 2	–	–	25,000	25,000
Project 3	–	14,000	18,000	32,000

The bonuses overall are lower than under the ROI scheme. However, it has not changed the manager's choice which still ranks them with Project 1 first, followed by Project 3 and then Project 2.

(c) Conflicts

The calculations made in (a) and (b) show that both systems of bonuses will result in the manager choosing the project which does not give the highest NPV. It is worth noticing that the bonuses based on RI would lead to the manager choosing Project 2 if the restriction of the bonus to £25,000 was lifted. This assumes that the manager is indifferent between bonuses in year 1 or year 3.

The bonus system should be aligned more closely with NPV, rather than ROI or RI, and should try to take a longer-term perspective.

(d) Investment and profit

Both ROI and RI use investment and profits, which can be partly inside and partly outside the control of the managers who are being assessed.

The investment decisions may be partly taken by the main board, but a large number of the decisions are likely to be taken by the divisional manager, and hence are controllable. It would be useful to try to separate those investments which are controllable from those that are not.

The profits can also be argued to be uncontrollable in the sense that the manager cannot alter the environment in which the business operates in the short term. This, however, removes all responsibility from the manager; part of the assessment of the manager's performance must be related to how they managed to deal with the situation they faced.

However, concentrating purely on profits and investment may not be addressing the various objectives of the company. A selection of targets which are more in line with the objectives, derived from stakeholder requirements, put together in a balanced scorecard would be a more comprehensive approach.

Question 2 Destroying value

(a) REPORT

To: Chairman

From: Management Accountant

xxx: xx of x 20xx

Value creation and destruction

This report will explain the principles of economic value added, in the light of the report by the analyst on the results of V plc, and in particular look at the treatment of R&D, advertising, interest and borrowings and goodwill.

1 General principles

   The principle is to calculate whether the profit generated by the business is sufficient return to the providers of capital for the risk they perceive in the operations. It adjusts the profits for a number of items (such as those below) to give what is felt to be a fairer measure of the profit generated. The return required is calculated from an estimate of the company's cost of capital applied to the long-term finance supplied to the business (shareholders' funds and long-term debt finance).

   This and similar measures have been developed because ratios taken directly from the financial statements can be manipulated more easily.

2 Research and development

   The analyst has assumed that the R&D expenditure will continue to generate revenue into the future, and so has capitalised the expenditure. Thus the profits are increased this year and the capital employed in the balance sheet is increased this year and the capital employed in the balance sheet is increased by the total of the last seven year's expenditure. Some assessment should really be made of its likely life so that it can be amortised approximately, but the analyst has not done this.

3 Advertising

   The analyst has, in a similar way assumed that advertising leads to increased revenues through brand awareness for some time and has capitalised the last five year's of expenses. Again, this should probably be amortised.

4 Interest and borrowings

As we consider the return to all long-term providers of finance, we need to assess the profit before interest. Hence interest is added back on to the profits, and long-term borrowings are included in the capital employed.

5 Goodwill

The goodwill represents the difference between the fair value of the net assets acquired in a business and the price paid, and should be related to the business reputation and its ability to make profits in the future. As such, it could produce benefits for some time (unless seriously impaired) and should be added back to the capital employed where it has been written off. Again, the value needs to be reviewed and amortised if it is found to have decreased.

If you have any further questions, I would be very happy to give more details.

(b) REPORT

To: Chairman

From: Management Accountant

xxx: xx of x 20xx

Divisional value

I attach as Appendix A a breakdown of the value creation or destruction reported by the analyst, split between the three divisions.

1 Results

The calculations show that A created value of £1m, while B destroyed £0.1m and C destroyed £2.3m. This is very different from the profits reported in the normal divisional performance assessment, which shows all divisions earning in excess of 20 per cent, and division C earning the best at 25 per cent.

2 Assumptions

Various assumptions have been made in the calculation to allow a split between divisions:

- Head office expenses are incurred in proportion to turnover.
- Tax paid/attributable to divisions is in proportion to profit after head office expenses and interest.
- Head office assets have been split on the same basis as head office expenses.
- Each division has been assessed using the same cost of capital.

3 Limitations

The most serious assumption is the last one, that all divisions have the same risk profile and hence cost of capital. It would be worth looking at this further to ensure that the return required from each division is appropriate to its risk. The 12 per cent cost of capital for the company is a weighted average across all divisions.

Appendix A

Adjusted profits

	A £m	B £m	C £m	Head office £m	Total £m
Reported profit	5.7	5.6	5.8	(1.9)	15.2
R&D		2.1			2.1
Advertising	2.3				2.3
Goodwill (1)		0.3	1.0		1.3
HO expenses (2)	(0.4)	(0.3)	(1.2)	1.9	–
Tax (3)	(2.0)	(1.6)	(1.2)	–	(4.8)
	5.6	6.1	4.4	–	16.1

Capital employed

	A £m	B £m	C £m	Head office £m	Total £m
Reported capital	27.1	23.9	23.2	3.2	77.4
R&D		17.4			17.4
Advertising	10.5				10.5
Goodwill		10.3	30.4		40.7
HO assets (2)	0.7	0.5	2.0	(3.2)	–
	38.3	52.1	55.6	–	146.0
Return required (12%)	4.6	6.2	6.7		17.5
Profit adjusted	5.6	6.1	4.4		16.1
Created/(Destroyed)	£1.0m	£(0.1)m	£(2.3)m		£(1.4)m

Adjustments

1. Goodwill for the year has been split in the same ratio as the goodwill write-offs.
2. Head office expenses and assets have been apportioned in the same ratio as divisional turnover.
3. Tax has been apportioned in proportion to profit after head office expenses and interest.

	A	B	C	Total
	5.7	5.6	5.8	
Interest	0.4	(0.7)	(0.9)	
HO expenses	(0.4)	(0.3)	(1.2)	
	5.7	4.6	3.7	14.0
Percentage	41%	33%	26%	

Question 3 M-HK

(a) Strategic information required by management

Customer demand

M-HK needs to determine the future demand so that it can plan sensibly. Although currently well used, the numbers may increase, decrease or remain steady. This is likely to depend upon the developments and economic well-being of the two largest cities. M-HK might look at any major expansion plans in the two cities, and any alternative transport to the ferries being considered.

Competition

M-HK needs to assess the strength of the competition. To do this, we must assess the current competition, in terms of quality and frequency of service, as well as any possible new competitors. The existence of barriers to entry, such as licensing required to set up a ferry service, may help to reduce this risk.

Competitiveness

M-HK needs to assess how it compares to the competition in terms of its current service, its pricing and its flexibility. It can do this by surveying current and potential customers. Its ability to alter its cost structure if demand fell might be hampered by the ownership of a large fleet of ferries.

Finance

M-HK should assess its likely financial needs in the future and be considering a number of possible sources. It therefore needs to consider the likely level of internally – generated funds, and obtain information on likely sources of additional external financing.

(b) Reports to senior management

The Chartered Management Accountant (CMA) needs to assess the management's requirements so that a sensible management information system can be developed. This will encompass financial and management accounting information as well as information for planning. The cost of development of such a system must be carefully balanced against the likely benefits.

Reports will be generated at two levels.

Operational level

This will look at the level of profits each service generates and so will give cost and revenue details. Some non-financial information such as number of passengers carried and the number of journeys made would also be useful to determine the least and most popular services offered.

Strategic level

The strategic level information will be more diverse, and will involve creating a database to record trends and customer patterns so that future services can be planned. An in-depth analysis of the competition, and their costs, revenues, prices and services will also be included.

To then make strategic plans, it would be useful to consider various different scenarios to assess the impact on M-HK and its competitors. This can then give the managers an idea of how to react in certain circumstances. This database will need reliable market information and will entail research. In addition, research into likely changes in legislation, covering all areas from safety to licensing would be helpful in trying to assess the impact of possible changes. Wider research into ferry operators in other parts of the world may also help managers in their strategic decision-making.

Question 4 Scorecard

The balanced scorecard was developed in order to achieve a balance between financial and non-financial, short-term and long-term measures of performance. It is concerned therefore with operational control rather than mission statements and corporate objectives.

The four main areas or perspectives used in the balanced scorecard, each of which may have a number of measures, are financial, customer, internal business process and learning and growth.

Financial perspective

For a profit-motivated organisation, the financial perspective, focusing on profits, revenue generation and cost control is very important as the ultimate objective is to maximise shareholders' wealth. However, financial measures will tend to be either historical or short term and do not give much idea of the long-term prospects of the business; these are covered in the other perspectives.

A not-for-profit organisation would only be concerned about the control of costs and keeping within the finance provided.

Customer perspective

This tries to measure the markets in which the organisation operates and considers customer retention and satisfaction, market share, number of new customers and customer account profitability. This is important for both the profit organisation to correctly target its market segments, and also for the not-for-profit in assessing the quality of its service.

Internal business process perspective

This looks at the internal processes and attempts to focus on those which add value to the service provided to the customers. Where the customer perspective identifies weaknesses in the service or additional features which are required, the internal business processes must be revised to provide the customer with what they require.

Learning and growth perspective

This perspective looks at how we can improve in the long term by considering what extra skills would benefit the business. Both the profit and the not-for-profit organisation will want to improve over time and identify new skills that would be useful.

The main problem with the balanced scorecard is that the different perspectives are likely to give different messages, and there is no overall summary performance measure.

Question 5 PAL

(a) Appropriate performance measures

   Benchmarking involves setting targets in various areas by reference to what is being achieved elsewhere – i.e. it is known to be an achievable, if stretching, target. This can be done in a number of ways but is often felt to be most appropriate by looking at the best performance amongst competitors in the same industry. This can sometimes be difficult to obtain if it relates to internal procedures.

In the case of home insurance, the performance measures might include the concerns of customers in the following way:

Price

The information is easy to obtain from competitors, but PAL must be careful to compare like with like in terms of cover provided, excess amounts on the policy, size of house and contents value, geographical location, and other services such as maintenance contracts added on. Once this is addressed, the benchmark targets can be set in financial terms.

Delivery

This presumably refers to the timescale between application and receiving the insurance cover note, and measures the efficiency of the processing. This can be determined by taking out policies with competitors and setting a benchmark in terms of days.

Technical content of literature

PAL can obtain copies of competitors' literature but judging the technical content is more subjective. Using simple language may be desirable but may fail to explain fully the insurance cover offered. Possibly outside consultants or sample customers could be used to assess this.

Customer service and correspondence

Some aspects of these can be objectively measured such as speed of response to enquiries and correspondence, but others are likely to be more subjective. The general area of customer satisfaction is more subjective in terms of how well the bank and its staff addressed the customer's needs. Again, a sample of customers with a questionnaire may indicate areas in which it falls short of its competitors.

(b) Strategies

(i) The strategy followed so far by PAL has been to compete on price offering the lowest rates it can to beat the competition. It therefore follows a cost-leadership strategy rather than one of differentiation and is focused on the area within 70 miles of the capital city. The benchmarking of competitors' rates is vital in supporting this strategy to ensure it has the lowest rates.

In home insurance, it is possible that PAL could follow a strategy of differentiation, emphasising its friendly local nature, quick processing and easily understood literature. However, given price as one of the major customer concerns, it seems likely that much of the operation will continue to be focused on delivering low prices.

There is some conflict between the areas used for benchmarking as an increase in customer satisfaction may involve time and expense, which in turn might have a detrimental impact on price.

However, if we view the core product as the home loans, we can view these additional services as being product development. These can be beneficial in their own right but could be viewed as helping to maintain its core market in loans. As such, the level of profit on these services is possibly less important and the level of customer satisfaction is more important in terms of tying customers into loans.

(ii) Benchmarking generally will, at the very least, improve PAL's understanding of how its competitors perform in these crucial value-adding activities, and will highlight its own deficiencies. How important PAL's customers or potential customers find these deficiencies depends upon the strategy being pursued by PAL and the reason its customers are attracted to it.

The benchmarking exercise also alerts the managers to changes in competitors' strategies, if carried out regularly, although the number of areas being benchmarked should be kept to a manageable level to avoid being overwhelmed by targets.

Question 6 RP manufacturing

(a) Strategy implementation and challenges

Generally, once an organisation has set its strategy, it may need to restructure itself in terms of its organisational structure and systems and staff. RP appears to be following this but may have problems in enforcing such changes from the top.

Staff usually are resistant to change and there seems to have been little effort made to manage the introduction of the new systems. It is likely there will be, therefore, problems in implementation. It might have been better to pilot certain ideas rather than trying to introduce everything at once.

The main challenges will be

- Overcoming staff resistance to the changes, which may mean having to re-timetable the introduction. The resistance may not only be due to dislike of change, but also to a lack of expertise or resources.
- Changing the role of head office so that it responds appropriately to the new system.
- A different management system will need to be introduced as much more outsourcing will mean less need to maintain motivation in the workforce and more emphasis on legal and quality considerations. The management will need to manage more of a network involving stakeholders outside the organisation.
- Achieving the savings envisaged in making these changes, even though in the short-term costs will probably increase due to such factors as redundancies.

(b) Traditional management accounting

Traditional management accounting suffers from a number of defects that might mean it is less appropriate for RP Manufacturing. The boundaries of the organisation are going to be less precise which might make a traditional reporting structure less useful.

Traditional accounting also focuses on historical information with a fixed view on cost structure rather than looking to the future and viewing all costs as manageable through the use of cost drivers and the review of outsourcing costs.

The traditional system focuses on financial costs, which are clearly still important, but fails to identify issues relating to quality, customers and markets. In addition, there is little attention paid to the strategic planning needs of the organisation, concentrating instead on operational and implementation issues. Finally, it is not suited to the partnership accounts and other information needed to run, assess and control its new structure.

(c) Information demands

In wanting to become more responsive to an ever demanding and fast-moving market while becoming more cost-conscious and thereby profitable, the information required from management accounting will change.

In particular, it is likely to mean

- value chain analysis and activity-based costing in order to analyse and identify areas where costs could be cut.
- Managing partnership arrangements and possibly inspecting the costs and profits of the partner organisations.
- Benchmarking information for new activities and for outsourced functions.
- Measurement of quality and delivery from outsourced facilities and comparison against contract agreements and benchmarks as well as trends.
- Measurement of performance of any subcontractors used, in terms of efficiency and production.
- Customer account profitability analysis, direct product profitability to ensure that all costs which relate to a customer or product are recognised.
- More environmental and market information so that RP can respond quickly to changes.

Question 7 Financial scandals

(a) Organisational objectives

Objectives fulfil a number of strategic functions which can be summarised as follows:

Planning

They translate the strategic intent into explicit targets towards which progress can be assessed.

Responsibility

By giving more explicit targets, these can then be delegated to the most appropriate business unit, department or individual, who can be given responsibility for particular areas. This might be for strategic objectives or they can be broken down into lower level tactical or operational targets.

Motivation

Motivation can arise through managers and others being included as a stakeholder group when setting objectives, so that they have a personal interest in seeing them achieved.

Evaluation

The main stakeholders in a company can assess its success by measuring its achievements against the objectives set.

Most of these functions will only be performed if the objectives are closely defined so that progress towards them can be assessed. This means that they need to be Specific, Measurable, Achievable, Realistic and Time-bound (SMART).

Private sector organisations see maximising shareholder wealth as their primary aim. Where this leads to the use of profit-related performance measures only, this can bring a number of problems:

- Increasing profits in the short term may lead to lower profits in the longer term as investments will be chosen which show early profits.
- Awarding bonuses which relate to the profits will lead to short-term investment decisions by managers as they seek to maximise their remuneration over the next 3 or 4 years.

- Other stakeholders, such as customers and employees, have a significant impact on the success of the business but are less interested in short-term profits. Instead measures of quality and reliability for customers and interesting work and good conditions for employees are more important. However, dissatisfied customers and de-motivated employees can quickly lead to falling profits for shareholders.
- Profits themselves can be manipulated in the short term, either through subjective judgements in areas like stock valuation or through creative accounting or fraudulent accounting.
- Profit generated does not take account of the risk which has been borne by the shareholders to achieve this profit. Thus profits could be enhanced by undertaking much riskier lines of business. In the same way, it takes no account of the value of the assets which have been used to generate this profit.
- Profit measures are hardly relevant for a variety of organisations in the public sector or not-for-profit area, such as charities, hospitals, schools or local authorities.

(b) Balanced scorecard

The balanced scorecard (BSC) looks to combine a number of performance measures which reflect the requirements of the main stakeholders. In this way it protects the long-term success of the business by balancing shareholders' short-term needs against those of groups such as customers. This reduces the need for what appear to be conflicting objectives being ranked and only the one of primary importance being pursued.

The BSC originally developed had four areas of concern, within each of which are set a number of performance measures and targets. These four "perspectives" are

- Financial perspective
- Customer perspective
- Internal business perspective
- Learning and growth perspective.

However, other perspectives could be incorporated as appropriate.

The BSC therefore helps to meet stakeholder needs by building in the aims of the major groups into the performance measures. It also helps to determine the business objectives by emphasising all the relevant areas of performance and measuring them in an objective manner. This will help in reviewing objectives and ensuring that all the areas covered in the BSC are included within the objectives. It also emphasises the interconnection between areas, between the financial and non-financial, the short term and long term, and ensures that a balance is maintained in the objectives.

Managers can be given objectives based on those performance measure areas which are relevant to the particular department under consideration.

The balanced scorecard is therefore very helpful in building in consideration of the needs of the key stakeholders, and in determining appropriate objectives which balance these needs.

Question 8   Royal Botanical Gardens

(a)

BRIEFING PAPER

To: The Management Board

From: Senior Management Accountant

The Balanced Scorecard

The balanced scorecard was originally developed to help commercial organisations and is a method of combining a number of different performance measures which reflect the requirements of the main stakeholders. It, therefore, helps to protect the long-term success of the business by balancing the traditional financial, possible short-term, measures against those representing longer-term interests. It also balances the competing demands on the resources of the organisation which may be complex if the organisation is involved in a number of different areas.

The four main areas or perspectives used in the balanced scorecard, each of which may have a number of measures, are financial, customer, internal business process, and learning and growth.

Financial perspective

For a profit-motivated organisation, the financial perspective, focusing on profits, revenue generation and cost control is very important as the ultimate objective is to maximise shareholders' wealth. However, financial measures will tend to be either historical or short term and do not give much idea of the long-term prospects of the business; these are covered in the other perspectives. In the case of The Royal Botanical Gardens, we would be interested in financial measures in those areas we control, such as our costs and receipts from the public.

Customer perspective

This tries to measure the markets in which the organisation operates and considers customer retention and satisfaction, market share, number of new customers and customer account profitability. This is important for both the profit organisation to correctly target its market segments, and also for the not-for-profit in assessing the quality of its service to the public.

Internal business process perspective

This looks at the internal processes and attempts to focus on those which add value to the service provided to the customers. Where the customer perspective identifies weaknesses in the service or additional features which are required, the internal business processes must be revised to provide the customer with what they require.

Learning and growth perspective

This perspective looks at how we can improve in the long term by considering what extra skills would benefit the organisation. Both the profit and the not-for-profit organisation will want to improve over time and identify new skills that would be useful.

Although the Balanced Scorecard was originally developed for use by commercial organisations, it has been used extensively by the not-for-profit sector, as the same perspectives are still important although measured in different ways.

The Royal Botanical Gardens would find such a process useful as it would help to balance its short-term and long-term objectives and involve all areas and personnel within the organisation in moving forward towards similar goals. It would mean that budgeting of the limited financial resources could be considered in the light of longer-term aims and hence the best use made of all the available resources. In addition, the central government is likely to be more amenable to any request for increasing funds if it can see the gardens are setting targets and measuring progress in all these areas, which together will help to show that we are producing value or money.

(b) Development of a suitable balanced scorecard

The balanced scorecard should be developed by a team comprised of individuals from all the different functional groups within the Gardens. The team should:

- Identify strategic themes
- Identify perspectives and desired outcomes
- Define performance measures and targets
- Develop strategic initiatives to achieve these targets.

The strategic themes should be developed from the mission statement and might include areas relating to research, display, conservation and national heritage.

In identifying the perspectives, we would need to think carefully how it might apply to the Gardens. For example:

Financial perspective might look at the government and some of the funding research foundations
Customer perspective might look at universities and the public
Internal perspective might look at botanists using the facilities
Learning and growth perspective might look more to the future and look for innovative ways to bring more people in.

The performance measures and target within those measures will be developed for each strategic theme and should consider the goals in each area. Measures in the strategic theme might include, for example:

Financial perspective
   Cost per sample provided
   Revenue generated from advice and consultancy
   Revenue raised by entrance fees paid by public.

Customer perspective
   Satisfaction surveys
   Amount of repeat business or return visits.

Internal perspective
   Published research
   Citations in other's research.

Learning and growth perspective
   Growth in visitor numbers
   New universities requesting samples.

Case Study Questions

11

✎ Exam focus

The compulsory case study question takes up 50 per cent of the exam and requires careful planning. The main problem is likely to be poor time management causing you to write very little, or nothing at all, on parts which could have given you easy marks.

The 20 minutes extra reading time at the start of the exam is particularly valuable here. Remember that you cannot write in the answer booklet or use your calculator, but you can use the time profitably to read the question and note in the margin your approach.

You need to break the requirements down into separate questions for timing purposes, but at the same time you don't want to be continually re-reading the scenario.

One approach would be as follows:

Read through all the requirements carefully; they are likely to cover a number of technical areas. Notice any parts that you can answer immediately, or that you have any ideas about and put some notes down on those.
Then scan the scenario quickly. Are there headings which help you find information; what industry and type of company is involved; are there any sections which are only relevant to one requirement?
Get an idea of where the information needed for each requirement is in the scenario (the information for making any calculation specifically required, for example, is likely to be grouped together) and mark it in the margin.
Then go back to the requirements and start working through them, reading the detail in the scenario as you need it. Watch your time carefully in the 3 hours of the actual exam, particularly in the case study question. Even if you haven't finished one requirement, go on to the next if the time is up. You can always come back if you have more time, but it's more important to get the easier marks at the beginning of each question than to make that final point!

On the following questions, be very strict with your time and see if you manage to make a reasonable attempt at all the requirements.

Questions

Question 1 G

Introduction

G plc is a long established divisionalised company with its origins in shipping. The company has been in existence for nearly 160 years and has developed a reputation for reliability and quality of service. Whilst the company obtains the majority of its turnover from various forms of shipping, its subsidiary interests extend into transport, construction and property.

The shipping activities in which G plc is engaged comprise four divisions – cruise, ferries, containers and bulk shipping. The cruise division is engaged entirely in the carriage of passengers and the ferries division carries passengers and vehicles. The vehicles carried by the ferries range from motor cars to articulated lorries and single deck buses. The containers and bulk shipping divisions are engaged in the carriage of freight only and do not carry any fare paying passengers.

Organisational aims

The company has stated over recent year that it aims to achieve the following goals:

1. Increase its emphasis on international businesses to achieve long-term profitability
2. Provide those businesses with the necessary capital investment to achieve their development
3. Continued development and training of the company's employees to achieve the organisational objectives.

Environmental policy

The company has established an environmental policy, which is monitored through an audit system, in an effort to ensure that its policies are being achieved. It is the aim of the company to have operational standards which at least equate with the best industry practice. Training of management, staff and specialist auditors is seen as a priority within the organisations environmental policy. This has become a major concern of the company which is aware of customer anxiety about travelling on roll on roll off (RORO) ferries following public debate about their safety.

Financial results

In the last financial year, earnings per share totalled £0.353 (35.3 pence) producing a dividend cover of 1.15. The dividend per share paid by G plc has remained at the same level for 5 years. Comparative values for divisional turnover and operating profit of each of the shipping divisions are as follows.

During this year, general inflationary levels in the shipping industry were approximately 5 per cent per annum.

	Turnover			Operating profit		
	This year	This year adjusted for inflation	Last year	This year	This year adjusted for inflation	Last year
Divisions	£m	£m	£m	£m	£m	£m
Cruise	856	815	735	96	91	88
Ferries	667	635	626	90	86	80
Containers	1262	1202	1051	42	40	40
Bulk shipping	125	119	112	(5)	(5)	(3)

Chairman's statement for the financial year

In his statement, the Chairman of G plc, commenting on turnover and profit before the inflation adjustment, said the company achieved encouraging results, particularly in the cruise division. The company has taken delivery of a new cruise liner, at a cost of £200 million and has two more on order. The chairman believes that this is an expanding market and considers the company to be in a good position to take advantage, as it is one of the world's largest cruise companies. With regard to the ferries division, the chairman expects continued growth, although there is an expectation of a sharp decline in the number of routes across the English Channel due to the opening of the tunnel link between the United Kingdom and France. Economic recovery, a continual reduction in costs and increased cargo volumes were all cited by the Chairman as reasons for the improved performance of this division. This contrasted with his view of the depressed containers and bulk shipping market which contributed to these divisions continuing disappointing results.

Market information

G plc commissioned some marketing research into its passenger shipping activities. The results of this research indicate that, in recent years within the cruise liner industry, there has been a change in customer appeal. Traditionally, the main customer base has comprised wealthy retire people. In the last 5 years, the cruise division has experienced an increase in younger customers. This stemmed from the late 1980s when the world's largest cruise company shortened the length of some cruises to appeal to American passengers who have only a short vacation period. This resulted in more affordable prices, other cruise companies, including G plc, followed the market leader. This, in turn, resulted in even more affordable prices and the market expanded, with a younger age range of customer being identified.

By contrast, the research showed a 15 per cent increase in passengers crossing the English Channel, but G plcs market share actually reduced by 4 per cent. In its other ferry services, G plc has seen the market holding steady.

The report indicates that the probability of the cruise market continuing to grow for the next 5 years at the current rate is 0.6, and that a growth rate of half that which it currently enjoys over the same period, has a probability of 0.3. There is no expectation of a decline in this market over the next 5 years, and the probability of the market remaining static is 0.1.

The report concludes that, in respect of the ferries division, the passenger market across the English Channel is expected to reduce by a further 5 per cent over the next year and then remain at this level for the next 4 years. This is given a probability of 0.7, whilst there is a 0.1 probability that the market will remain at its current level, and a 0.2 probability that it will fall by a further 10 per cent next year and then remain static. The report concludes that the other ferry routes should maintain their current market levels.

Requirements

(a) With reference to the organisational aims set out above, state what G plc's corporate objectives should address.

(5 marks)

(b) It has been argued that an organisation which operates in a turbulent environment should include flexibility as an objective in order that it can be responsive to changing environmental conditions.

Explain how G plc could achieve flexibility in its operations, AND discuss potential areas of stakeholder conflict which may occur in satisfying its organisational objectives.

(15 marks)

(c) Discuss the change in turnover and profit of the shipping divisions within G plc in the last financial year, AND state, with reasons, whether you consider the chairman's statement reflects the divisional results achieved.

(10 marks)

(d) With reference to Porter's five competitive forces model, assess the nature of the cruise and ferry shipping market in which G plc is engaged, AND discuss what opportunities and threats exist in respect of its market share.

(15 marks)

(e) Discuss how monitoring through an audit system can be implemented to ensure that G plc's environmental policy is being achieved.

(5 marks)
(Total = 50 marks)

Note: CIMA's rules do not normally allow two verbs under one mark, but this old exam question has been left as it was set in order to avoid an eight part question!

Question 2 FNJ and WT

Background

FNJ is a company which has developed business interests in the very competitive music industry. It produces and sells compact discs (CDs) and traces its history back to when it manufactured vinyl records. It is contracted to produce CDs for many famous recording artists which it is able to distribute through its own worldwide chain of retail music stores.

A new Chief Executive (CJ), who came from an unrelated business, was appointed to run FNJ about 12 months ago. The financial situation for the company has become perilous with falling worldwide sales and difficult trading conditions. The company has issued a number of profit warnings and experienced severe management disputes which have been made public. The result of these factors has been a low share price. CJ implemented cost reductions at FNJ and developed a strategy which focuses the company's attention on the provision of music to customers via the Internet, with the eventual aim of replacing CDs with Internet sales in the years to come.

WT is a large entertainments group which has growing business interests in producing motion pictures (movies) and retail outlets (trading under its own brand name of WT). The company is well regarded worldwide within its industry. It has augmented the product range with, for example, soft toys (related to its popular movie characters) which are sold through its retail outlets.

The merger

A merger deal has recently been agreed between the directors of FNJ and WT. This has yet to be ratified by both sets of shareholders, but it is expected to be accepted. The new group (FW) aims to achieve a high market share of total world-wide music sales. Following the merger, it is expected that the two companies will shed jobs throughout the world in the interests of improving efficiency. The contracts for some of the recording artists who are not achieving high sales will not be renewed.

Financial summary of the merger

The following details highlight the main points relating to the merger:

1 The merger is worth $10 billion in terms of total asset value.
2 WT has 8 seats while FNJ has 7 seats on the new board of FW.
3 CJ will be the Chief Executive of FW.
4 Shares in FW will be allocated in proportion to the current shareholdings. This will result in each company's shareholders holding 50 per cent of the shares.
5 Directors' share options come to fruition on completion of the merger.
6 The share price of FNJ rose by 11 per cent after the merger was announced.

Selected details relating to FNJ and WT before the proposed merger

CDs (FNJ):

	Last year	2 years ago
Actual sales	$90 million	$95 million
Budgeted sales	$100 million	$100 million
Average actual price per CD	$20	$20
Average actual cost per CD (1/3 of this is variable cost)	$12	$12
Average budgeted price per CD	$22	$20
Average budgeted cost per CD (1/3 of this is variable cost)	$15	$10.5

The average annual sales of CDs over the last 5 years were $100 million. The trend of changes in sales levels for CDs which has been apparent over the last 2 years is expected to continue.

Motion pictures (WT):

	Last year	2 years ago	3 years ago	4 years ago
Total revenue	$2,000 million	$1,800 million	$1,400 million	$1,000 million
Total costs	$1,900 million	$1,600 million	$1,100 million	$700 million

Retail music stores (operated by FNJ):

	Last year	2 years ago	3 years ago	4 years ago
Total revenue	$140 million	$138 million	$136 million	$135 million
Total costs	$136 million	$131 million	$134 million	$135 million

The resale value of FNJ's retail music stores is reducing because of the increasing popularity of alternative methods of shopping.

Strategic development of FW

CJ has forecast that next year sales of music will be available through the Internet with digital downloading to the customer's own personal computer. At the moment, most of the FNJ retail music stores' revenue is generated by the sale of FNJ-produced CDs. He believes that by supplying customers through the Internet, overall sales revenue (combining Internet sales with CDs), will increase by 20 per cent. The average variable costs for Internet sales will reduce by 25 per cent on that currently incurred in CD production. This cost reduction is expected as a result of not needing to employ expensive recording studios which are currently required to produce a CD. The average selling price and average variable cost of a CD are expected to remain at $20 and $4 respectively throughout next year. The average selling price of each Internet sale is also expected to be $20.

Independent research has revealed that the market for digitally downloaded music is forecast to grow next year. Customers will have the opportunity to create their own "do it yourself" compilation albums.

Some of FW's competitors have already made effective use of the Internet to distribute CDs and videos, undercutting high-street retailers on price. However, digital download through the Internet is still experimental.

Requirements

(a) Discuss the dynamic nature of the business environment experienced by FNJ and WT, and explain the rationale for the merger.

(10 marks)

(b) (i) Analyse the business performance of CDs, motion pictures and FNJ's retail music stores over the period contained in the scenario. Include calculations on the projected change in contribution each year for CD and Internet sales if CJ's forecast is accurate.

(14 marks)

(ii) Calculate and analyse the contribution volume variance relating to CD sales for last year and 2 years ago.

(5 marks)

(iii) Recommend ways in which the directors of FW should pursue the strategic development of the CD, motion pictures and FNJ's retail music stores businesses.

(12 marks)

(c) Briefly explain the theory of shareholder value and discuss how shareholder value may be increased by the merger.

(9 marks)
(Total = 50 marks)

Question 3 Y-Land FE

Introduction

The Y Corporation is based in the United States of America (USA). It was founded in the early part of the last century when Mr Y produced cartoon films. These soon proved very popular as a form of family entertainment and the characters in the films became household names.

The Corporation established a theme park (based around the film characters) in the southern USA, where there was a warm and mainly dry climate. The theme park, known as Y-land, proved to be an immediate success, attracting millions of visitors each year. A whole range of family entertainment flourished, based on the original theme of the cartoon characters. These included shops, restaurants, hotels and amusement rides.

Following the success of Y-land in the USA, the directors of the Corporation established another Y theme park based in Northern Europe. The rationale behind this was that although many Europeans visited Y-land in the USA, the cost of travel made visiting the attraction very expensive. The directors believed that establishing a Y-land in Northern Europe would enable European people to visit the attraction without incurring high travel expenses. Y-land Europe was built in a highly populated area of Northern Europe which is easily accessible. A factor which differentiates Y-land Europe from the theme park in the USA is that it is located in a region which is frequently affected by rain and it does not enjoy a guaranteed warm climate. Y-land Europe did not in fact attract the volume of visitors that were expected and almost went bankrupt before receiving a massive cash injection from a wealthy donor who took part shares in the theme park.

Further strategic development

The Y Corporation is now considering building another theme park, this time in a tropical area in the Far East. Y-land FE will be part-funded by the host government in the Far East, which will take a 60 per cent share in the park. The Y Corporation will fund the remaining 40 per cent. Profits and losses will be shared in direct proportion to the shareholding of each of the joint venture partners.

It is believed that local tourism and related sectors of the entertainment industry will benefit from the development as the theme park will attract more visitors to the region. Similar to the other two Y-land theme parks, the development will include many facilities such as hotels, bars and restaurants as well as the entertainment attractions.

It will take 2 years to build Y-land FE before any paying visitors enter the park. The Y Corporation has based its estimates of visitors in the first year of operation (that is, after the 2 years of construction) on the following probabilities:

	Visitors	*Probability*
Optimistic	8 million	0.25
Most likely	3 million	0.50
Pessimistic	2 million	0.25

After the first year of operation, it is expected that the number of visitors will increase by 50 per cent in the next year. The Y Corporation directors consider that this number of visitors will be the maximum and after that the theme park will suffer a reduction in the number of visitors (marketing decay) of 5 per cent compound each year for the next 2 years. After 2 years, the directors expect the number of visitors each year to remain constant at this level.

The host government believes that the theme park will create about 15,000 new jobs in the area through servicing the facilities. It expects the construction of the park to create about 5,000 jobs in addition to the 8,000 who will be employed in land reclamation and other necessary infrastructure work associated with the project.

Cost and revenue estimates

It is expected that the overall capital cost of the theme park will be $2,200 million. This sum will be spread evenly over the construction period and, for the purposes of calculation, the actual cash outflow may be assumed to arise at the end of each of the 2 years. The Y Corporation will be responsible for raising 40 per cent of this sum.

In any year, the visitors are expected to be in the proportion of 40 per cent adults and 60 per cent children or people who will obtain a concession (reduction) on their entrance fees. For simplicity, the entrance charges will be set at a flat rate of $50 for each adult and $30 for each child or concession. There will be no further fees for entertainment after the entrance charge has been made to the visitor.

Past experience has shown that running expenses of the theme park show a certain level of consistency. In terms of labour, the costs follow the pattern of a 90 per cent learning curve which applies on average to every 1 million visitors. This lasts for the first 2 years, after which the labour costs for each visitor become constant. The cost of labour at the time the park will open is expected to be $3 for each visitor. The effects of this are that the cumulative average direct labour costs in the first year of operation (i.e. year 3 of the project) are estimated to be $9.72 million (after being multiplied by the number of expected visitors in that year). The cumulative average labour costs for both the first and second years of operation (i.e. years 3 and 4 of the project) are expected to be $21.14 million (after being multiplied by the total number of visitors for the first 2 years of operation). After this point the learning effect is expected to cease.

The other direct costs, which are not subject to learning, can be assumed to be incurred at the rate of $2 for each visitor. Attributable fixed running expenses are estimated to be $100 million each year in cash terms.

In addition, the Y Corporation expects that its joint venture with the host government will earn average net contribution of $10 from the sale of souvenirs and refreshments and $100 from accommodation charges for each adult, child or concessionary visitor each year.

The cost of capital for the whole project is expected to be 15 per cent.

Shareholder value

The Y Corporation believes that its main objective is to increase the wealth of its owners. The Corporation requires a gross return on investment of 22 per cent after 8 years of income generated from the venture. It has been recommended to the directors of the Y Corporation that the return is calculated by taking the net present value of the project after 8 years of operation and dividing this by the gross initial undiscounted capital outlay of $2,200 million.

Ignore taxation, inflation and variations due to exchange rates.

Requirements

(a) Evaluate the usefulness of Porter's Diamond Theory (the Competitive Advantage of Nations) in helping the directors of the Y Corporation to determine whether or not it should proceed with establishing Y-land FE.

It is not necessary to draw a diagram of the Diamond Theory.

(10 marks)

(b) (i) Produce a discounted cash flow (DCF) calculation for Y-land FE from the start of building work in the first year until 8 years of cash inflows have been generated (i.e. 10 years in total).

(12 marks)

(ii) Calculate the return on investment in accordance with the method recommended.

(3 marks)

(iii) Analyse and critically appraise the DCF calculation and the resulting return on investment as defined by the method recommended to the directors of the Y Corporation.

(6 marks)

(iv) Advise the directors as to whether they should proceed with Y-land FE. You should consider financial and non-financial factors in providing your advice.

(7 marks)

(c) Discuss how the directors of the Y Corporation can use Shareholder Value Analysis to determine the development of its portfolio of products and services.

(10 marks)
(Total = 50 marks)

Question 4   ICS

ICS was established 10 years ago. The company began by providing computer software programs to local businesses. This is an industry which is dynamic. Rapid technological development constantly causes fast changes within the industry.

The demand for ICS's services grew. After 2 years of operation, ICS had almost doubled its turnover and had taken on more staff. In addition to software programming, ICS then diversified into providing emergency computer data retrieval services. This necessitated obtaining some specialist equipment and hiring specifically trained staff. Rapid growth in turnover continued until the mid 1990s, but has reduced in recent years.

ICS is managed by a board of directors, and the company is financed by equity (mostly held by private investors) and debt. The current gearing ratio is in the proportion of 60 per cent equity to 40 per cent debt. The shareholders are becoming concerned about ICS's recent poor performance.

Financial results:

The financial results for the last five years of trading are shown below.

Year ended 31 December	1997 $'000	1998 $'000	1999 $'000	2000 $'000	2001 $'000
Sales	6,300	6,400	6,600	6,500	6,300
Variable costs	4,621	4,732	4,881	4,891	4,778
Fixed costs	1,481	1,489	1,730	1,750	1,900
Capital employed	2,400	2,500	2,500	2,600	2,600

Turnover provided in percentage terms each year to different types of customer sector:

	1997	1998	1999	2000	2001
% retail	70	65	65	55	50
% industrial	23	26	26	30	33
% other	7	9	9	15	17

Comparative figures for each of the three sectors served by ICS for the years 1997 and 1998 are as follows:

1997	Retail $'000	Industrial $'000	Other $'000	Total $'000
Contribution	1,323	290	66	1,679
Profit before interest charges and tax	221	0	(23)	198

1998	Retail $'000	Industrial $'000	Other $'000	Total $'000
Contribution	1,249	333	86	1,668
Profit before interest charges and tax	209	0	(30)	179

Developments:

ICS is looking to develop the services it provides. It has the opportunity to place a bid for a contract with a customer in the industrial sector which will initially have a probationary period of one year. The contract will take effect from 1 January 2003 and may be renewed after the first year for a further 5 years. If the bid is successful, it will be necessary for ICS to obtain some new capital equipment which it will rent for the probationary year at a hire charge of $100,000. This sum will be paid at the beginning of the contract.

It is anticipated that the contract will increase turnover by 40 per cent over the Industrial Sector level for the year ended 31 December 2001 in each year of its operation. The variable cost ratio for the contract will be slightly lower than for 2001. It is estimated that the variable cost ratio for the contract will be 77.5 per cent of the 2001 level in the Industrial Sector. Fixed costs, however, are expected to increase by a total of 20 per cent over the amount incurred on the Industrial Sector for the year ended 31 December 2001 directly as a result of taking the contract.

Z, the Managing Director of ICS, is very keen to place a bid for the contract as he has recognised the decline in profitability in recent years. He believes that the only way to return to profitability is to continually expand the company's service provision.

Management information systems:

ICS has never made any provision for management information. Z uses a local accountancy firm, Y & Partners, which produces only the statutory information and returns. It was A, an accountant from Y & Partners, who provided the financial and turnover percentage information given above.

While it is not possible to be fully accurate, A estimates that the variable costs and fixed costs as a proportion of turnover for each type of service provided were:

	Variable costs: % of turnover	Fixed costs: % of turnover
Years	1997–2001	1997 and 1998
Retail	70	25
Industrial	80	20
Other	85	20

A calculates the fixed costs in each of these sectors over the last 3 years to have been as follows:

Year ended 31 December	1999 $'000	2000 $'000	2001 $'000
Retail	1,070	890	790
Industrial	470	590	800
Other	190	270	310

For some years, A has tried to explain to Z the necessity for ICS to be provided with regular management information, in particular management accounting information. However, Z has always rejected this advice, saying that it would be too expensive and that the board of ICS should not "waste its time on detail".

"In any case", Z says, "I know the business we are in. I am able to see what work we should be taking on. I know the way to be successful and profitable is to expand the services we provide. This worked in the early 1990s and will work again."

A has expressed concern to Z over ICS's cash flow.

Note: Net present value calculations are not required in answering this question.

Requirements

(a) Discuss how setting corporate objectives can help and/or obstruct ICS in satisfying the demands made by its shareholders.

(10 marks)

(b) Discuss the relevance of the provision of management information to a company such as ICS in the 21st century when the business environment is always changing so fast.

(10 marks)

(c) (i) By analysing the turnover and costs for the years 1999–2001 across the three main sectors in which ICS operates, advise the board of directors what management accounting information should be provided to them.

(12 marks)

(ii) Identify the priorities which should be addressed, given the current financial circumstances of ICS.

(8 marks)

(d) Advise Z whether ICS should bid for the new contract. Include any reservations you may have about whether or not the bid should be made, and support your answer with calculations.

(10 marks)
(Total = 50 marks)

Question 5   C

Introduction

C is a company which is engaged in synthetic fibre production. It is situated in Home country where it operates two production plants. C pipes raw material from an oil refinery (which it does not own) to its own production plant where it manufactures a single product which is a special grade of polymer. The polymer is then transferred to a second production site which produces two products, "Synfib" and "Thetfib". As the polymer is of a special grade and manufactured specifically for the production of Synfib and Thetfib, there is no intermediate market for it. The transfer price for the polymer has been set at $40 per litre.

Mission and objectives

C's Chairman has declared that the firm's mission is to "provide its customers with the highest quality product at a reasonable price". The organisational objectives are to satisfy the demands of the shareholders, reduce pollution to a minimum, maintain secure employment and to sell a product of high quality which satisfies customer requirements. The objectives also make reference to maximisation of shareholder wealth while at the same time keeping the shareholders' exposure to financial risk to a minimum. Approximately 75 per cent of the shares are held by large financial institutions. The remainder are held by individual investors including employees and the directors.

The final products

While Synfib and Thetfib are both produced at the second production site in Home, they are produced in different processes. There is strong demand for both of these specialist products worldwide and C is the only producer. However, substitute products are available and may be used in place of them. The following schedule shows the monthly demand for each product at various selling prices:

Synfib		Thetfib	
Litres (millions)	$ per litre	Litres (millions)	$ per litre
75	200	200	70
100	175	400	60
125	150	600	50

The divisional manager (M) of the second production site has autonomy to choose the level of output, and always selects that level of output which maximises divisional contribution.

Output of Synfib is produced in batches of 25 million litres. The minimum monthly quantity produced is 75 million litres. Thetfib is produced in batches of 200 million litres with the minimum monthly quantity being 200 million litres. Sales of each product are made in these batch quantities and it can be assumed that they are indivisible. The maximum monthly demand is 125 million litres for Synfib and 600 million litres for Thetfib, and these are the maximum quantities of each product that can be produced each month.

As a result of its production processes, Thetfib emits waste products which pollute the atmosphere. The government of Home has introduced strict regulations in recent years to control waste emissions and C estimates that the firm incurs a fixed monthly cost of $2,000 million in order to comply with these regulations.

Transfer of production of Thetfib to another plant in Foreign country

The directors of C are considering transferring production of Thetfib to another plant which the firm owns in Foreign. The plant is already established in Foreign and could produce Thetfib in the quantities required without any other costs being incurred except for those shown in the table below. Foreign is a developing country which encouraged the directors of C to build a plant there by offering grants and loans at a very attractive interest rate. Foreign's government also takes a more relaxed view of pollution and, while it does have regulations in place, these are less strict than those which apply in Home. The directors of C estimate that compliance with the regulations applying in Foreign would cost the company $600 million per month.

Information relating to Synfib and Thetfib

	Synfib $ per litre	Thetfib in Home $ per litre	Thetfib in Foreign $ per litre
Transfer price of polymer	40	40	To be decided
Costs			
Direct labour	12	8	3
Additional materials	2	2	2
Direct processing	6	3	3
Transport	4	2	14

The marginal costs of C's plant which supplies the polymer are $12 per litre. The corporation tax-rate in Home is 35 per cent and in Foreign it is 20 per cent. Foreign tax neutrality applies between Home and Foreign. This means that C would pay tax at the rate of 35 per cent on net contribution generated by its production in Home and 20 per cent on its contribution from production in Foreign.

Output of the receiving plant in Home

Recently, M has argued that the transfer price which is charged is too high at $40 per litre. She believes that a transfer price set at the supplying division's marginal cost would result in increased contribution for C as a whole. M has presented the following schedule relating to Synfib to support her view.

Output of Synfib and total contribution per month at a transfer price of (i) $40 per litre and (ii) $12 per litre:

	(i) Transfer price of polymer at $40 per litre			(ii) Transfer price of polymer at $12 per litre		
Output of synfib	Total revenue	Marginal costs	Total contribution	Total revenue	Marginal costs	Total contribution
Litres (million)	$ million	$ million	$ million	$ million	$ million	$ million
75	15,000	4,800	10,200	15,000	2,700	12,300
100	17,500	6,400	11,100	17,500	3,600	13,900
125	18,750	8,000	10,750	18,750	4,500	14,250

M has produced the following statement indicating the after-tax increase in contribution if the transfer price was set at $12 and production increased from 100 million litres to 125 million litres.

Synfib	Revenue	Marginal costs	Contribution
Transfer price $12 (125 million litres)	18,750	4,500	14,250.00
Transfer price $40 (100 million litres)	17,500	6,400	11,100.00
Increase in total contribution	–	–	3,150.00
Less tax liability at 35%	–	–	1,102.50
Increase in after tax contribution	–	–	2,047.50

Requirements

(a) Produce a critical appraisal of the content of the mission statement and objectives of C as they are presented to you in the scenario. Recommend what changes should be made to their content.

(10 marks)

(b) (i) Produce an analysis of the contribution from Thetfib which would be made in Home by using the existing transfer price of $40 per litre. Show, with supporting calculations, whether contribution could be increased by changing the transfer price and/or varying the level of output.

(12 marks)

(ii) Compare the expected profitability for C if production takes place in Home or alternatively in Foreign after your recommended transfer price has been applied.

(8 marks)

(c) With reference to the results of your calculations in requirement (b), discuss the effect transfer pricing would have on C's management accounting systems in helping it to achieve its organisational objectives.

(10 marks)

(d) Advise the directors of C what action they should take to establish appropriate measures for the assessment of overall divisional performance in order to meet the organisational objectives.

Note: The actual measures which C could use are **not** required.

(10 marks)
(Total = 50 marks)

Question 6 PC airlines

Introduction

PC Airlines was founded nearly 60 years ago by two pilots. The airline began flying from its home base in Asia to local destinations. It soon grew and now has acquired routes to many worldwide locations. The company was listed on its home stock exchange 15 years ago. Now, a conglomerate group holds 45 per cent of the airline's shares while a further 25 per cent are held by an Investment Corporation.

Four years ago, PC Airlines entered an alliance with other airline companies. The alliance took the name "Worldair" as this reflects its composition, which is made up of airlines based in the USA and Europe, as well as Asia. The three airlines in the alliance are PC, AB and US. They operate out of the following geographic regions of the world:

    PC   Asia
    AB   Europe
    US   USA

Aims of Worldair

The Worldair Alliance was formed in response to increasing competition from other airline alliances. These competing alliances threatened to attract customers (passengers) from the Worldair members. The Worldair Alliance members have agreed to co-operate with each other on route destinations. The members also enjoy economies of scale in satisfying their customers' demand by reducing the overall number of flights and increasing the seat occupancy of member airlines. This means that a customer may book a seat with one member of the Alliance and be allocated to another member's flight which is travelling to the same destination. Senior managers of the members of the Alliance claim that by rationalising the number of flights, they are able to pass on economies to customers in terms of seat prices and also reduce aircraft traffic congestion and pollution emissions.

The financial aim of Alliance members is to increase their shareholders' wealth by providing a better service than their competitors. To achieve this aim, it is essential that all members improve profitability by increasing their popularity with customers. All senior managers of the Alliance have agreed that it is very important for the members to establish consistent policies and that each must not deviate from these in any way. In order to co-ordinate the activities of the Alliance, a Worldair management team, drawn from senior managers of the members, has been appointed.

Recent bad publicity

Much publicity has recently been given to lack of passenger space associated with travelling in economy-class seats on long-distance (known as "long-haul") flights. (Short distance flights are known as "short-haul".) The publicity has centred on the fact that many economy-class passengers feel discomfort on long-haul flights because the seats are too close to each other.

An expected level of growth of 5 per cent in passenger numbers for Alliance members next year was anticipated by senior managers of the Alliance airlines. However, as a result of the recent bad publicity, they do **not** now think there will be any growth next year in long-haul economy-class passenger numbers. Turnover levels from long-haul economy-class passengers of Alliance members are expected to remain at the current year's level. There is also expected to be a depressing effect on the rate of growth of short-haul passenger numbers for next year, but this is not thought by the senior managers to be as severe as for long-haul passenger forecasts.

In a measure to counter the potential threat resulting from the bad publicity, all members of the Alliance have established a programme to increase the amount of space available for each economy-class customer. This will be achieved by reducing the number of this type of seat in its aircraft which undertake long-haul flights. AB favoured delaying this and waiting to see whether the bad publicity actually resulted in reduced customer numbers. The other Alliance members, however, were not willing to wait. They wanted to assure customers of their serious concern for customer safety and comfort while on a long-haul flight. Additionally, it was felt prudent to take some positive action on restricted leg room to calm possible fears among customers and before legislation was passed forcing airlines to comply with minimum space requirements between economy-class seats on long-haul aircraft.

Financial and customer information relating to the Alliance.

(Last year actuals and current year forecasts)

	PC	AB	US	Total
Last year:				
Passengers carried	2 million	5.5 million	7 million	14.5 million
	$ million	$ million	$ million	$ million
Turnover	1,000	2,500	3,000	6,500
Gross profit	200	350	450	1,000
Net profit	25	30	50	105
Current year:				
Passengers carried	2.3 million	5.4 million	7.5 million	15.2 million
	$ million	$ million	$ million	$ million
Turnover	1,200	2,540	3,300	7,040
Gross profit	250	330	500	1,080
Net profit	30	15	56	101

Other information for current year:

	PC %	AB %	US %
Gross contribution to sales ratios:			
Economy class	25	10	17.5
Other classes	70	85	80
Proportion of total turnover from economy-class seats	75	50	80
Proportion of economy-class turnover coming from long-haul passengers	70	80	60

All aircraft within the Alliance currently fly on average at 95 per cent of passenger capacity.

Impact of bad publicity

For each Alliance member, the net contribution levels for next year which were expected to result if the effects of the bad publicity had **not** been felt by the airlines are as follows:

PC	AB	US	Total
$ million	$ million	$ million	$ million
456.75	1,266.8	1,039.5	2,763.05

Information for next year

- A marketing forecast for the Alliance has predicted that customer numbers will grow on average by 5 per cent for each Alliance member next year for all classes **except** long-haul economy-class.
- Turnover from long-haul economy-class passengers for Alliance members next year is expected to be at the current year's level.
- It may be assumed that customer growth will be the sole cause of a change in turnover next year.
- The possible effect of the bad publicity has also been estimated as having a depressing effect on short-haul economy-class marketing growth forecasts for next year, as follows:

    10 per cent reduction on growth forecast – probability of 0.3
    20 per cent reduction on growth forecast – probability of 0.4
    30 per cent reduction on growth forecast – probability of 0.3

- Senior managers of the Alliance estimate that it will be necessary to reduce the number of economy-class seats in long-haul aircraft operated by all Alliance members by 5 per cent from the current average of 400. Next year the cost of this refit will be:

    PC $30 million
    AB $50 million
    US $80 million

    In other classes, seating will be unchanged.

- Research and development (R&D) and publicity costs into customer preferences on long-haul flights are estimated to be $50 million and $20 million respectively next year. This will be charged to each Alliance member in proportion to current year turnover.

Requirements

(a) Discuss the benefits and disadvantages of Worldair Alliance membership to PC Airlines in determining its future aims and objectives.

(10 marks)

(b) Discuss what action the Worldair Alliance management team should take regarding the potential threat from the bad publicity. Explain the possible implications for members of the Alliance of **not** taking any action. In answering this question, you should consider the availability and quality of data provided in the scenario on space between seats in economy class on long-haul flights.

(10 marks)

(c) Produce an analysis of the net contribution for **next year** for each of the Worldair Alliance member airlines. The net contribution should be calculated after the deduction from total gross contribution of costs relating to seat conversion, R&D and publicity. Explain the value of such an analysis for strategic decision-making by the Worldair senior management team.

(20 marks)

(d) Discuss the different attitudes of Worldair Alliance members towards the implementation of an operational policy to address the bad publicity and discuss how disagreements between Alliance members on operational policy issues may be reconciled.

(10 marks)
(Total = 50 marks)

Question 7 CG

Background

CG is a publicly funded development organisation. It allocates money which it receives from the government to overseas organisations for the purpose of business development. The directors of CG do not aim to maximise profits. The government expects the directors of CG to make a return on capital employed (ROCE) of just 5 per cent. This is the only directive given to CG by the government.

Strategic objectives

In its 20-year history, CG has provided development funds to many organisations around the world. Its main objective is to provide funds to organisations in poorer regions of the world so that they may use them to generate their own future growth and become financially self-sufficient. The main approach employed by CG is to provide start-up funds or loans and expertise to local businesses to the point that they are providing employment locally and contributing to their own national economy. CG's initial outlay is recovered from income derived from operations carried out by local businesses receiving the start-up funds. Once the project is viable without further support, it is passed over for the local business to continue to run. The only criterion set by CG for the type of business to be supported is that it must be engaged in legal activity. After the initial outlay has been made and the ROCE (relating to the period for which the funds have been committed) has been paid, there is no further payment to CG from the local business.

The directors of CG have employed the rational planning model in developing their strategic plans. In recent years, the directors have been criticised for being too inflexible in the provision of development funds by concentrating in business areas which are too narrow and focusing too frequently on particular areas of the world.

Performance measures

CG operates on a divisionalised basis with regional managers having responsibility for particular overseas regions. The regional managers have discretion to allocate funds up to a limit. In the event that they identify a funding proposal which exceeds their discretionary limit, the regional managers may make a business case and apply to the directors of CG for the larger sum to be made available. The directors measure the performance of the regional managers by determining their ROCE using the net book values of capital employed. The operating surplus or deficit is divided by the net capital employed to arrive at the ROCE. The method of determining the ROCE is in accordance with government regulations with depreciation being charged within the fixed administration costs. CG apportions its own headquarters costs across the regions on a flat rate which has worked out to be $300,000 in each region in the last reporting period. Regional divisions of CG provide technical services (for example advice on environmental pollution) to each other and make a charge accordingly. This avoids duplication of technical expertise within each of CG's regions. Income received from inter-regional transfers is included in the ROCE calculations.

The directors of CG are now considering the ROCE of two regions, M and Z. In addition, they are considering two possible development proposals, one in each region. Region M was established 9 years ago. Region Z is a new area of activity for CG and has just produced its first set of accounts. The performance of the two regions in 2002/3 is set out below.

	Region M $'000	Region Z $'000
Income generated in regions M and Z:		
From development projects funded by CG within the region	3,500	700
From other CG regions	100	2,100
Expenditure incurred in regions M and Z:		
Variable service costs	450	200
Fixed service costs	380	600
Variable administration	250	80
Fixed administration	1,470	1,270
CG headquarters (apportionment)	300	300
Capital employed:		
Gross book value	12,000	10,000
Depreciation	9,000	1,000
ROCE	25.00%	3.88%

After another 3 years for region M and 9 years for region Z, the assets will be fully depreciated. In the next financial year, the depreciation charge will be $1 million for each region.

Development proposals

The details of the two development proposals are

	Region M $'000	Region Z $'000
Initial cost (to be added to capital employed)	300	400
Scrap value	0	10
Annual net cash inflow	100	
Revenue from annual production of 500 units		200
Annual cash costs incurred by region Z for 500 units		95
Estimated life	4 years	6 years

Depreciation is calculated on a straight-line basis. The development proposal for region Z involves the annual production of 500 units of a single product. Each unit of the product sells at the same unit price and each incurs exactly the same costs.

152 Exam Practice Kit: Business Strategy

The nominal Cost of Capital for CG is 10 per cent and the regional manager of M has calculated that his proposal has an NPV of $17,000. In addition, he has calculated the expected impact on ROCE in 2003/4 as follows (assuming all other revenues and costs remain the same next year).

	$'000
Operating surplus without the proposal	750
Net operating surplus from the proposal (after depreciation)	25
Revised operating surplus	775
Net capital employed without proposal	2,000
Gross cost of proposal	300
Depreciation on proposal	(75)
Revised capital employed	2,225
ROCE	34.8%

The regional manager for region M is concerned about the risk associated with the proposal. He has identified that any of the following situations could result in a zero NPV:

(i) the initial cost needs to rise by only 5.66 per cent ($17,000/$300,000);
(ii) net cash inflows need to fall by only 5.36 per cent [($17,000/3.17)/$100,000];
(iii) the cost of capital needs to rise to only 12.5 per cent.

Therefore, he thinks the proposal is very sensitive to any of these situations occurring. The directors of CG are also becoming concerned about the high level of ROCE being achieved by region M given its target set by government.

Ignore inflation and tax.

Requirements

(a) Advise the directors of CG on the method which is most appropriate for them to formulate strategy. Your advice should include a critical appraisal of the current method (rational planning model) employed.

(10 marks)

(b) (i) Evaluate the performance of the regional manager for region Z (making whatever comparisons with region M you think are appropriate)

(12 marks)

(ii) Advise whether the development proposal for region Z should go ahead. Your advice should take account of the expected NPV of the proposal, its impact on ROCE in 2003/4 (assuming all other revenues and costs in 2003/4 are the same as for 2002/3 except for the effect of depreciation on any new proposals) and include calculations demonstrating its sensitivity to the possibility of returning a negative NPV.

(18 marks)

(c) As stated in the "Performance measures" section, the directors measure the performance of the regional managers by determining their ROCE using the net book values of capital employed. Discuss the method employed by the directors of CG to evaluate the performance of its regional managers and advise on alternative approaches which may be used. Your discussion should also take into account the effect on the performance of the regional managers of the government target ROCE of 5 per cent.

(10 marks)
(Total = 50 marks)

Question 8 MW and FS

Background

MW and FS are both supermarket chains which operate in different parts of a country. Both are listed on the country's Stock Exchange. MW operates in the north of the country while FS stores are located predominantly in the south. Recently the Chairman of FS has approached the Chairman of MW and suggested that MW may wish to present a take-over bid for FS. The Chairman of FS has indicated that such a bid would be favourably received by his Board of Directors and would pre-empt a bid being made by other less desirable predators in the industry. According to the Chairman of FS, there would need to be some staff rationalisation and about 10 per cent of the total number of stores of the combined group would need to be sold as a result of demands which would be made by the country's competition regulatory organisation.

However, he believes that there would be increased profitability for the combined group as a whole which would lead to improved shareholder value. At this stage, no public announcement of the possible take-over has been made and all the information relating to it is being treated as strictly confidential.

MW

MW was established over 100 years ago by Mr W. His son (KW), who is now over 70 years old, is the Chairman of the company. The W family has maintained strong control over the business and still owns nearly 40 per cent of its shares. The main principle established by Mr W was that of offering quality products at a reasonable price and this principle has been rigidly maintained throughout the company's history. Organisationally, MW stores are split into two operating areas – the North West and the North East, although it is controlled from its head office by KW and his management team. Each individual store is managed locally by a Store Manager and an assistant. In addition, there are supervisors, till checkout staff, storekeepers and shelf stackers working in each store. Other skilled trades staff are also employed including butchers, bakers and fishmongers.

Recent results have shown that MW has increased its sales by 8 per cent and its net profit by 15 per cent over the previous year. MW has become a popular share as a result of the company's ability to cut its operating costs and increase its profitability each year. MW's current share price is $3. Its market capitalisation is $4,500 million. Two years ago its price/earnings ratio was 10.

KW follows the sound principles of business development established by his father. He prefers to rely on a capital structure which is low geared and has generated organic growth rather than undertaking large take-overs. The last time MW undertook a take-over was 25 years ago when it bought six supermarkets. If a bid is made for FS then it is most likely that KW will wish to offer a share exchange rather than pay any cash. He is acutely aware of competition in the industry within the country and has been advised by the Finance Director that there are two other main competitors which may put forward counter-bids if MW makes an offer for FS.

FS

FS's stores operate within the South West and South East of the country. Approximately 55 per cent of its shares are held by ten major institutional shareholders which have been disappointed in recent performance. These institutional shareholders have been impressed by the success of MW and instructed the Chairman to begin take-over negotiations with KW. FS's share price currently stands at $2 with a market capitalisation of $4,000 million. Two years ago its price/earnings ratio was 30.

Performance of both companies for the last financial year

For simplicity, the data supplied below represents the average *for each store* in the relevant area. All stores for each company are built to a standard layout. On average, FS stores are 20 per cent smaller in terms of area than MW stores.

	MW		FS	
	North West $ million	North East $ million	South West $ million	South East $ million
Turnover	10.0	8.0	6.0	5.0
Cost of sales (excluding wages)	4.0	3.0	2.0	1.8
Overheads				
Managers and supervisors salaries	1.0	1.0	0.7	0.6
Non supervisory staff wages	1.0	0.7	0.7	0.6
Other overheads	1.0	1.1	1.1	0.9
Local taxes	1.0	0.8	0.7	0.6
Net profit	2.0	1.4	0.8	0.5

Additional information	MW		FS	
	North West	North East	South West	South East
Total square metres per store	6,000	6,000	4,800	4,800
Average number of customers visits per store	0.3 million	0.2 million	0.15 million	0.1 million
Managers and supervisors per store	15	12	14	12
Total staff per store	69	56	56	51

The profit attributable to ordinary shareholders in the last financial year was $225 million for MW and $200 million for FS. Stock is held centrally by each company in its own secure warehouse. It is issued on a daily basis to each store. On average, each MW store has a stock turnover of 2 days while each FS store has a stock turnover of 3.5 days.

MW's strategy

KW has recognised the need to obtain support from shareholders and therefore will need to maintain enhanced shareholder value. The Finance Director has acquainted him with the seven value drivers which Rappaport believes affect shareholder value. These are as follows:

(i) sales growth rate;
(ii) operating profit margin;
(iii) the planning period;
(iv) the rate of cash income tax payments;
(v) incremental fixed capital investment;
(vi) working capital investment;
(vii) the cost of capital.

Requirements

(a) Produce (i) a SWOT analysis for MW and (ii) explain how such an analysis can assist the company in achieving its organisational objectives.

(13 marks)

(b) Discuss the usefulness of Rappaport's seven drivers to the directors of MW in helping the company to improve its shareholder value.

(10 marks)

(c) In your capacity as Management Accountant for MW, produce a report to KW which outlines the benefits and risks of acquiring FS. Your report should include

- an analysis of the data provided in the scenario by making whatever calculations you think appropriate;
- an analysis of the potential impact of the take-over on shareholder value;
- a statement regarding any strategic issues which you think should be considered by the Board of MW before a bid is made.

(17 marks are available for the calculations and 10 marks are available for the narrative part of this requirement, including 2 for the specified format)
(Total for requirement (c) 27 marks)
(Total = 50 marks)

Question 9   ACEP

ACEP plc (ACEP) is a UK listed company which started as a publishing business over 50 years ago and has grown into a company involved in consumer magazines, radio broadcasting, television production and recorded music production. The company is currently based exclusively within the UK. Each industry is represented by a separate division within the company, each of which has been added, and grown, by a series of acquisitions of small companies. All have been successful with the exception of the music business, which was acquired 6 years ago.

ACEP entered the music industry believing that the music division would grow to rival the larger companies, despite continuing to focus on less well known artists and groups who had a specialist following of fans. Although there have been successful court cases against the suppliers of file sharing software, illegal music copying is still a big issue for the industry. The losses of royalties are claimed to be considerable.

The regulation of the broadcasting industry has, traditionally, focused on audience size but over the past 10 years there has been considerable deregulation and consolidation. ACEP has the maximum number of radio licences possible, as have the other two major industry players. This division regularly runs concerts at popular tourist venues where its target market tends to spend its summer vacation.

The magazine publishing industry structure is similarly concentrated and, although there is no equivalent regulation based on audience size, it is unlikely that further acquisitions of companies would be allowed on competition policy grounds. The development of new titles by organic growth would, however, be permitted. ACEP has been successful with this approach and has two titles in the top five lifestyle magazines and six in the top 10 teenage titles. Both magazines and radio earned 70% of their revenue from advertising in 1999 and 2000. Across the industry, advertising revenue has been depressed for the past 2 years.

The television production division produces music programmes for satellite and cable television under the Masthead (collective brand name) of *Taste*, which is the same name as that used for the radio stations and some of the magazines. Although this presents cross-marketing opportunities in the market segment of 13–30 year olds, who have considerable spending power, the division is a relatively small player within the industry.

With the exception of the finance director, who was recently brought in from a commercial radio station, each member of the board has a publishing background and has been with the company for a number of years. These individuals have a reputation within that industry for achieving major post-acquisition cost savings.

There are five institutional shareholders, all with significant holdings, who have become more publicly critical of both the share price of the company, which has been falling, and the size of the dividend which has been maintained at its present level for the past four years. They have said that both television and music should be sold off; these could realise £20 million and £10 million, respectively. The balance of the shares in issue are broadly held. The results for the past 4 years are shown in Appendix A.

Since the company is market leader in its target market, it has been considering expanding magazine publication into mainland Europe. A potential acquisition has been identified at a cost of £10 million. It is felt that, in the first year only, contribution would increase by £3 million and fixed costs would rise by £1 million. Alternatively the company is considering an approach from a significantly larger European publisher and broadcaster, whose organisation is privately owned, to form a joint venture in the latter's country. Discussions have suggested that an initial investment by ACEP of £20 million would give rise to an increase in contribution to ACEP of £4 million. Fixed costs for ACEP would again rise by £1 million for the first year. In both cases, ACEP's Board feels that there would be considerable opportunities for cross marketing to its existing market.

The company has also had discussions with a firm which supplies equipment to be installed in retail outlets which downloads music to CD on demand. In addition to the cover charge for the CD advertising, revenue is earned depending on the number sold. A major retail chain has expressed an interest in installing the equipment in its 50 stores across the country. The equipment could be hired by ACEP for a cost of £2 million for the 50 sites. The board is impressed that the project, based on figures supplied by the equipment vendor, has an expected annual net profit of £1.182 million. This option will not be viable if the music division is sold off. A marketing research exercise by the equipment supplier has provided the projections shown in Appendix B.

Appendix A

£ millions	*2002*	*2001*	*2000*	*1999*
Sales				
Publishing	425	500	523	419
Radio	350	375	380	320
Television	65	75	80	70
Music	20	30	40	44
Total	860	980	1,023	853
Profit before interest & tax	166	256	281	205
Capital employed	900	900	870	805

Variable costs/sales ratio

Publishing	0.49	0.45	0.45	0.45
Radio	0.26	0.25	0.25	0.25
Television	0.18	0.25	0.25	0.26
Music	0.20	0.20	0.20	0.20

Fixed costs/sales ratio

Publishing	0.38	0.32	0.31	0.37
Radio	0.43	0.40	0.39	0.40
Television	0.62	0.53	0.50	0.50
Music	1.50	1.00	0.80	0.73

Appendix B

With promotional costs per month of £12,000 and a CD retail price of £2.00 it is expected that monthly sales will have the following pattern:

Probability	Sales (units)
0.4	10,000
0.5	12,000
0.1	14,000

For sales up to and including 11,000 units, advertising revenue is predicted to be £17,000 per month if sales are over 11,000 units. Advertising revenue is predicted to be £18,000 per month. Combined monthly fixed costs of production and distribution will be £16,000 and variable costs will be £0.45 per CD. Retailers will receive a 25% margin on sales.

Requirements

(a) Regarding the proposal to download CD's in retail outlets, demonstrate how the equipment supplier has calculated the expected annual net profit, and evaluate whether it gives a complete picture of the project.

(10 marks)

(b) Discuss the concept of portfolio planning models and, in the light of the comments of the institutional shareholders, analyse the portfolio managed by ACEP.

(8 marks)

(c) (i) Evaluate the risks involved in entering the magazine publishing market in mainland Europe.

(8 marks)

(ii) Discuss the merits of each of the two proposed methods for entering the mainland Europe market.

(9 marks)

(d) The Board of Directors has asked you, as Financial Controller, to prepare a report which produces

(i) recommendations regarding the options to purchase the CD download equipment, move into Europe and/or dispose of the television and music divisions;

(ii) a response to the institutional shareholders explaining how these recommendations will contribute to sustained business growth for ACEP, recognising any concerns these shareholders might have.

(15 marks)
(Total marks = 50)

✓ Answers

Question 1 G

(a) Corporate objectives

Objectives should be SMART, that is specific, measurable, achievable, relevant and time-bound so as to form sensible targets against which performance can be judged.

Corporate objectives would normally cover three or four main aims over the medium term of 3–5 years. At the business unit level, more specific objectives, relating to the particular matter in which they operate, might be set.

The organisational aims stated appear to be more actions than targets. Objectives need to be set which state the target in some measurable form so that the organisation can check its performance towards them. The areas referred to in the aims would suggest profitability and development and training of employees as two possible subject for objectives.

(b) Flexibility

Flexibility can be beneficial to the organisation so that it can respond quickly to changes in customer demand or requirements, competitor's actions or other external influences. It effectively means having internal resources that can easily be increased, decreased or switched across the business as external circumstances require. It is possibly a desirable state for an organisation but is difficult to classify as an objective as it lacks many of the SMART attributes; it would be hard to devise a sensible measure of flexibility for example.

G might find it difficult to make its resources much more flexible as it might involve

- Changing job descriptions and the working culture to allow staff to be transferred quickly between divisions.
- Having sufficient credit lines in place to increase marketing and investment in areas as required.
- Sharing maintenance and repairs between divisions and possibly even trying to make ships interchangeable between some of the divisions.
- To reduce the impact of major swings in markets, it would be sensible for G to keep and maintain its diversification between markets.

Stakeholders are those with an interest in the organisation, and for some increasing flexibility of operations in G may not be in their interest. In particular:

- Employees may find the flexibility of job roles, both in and between divisions, difficult to manage.
- Customers may feel that they are receiving less attention as the staff and other resources no longer specialise in a single market.
- Shareholders who are already diversified may not welcome additional diversifications by G.

Other objectives may also cause conflict between stakeholder groups, such as:

- Customers requiring additional services and safety measures which reduces the profits for shareholders.
- Managers may prefer to safeguard the company and their jobs rather than pursuing the maximum profits required by shareholders.
- Individual unit managers will want the best resources for their unit, which will bring them into conflict with other managers.

(c) Performance

Division	Turnover	Profit	Profit margin
Cruises	+10.9%	+3.4%	11.9 → 11.2%
Ferries	+1.4%	+7.5%	12.8 → 13.5%
Container	+14.3%	0	3.8 → 3.3%
Bulk	+6.3%	−66.7%	−2.6 → −4.2%

Cruises. Although turnover has increased by about 11 per cent, profits have only increased by 3.4 per cent, meaning that profit margins have deteriorated. G does appear to be expanding in this area, as the Chairman says, but either it is having to lower prices in this competitive market or costs have not been kept under control.

Ferries. The turnover has increased slightly but profits have increased by 7.5 per cent, suggesting the Chairman is correct in identifying continuing cost reductions. The reduction due to the tunnel link seems likely but has not shown on these numbers.

Container. This appears to be a highly competitive market as turnover has increased by 14 per cent with no impact on profit, suggesting a general price decline. The division has done well to increase its turnover in such a market and appears to be holding its own. The Chairman is perhaps a little harsh in condemning them as disappointing.

Bulk. The bulk shipping is making losses and, despite increasing turnover the situation has worsened in the year. It seems likely that this is a competitive, price-driven, market and the Chairman is correct in describing the results as disappointing.

(d) Cruise and ferry market

The cruise and ferry markets are fundamentally different from the container and bulk shipping as the first two operate in markets in which differentiating the service provided can help to maintain and gain competitive advantage. The latter two are likely to be operating in markets in which the service is treated as a commodity and those with the lowest prices, usually those with the lowest cost structure, will own the greatest share.

Cruises

Substitutes for a cruise might be package tours, particularly those which take people to two or three countries. There are a lot of alternative holidays to cruise and this is a powerful competitive force.

Suppliers provide the workforce, maintenance and shipyards building new ships. None of these are particularly powerful even with union power and few shipyards as both will be looking for work and prepared to compromise on price.

Customers could be the ultimate consumers or travel agents. Individual customers do not have sufficient power to negotiate price reductions and are not powerful in their own right. A holiday company that contracted a large number of places might have more bargaining power.

It is unlikely that new entrants form much of a threat as it requires a large investment (£200m) to acquire a new cruise liner to enter the market.

The level of rivalry in the market, however, appears to be high with a reasonably mature market, very little segmentation and high fixed costs. These all suggest a highly competitive market.

The main opportunities and threats therefore relate to substitutes in the form of other holidays, and the level of rivalry from other cruise operators. The threat is that G loses business to both these.

The opportunities are to counter these threats by differentiating a cruise in its marketing from other types of holiday, emphasising convenience and quality of service, and differentiating its cruises from those of competitors, using its new ships, motivated staff and superior service and facilities as possible promotions.

Ferries

The competitive forces analysis for ferries is very similar, with suppliers (workforce, maintenance, shipyards), individual customers and new entrants not being particularly powerful forces.

Substitutes in terms of plane and train through the tunnel present a more powerful threat, as does the rivalry between ferry operators as they compete for a shrinking market with surplus capacity.

The main threats are therefore a further reduction in the market due to substitute methods of travel, and a subsequent collapse in prices as rivals try to secure market share with their surplus capacity.

The opportunities are to differentiate a ferry from other travel by emphasising the ability to wander around the ship, to shop, eat and watch films or simply relax and watch the sea, compared with the stress of travelling by car, plane or train. G could also try to differentiate itself from other ferry operators by adjusting its timetable and possibly routes, to be more appealing and emphasising the quality of its service over competitors. One possibility is to offer a restricted number of cheap tickets so customers can sample its quality without reducing prices across the board.

(e) Monitoring environmental policy

To be implemented effectively, we will need:

- Specialist staff who are able to undertake environmental testing.
- A change in culture of the organisation so that all staff are aware of the environmental consequences of their actions.
- Some idea of the targets that can be set in this area which are achievable. This may involve looking at best practice and benchmarking.
- Training, either for all staff or managers or for a certain core spread throughout the organisation who can then disseminate the information.
- A reporting structure in which the assessment of performance can be collected and summarised.

Question 2 FNJ and WT

(a) Business environment and rationale

FNJ is particularly exposed to rapid changes in technology both in terms of how music is recorded and in how easy it is becoming to download music from the Internet without payment, coupled with the growth in pirated copies. A subsidiary issue is changing consumer tastes, which could lead over time to a catalogue of music and artists for which there is no demand.

WT is more susceptible to consumer taste changes as new films cost a huge amount but can produce very little revenue if the critics and public dislike them. The growing catalogue of tried and tested characters in popular films and the accompanying merchandise help to stabilise its income. To a lesser extent, WT is affected by changes in technology as new techniques in filming and computer graphics are introduced.

The rationale for the merger is that shareholder value will be increased by boosting revenues and reducing costs. Together, they may be able to develop the distribution of music and films via the Internet, market the music from the films using their own artists, and combine their retail outlets. The costs associated with duplicated stores, and longer term with the production of CDs, will be reduced.

(b) (i) Analysis of performance

CDs

To date
Total for last 5 years' revenue = 5 × $100m   = $500m
So average for first 3 years   = (500 − 185)/3 = $105m per annum
Therefore sales revenue has dropped by 15/105 = 14% over the last 2 years

Projections

Sales revenue = $90m × 1.20 = $108m per annum
No. of sales = $108m/20 = $5.4m per annum

	CD	Internet
Price	20	20
V/C	(4)	(3)
	16	17
Volume*	4.263m	1.137m
Total contribution	$68.208m	$19.329m = $87.537m

This is an increase of (87.537 − 72)/72 = 21.5%

* Last year   90/20   = $4.5m sales
  Previous year   95/20   = $4.75m sales
  This year estimate = 4.5 × 4.5/4.75 = $4.263m

Motion pictures

The revenue has increased by about 26 per cent per annum over the last 4 years, while the costs have risen by about 40 per cent per annum. This trend cannot continue as it will soon eliminate the profit and WT needs to review its cost base as a matter or urgency.

Retail music stores

The music stores show a steady rise in revenue (1.2 per cent per annum) and a very small increase in costs (although a larger increase in the last 2 years). However, the future of the music stores may be threatened by the growth in Internet sales.

(ii) Contribution volume variance

	Last year	2 years ago
Budgeted volume	4.545m (100m/22)	5m (100m/20)
Actual volume	(4.5m)	(4.75m)
	0.045m	0.25m
Budgeted contribution	$17	$16.50
Volume variance	$0.765m (Adverse)	$4.125m (Adverse)

(iii) Recommendations

The CD business must pursue the sale of music by the Internet to keep its market share. The projections show the benefit this would bring, although more analysis should be undertaken on the assumptions made.

The motion picture business is producing steady revenues but its costs appear to be out of control and need to be severely curtailed if this is to remain a profitable business.

The distribution of films via the Internet and other personal pay-to-view channels should be investigated.

The retail music stores are likely to see a steady decline in the future as less music is sold through shops. Whilst sales of CDs are likely to continue for some time, the retail space should be gradually turned over to other group sales including the movie merchandising. Where they are surplus to requirement, or duplicate the WT retail outlets, they should be sold.

(c) Shareholder value

Shareholder value was developed to assess the performance of a business and link it to the increase in the value of the business. It started with the premise that it depended not only on the profits generated but also on the investment base managed by the business, the potential sales growth and the cost of capital, representing the return required for the risk perceived.

In the proposed merger, profits will increase as costs are cut and stores closed and revenue boosted as the music and film businesses sell each other's products. The cost of capital will potentially reduce as investors feel the merged enterprise is less risky, and that it will have the market strength to push ahead with Internet sales of music, leading to growth.

However, the outcome may be different from that predicted by the theory as it requires management skill to run the enlarged business.

Question 3 Y-Land FE

(a) Porter's Diamond theory

Porter's Diamond looks at national competitive advantage to establish why the most successful companies in certain industries are located in a particular country. The Diamond looks at four key areas which can be used to assess the attractiveness of a country for establishing a base.

Demand conditions

The high demand in its home country has allowed Y to generate good returns and to gain experience in running an efficient attraction. However, their experience in Europe shows that this cannot be assumed to work in other countries and the demand, requirements and tastes of visitors in the Far East needs to be examined very carefully.

Related and support industries

It is important that the area has appropriate infrastructure and that supplies and services needed can be easily accessed. The partnership arrangement should help in this respect as presumably the government will ensure the infrastructure is in place.

Factor conditions

This looks at the resources required, and means that the directions must be satisfied that both the site and the labour force are suitable; this may involve substantial training.

Firm structure, strategy and rivalry

The directors need to consider the appropriate structure of the joint venture as well as any competing attractions in the area. Y would like to see barriers raised against other attractions being built once it was established, so they should discuss the government's intentions in this area (and also their attitude towards an expansion of Y-land FE).

Overall, the model points out some crucial aspects that need to be discussed before going ahead, particularly in the area of customers and competition.

(b) (i) Average visits in year of operation = (8 × 0.25) + (3 × 0.50) + (2 × 0.25) = 4 million (increases 50 per cent for one year then 5 per cent per annum down for 2 years)

Average rate = (40% × $50) + (60% × $30) = $38

Net Revenue (excluding labour) = 38 − 2 + 110 = $146/visitor

(In $m)	T_0	T_1	T_2	T_3	T_4	T_5	T_6	T_7	T_8	T_9	T_{10}
Build	(1,100)	(1,100)									
Fixed costs				(100)	(100)	(100)	(100)	(100)	(100)	(100)	(100)
Net revenue (ex labour)				584	876	832.2	790.6	790.6	790.6	790.6	790.6
Labour				(9.7)	(11.4)	(10.8)	(10.3)	(10.3)	(10.3)	(10.3)	(10.3)
		(1,100)	(1,100)	474.3	764.6	721.4	680.3	680.3	680.3	680.3	680.3
DF	1	0.870	0.756	0.658	0.572	0.497			(5.019 − 3.352)		
PV		(957)	(831.6)	312.1	437.4	358.5			1,134.1		

Net present value = $453.5m

(ii) Return on investment = $\frac{453.5}{2,200}$ = 20.6%

(iii) **Results**

All cash flows have been estimated and it is particularly difficult to assess demand in 10 years time in another country. The probabilities attached to demand and to the split between different types of visitors have been averaged, but this results in 4 million visitors in year 1, which is not one of the possibilities. The pessimistic view is only half this, and yet there is apparently a 1 in 4 chance of this occurring. It would be sensible to carry out sensitivity analysis in all the estimates, particularly to assess the impact if the learning curve did not materialise.

(iv) **Assessment**

The return on investment would suggest a viable project, but the directors should consider a number of other, non-financial factors. The estimate of visitors will be very dependent upon the competing attractions in the area and on whether the Y Corporation brand will appeal enough to the local people, who have a different culture and social outlook. The surrounding area and its population density is likely to have an impact both on visitors and on any restrictions placed on its operation and any later expansion.

The financing of the investment has not been mentioned, but if external funds are raised the directors need to consider if the investment will cover the cost sufficiently with a discount rate of 15 per cent.

The directors need to study the experience of the park established in Europe and ensure that robust, possibly pessimistic, estimates have been built into the visitor numbers and revenue. The directors therefore need to consider the revenue estimates very carefully as they are based on a number of assumptions which may not prove correct.

(c) Shareholder Value Analysis (SVA)

SVA looks at how to increase shareholder value by considering not only the profit generated but also the investment required, the risk as represented by a discount rate, and the likely growth. However, it is still focusing on financial measures and as such only looks at non-financial areas by implication.

In this situation, it is crucial that the directors also consider non-financial measures such as customer/visitor satisfaction and employee motivation as they will have a direct impact on the revenues and costs.

The directors also need to consider the impact that a failure at this park would have on the rest of the corporation. Strategically it would be viewed as a disaster and the image of the company and its value would suffer far more than the financial results warranted as shareholders lost confidence in the management.

Question 4   ICS

(a) Corporate objectives

Objectives, and targets generally, are set by organisations in order to

- enable plans to be made which help achieve the objectives
- co-ordinate activities and encourage goal congruence

- motivate staff and management
- communicate plans and targets to staff and management
- evaluate performance of managers against target.

All of these will help ICS as, for example, setting objectives will help it in bidding for the new contract. It will mean establishing a plan of action, co-ordinating the various elements, motivating the staff and communicate the company's intentions to them.

This will help ICS satisfy the demands made by its shareholders by clearly identifying its priorities, such as maximising shareholder wealth, and translating this into achievable plans of action.

The main problem that can mean setting and pursuing objectives obstruct ICS is to do with the nature of its industry. Corporate objectives to be fairly long term but the computer software industry is very dynamic and fast-moving. As a result, there is a danger that ICS will set objectives which result in pursuing markets or products to the detriment of opportunities that suddenly arise elsewhere. There would therefore be some benefit in either setting objectives for a shorter time frame than might be usual, or for allowing sufficient flexibility within the plans for achieving them, so that ICS can take advantage of any opportunities that present themselves.

(b) Management information

The business environment in which ICS operates certainly changes very rapidly, but that is not a good reason for management to be making business decisions without relevant, accurate information. Management information is to help management, so they must first of all decide what would be useful before a system can be designed. The requirements will need to be balanced against the time, effort and cost of obtaining the information.

Management information can be used for all levels of decisions – strategic, tactical and operational – but each will require different information. Typical strategic information might include analysis of competitors and particularly of their new products and those of any new entrants in this rapidly changing markets. This may prompt ICS to review the expected life cycle length of existing products and give them ideas for new products and other opportunities.

The management information system itself will need to be flexible and fast as it needs to provide different details as the environment changes. This will make it even more valuable to management in their decision-making, as long as the information produced can be relied upon.

However, a management information system must be selective in the information it provides or the manager can become overwhelmed by data. It is important that data is presented which gives the manager the information needed for the decision so it is sensible for the managers themselves to refine the reporting requirements of the system over time.

(c) (i) Analysis

	1999 $'000s	2000 $'000s	2001 $'000s
Retail			
Sales	4,290	3,575	3,150
Variable costs (70%)	(3,003)	(2,502)	(2,205)
Contribution	1,287	1,073	945
Fixed costs	(1,070)	(890)	(790)
Profit pre interest and tax	217	183	155
Industrial			
Sales	1,716	1,950	2,079
Variable costs (80%)	(1,373)	(1,560)	(1,663)
Contribution	343	390	416
Fixed costs	(470)	(590)	(800)
Profit pre interest and tax	(127)	(200)	(384)
Other			
Sales	594	975	1,071
Variable costs (85%)	(505)	(829)	(910)
Contribution	89	146	161
Fixed costs	(190)	(270)	(310)
Profit pre interest and tax	(101)	(124)	(149)
Total			
Sales	6,600	6,500	6,300
Variable costs	(4,881)	(4,891)	(4,778)
Contribution	1,719	1,609	1,552
Fixed costs	(1,730)	(1,750)	(1,900)
Profit pre interest and tax	(11)	(141)	(378)
ROCE (in %)	(0.44)	(5.4)	(14.5)

This supports the need for an accurate and fast management information system which will allow managers to track actual revenues and costs and compare them to budget, prompting immediate corrective action. Information on market size and share would also help to highlight areas in which competitive advantage was being eroded.

(ii) Priorities

ICS clearly has problems as it has made a loss for the last 3 years and its position is deteriorating rapidly. It can be seen that the retail sector is the only one which has a profit before interest and tax, and has supported the loss making industrial and other sectors.

However, it would not necessarily be beneficial to close the two loss making sectors as they make a positive contribution towards the fixed costs. ICS needs to examine the fixed costs associated with them carefully and ascertain the extent to which they would reduce if the sectors were closed.

Even in the retail sector, the profits are reducing and the contribution margin is being squeezed. Management needs to investigate the cause of this, which may be competitive pressure on pricing or a lack of cost control.

168 Exam Practice Kit: Business Strategy

The fixed costs appear to be reducing in the profitable retail but increasing in the loss making industrial and other sectors. A move to an activity-based costing system, identifying cost drivers and apportioning costs accordingly might change the cost split, and hence profitability significantly.

(d) New contract

	$'000s
Extra revenue (2,079 × 40%)	831.6
Variable costs (80% × 77.5%)	(515.6)
Contribution	316
Fixed costs (800 × 20%)	(160)
	156
Hire of equipment	(100)
	56

The calculations would suggest that the new contract is viable, with the following caveats:

- it would be usual to take account of the time value of money, which would show the hire of equipment occurring at the start of the year while contribution was earned later
- as the industrial sector has been unprofitable for the last 3 years, it seems surprising that this contract is profitable
- it relies upon the variable costs being at a lower rate than normal; applying the current rate would result in a negative position of $94,000
- it does not take into account the possibility of subsequent years being renewed.

Given that at such an early stage ICS would not be committed, it is worthwhile making a bid while using the newly established management information system to ascertain the cost structure with more certainty.

Question 5 C

(a) Mission statement and objectives

A good mission statement will reflect the needs of the main stakeholders, define the business the firm wants to be in, and try to differentiate the organisation from its competitors.

C's mission statement does not appear to address any of these aims as it says nothing about the business it is in and only addresses the needs of its customers. The vague terms "highest quality" and "reasonable price" do not differentiate it and may be contradictory. A mission statement should ideally inspire those who come into contact with, or work for, it but it is unlikely that this will inspire staff.

Objectives should be SMART, that is, specific, measurable, attainable, relevant and time-bound. The objective to maximise shareholders' is traditionally the primary objective but needs to be carefully defined and targets set within a timeframe. The reference to keeping risk to a minimum needs to be quantified and targets set accordingly. In the same way, the objectives dealing with pollution, employment and quality and customer requirements need to have specific targets set after being more closely defined. The satisfaction needs to be tied into the mission statement's aim of "highest quality" to decide on the level required to reach this aim.

(b) (i)

Price of Thetfib	$70	$60	$50
Output level (million litres)	200	400	600

Transfer price = $40

Revenue	14,000	24,000	30,000
Costs (15 + 40)	(11,000)	(22,000)	(33,000)
Thetfib contribution	3,000	2,000	(3,000)
Polymer contribution (40 − 12)	5,600	11,200	16,800
Total (company)	$8,600m	$13,200m	$13,800m

Transfer price = $12

Revenue	14,000	24,000	30,000
Costs (15 + 12)	(5,400)	(10,800)	(16,200)
Thetfib contribution	8,600	13,200	13,800
Polymer contribution	–	–	–
Total	$8,600m	$13,200m	$13,800m

At a transfer price of $40, M will choose to produce 200 million litres and sell at $70 as it gives maximum contribution. However, the company would make more by selling 600 million litres at a price of $50. Changing the transfer price to $12 would mean that M would also choose this level.

For the receiving division

Transfer price	$40	$12
Contribution	3,000	13,800
Fixed costs	(2,000)	(2,000)
	1,000	11,800
Tax (35%)	(350)	(4,130)
	$650m	$7,670m

There would be an increase in profit of $7,020m per month for the receiving division.

(ii) Overseas production with transfer price = $12

Price	$70	$60	$50
Output (m)	200	400	600
Revenue	14,000	24,000	30,000
Costs (22 + 12)	(6,800)	(13,600)	(20,400)
Contribution	7,200	10,400	9,600

This implies a production level of 400 million litres if overseas

Contribution	10,400
Fixed costs	(600)
	9,800
Tax at 20%	(1,960)
	$7,840m

This exceeds the best achieved in home country by $170m per month.

(c) Impact on management accounting

The best production plan is to produce 125 million litres of Synfib in house and 400m litres of Thetfib in Foreign which will maximise contribution. Assuming there is no reduction in customer satisfaction or quality, this will help in maximising shareholder's wealth.

The management accounting system needs to ensure that the managers come to the best decision for the company. This would therefore suggest the transfer price should be set at $12 to ensure this. However, this would take away any negotiating power from the managers and would leave the supplying division with no profit at all as it would only cover its marginal cost. This will have a serious impact on motivation and will not inspire them to meet the objectives.

One possibility to ensure that managers take a wider view of the entire organisation is not to divide the company up on divisional lines. This will mean redesigning the structure and remuneration system.

The management accounting system also needs to capture and monitor the information which led to the decision to go overseas with Thetfib. Changes in transport costs, taxes or employment costs may bring the decision into question as might any other costs such as redundancies in the Home country. Government policy changes on areas such as import barriers and currency restrictions in Foreign also need to be monitored as the strategy to produce in Foreign assumes that the status quo is maintained.

(d) Assessment of divisional performance

In order to achieve its organisational objectives, the directors of C need to set SMART targets and to measure the progress towards these targets. This will inevitably mean that the performance of the divisions needs to be assessed, as the objectives can be broken down into operational targets for each business unit.

In particular the directors need to set a target and measure

- the level of profits achieved by each division
- the quality of the product produced
- the overall level of costs
- the economical and efficient use of resources
- the level of pollution produced by the different plants
- training and staff turnover
- output per employee.

The reporting systems as well as the areas being measured, along with their targets, need to be carefully monitored to ensure that all the useful management data is being captured.

Question 6 PC airlines

(a) Benefits and disadvantages

The main impacts on PC Airlines in determining its future aims and objectives are as follows:

Benefits

The aim of increasing members' shareholder wealth is likely to be in line with its own aims and objectives both now and in the future. Membership of the alliance is intended to increase revenues and decrease costs through economics of scale, which should help achieve this aim.

The last 2 years have seen growth in turnover and contribution enjoyed by PC, which presumably is partly due to membership of the alliance.

Disadvantages

Membership of the alliance will continue to benefit PC only as long as the objectives coincide with the companies. Although it is unlikely that the main objective of shareholders' wealth will conflict, supporting objectives relating to staff and customer service or environmental issues may be at odds with PC's objectives.

PC may have to consult the members of the alliance before implementing policies and this could place limitations on its operations. The disagreement over the action to take regarding the bad publicity shows how operational decisions, or the implementation of the objectives as the senior management of Worldair see them can be against the wishes of individual members.

Overall, PC must abide by the rules of the alliance and must balance the benefits of its continuing membership against the potential disadvantages of conflicting views on implementation of strategy. PC is the smallest member but has seen increasing turnover and contribution within the protection of the alliance.

(b) Action and implications

A commercial business needs to react to changes in its environment and the bad publicity will affect Worldair if no action is taken. Its competitors will undoubtedly take action, so the impact may be more than an industry-wide reduction as customers desert to airlines that address the issue.

It is unclear how reliable the estimates on the reductions due to the bad publicity is, and more research needs to be done to establish this. It may not be a major public concern that influences their choice of airline, despite media reports. The research needs to be among Worldair's current customers to assess the impact.

If the discomfort leads to medical issues, or the lack of room to safety issues, the governments in various countries may legislate, driving all airlines using those destinations to comply. Where regulation is considered, the alliance should present well-researched data to back up their recommendations to governments and other regulatory authorities.

It may well be, on analysis of the data, that more leg room is necessary and the seats would be readjusted. This needs to be widely broadcast to the public, and may form the rationale for a price increase if other airlines have not followed suit.

The research needed will have to be funded by the alliance members and may exceed the amount allowed for.

(c)

	PC $m	AB $m	US $m	Total $m
Turnover this year	1,200	2,540	3,300	7,040
Economy (75%, 50%, 80%)	900	1,270	2,640	
Other classes	300	1,270	660	
Economy long haul (70%, 80%, 60%)	630	1,016	1,584	
Economy short haul	270	254	1,056	

NEXT YEAR

Other class revenue (5%)	315	1,334	693	
Economy long haul	630	1,016	1,584	
Economy short haul (4%)*	281	264	1,089	
	1,226	2,614	3,375	

CONTRIBUTION

Other class (70%, 85%, 80%)	221	1,134	554	
Economy long (25%, 10%, 7.5%)	158	102	277	
Economy short (25%, 10%, 17.5%)	70	26	192	
	449	1,262	1,023	2,734
Seat conversion	(30)	(50)	(80)	(160)
R&D & publicity	(12)	(25)	(33)	(70)
NET CONTRIBUTION	407	1,187	910	2,504

* Average reduction = 20%
Growth now predicted as 5% × 80% = 4%

The benefits of this analysis are that it shows the Worldair management how the revenues and contributions are divided between the airlines in the alliance and they can measure the impact of the bad publicity and other issues on the contribution to assess its importance.

	PC	AB	US	Total
Currently predicted	407	1,187	910	2,504
Without publicity	457	1,267	1,040	2,763
Decrease	$50m	$80m	$130m	$259m
Percentage	11%	6%	13%	9%

This shows a significant impact of a 9 per cent reduction in contribution across the alliance and 13 per cent for us. This will therefore need to be addressed by the Worldair senior management.

(d) Attitudes to implementations

AB appears to be less anxious than the other two airlines to implement the suggestions to counter the adverse publicity; this is probably due to two reasons.

Firstly, the impact on AB of the publicity is less severe as can be seen by the calculations above. AB are expected to lose 6 per cent of their contribution and this would be reduced to only 2 per cent if the seat conversions were not implemented. This is in contrast to PC (11 per cent) and US (13 per cent) who will be more concerned to mitigate the problem.

Secondly, AB has been suffering a deterioration in profits and revenues between last year and this year, in contrast to the growth experienced by PC and US. It may feel it cannot really afford to implement such a programme.

In an alliance, decisions reached must be on a consensual basis, either through majority voting or by dictating the requirements for decision-taking in the rules of the alliance. There is no point in having an alliance if each member will only follow the decisions of the alliance when it can see direct advantages to itself. In this instance, AB must be persuaded of the benefits to the whole alliance and in the longer term to itself rather than only considering its own short-term position.

It is worth pointing out that the estimates do not take into account the impact on the turnover and contribution if the mitigating actions were not taken. In that sense the 6 per cent drop for AB is misleading as it compares results to what might have been rather than the result, given the publicity, if no action is taken.

Question 7 CG

(a) Strategy formulation

The rational planning model follows a logical approach from objectives, position and environmental analysis through to identifying a strategy for maintaining or increasing competitive advantage. However, CG does not compete in the commercial sense and has less control choice over its "markets". Applicants for funding will approach CG rather than CG targeting particular organisations.

As a result, the rational planning model may be too inflexible and unable to adapt to environments and circumstances which change quickly, as may well be the case in developing countries. Although it has benefits in allowing managers to understand the strategic direction of CG, they need to recognise that the output from the rational planning model may need to be modified over time as strategies emerge, driven by the environmental changes and the vagaries of rational resource analysis.

(i) Analysis of performance

	$'000s	% of Income
Income		
External	700	25% (M: 97%)
Other regions	2,100	75% (M: 3%)
	2,800	
Variable costs		
Service	200	7% (M: 13%)
Administration	80	3% (M: 7%)
	280	
Contribution	2,520	90% (M: 80%)
Fixed costs		
Service	600	22% (M: 11%)
Administration	1,270	45% (M: 40%)
	1,870	
Surplus	650	23% (M: 29%)
CG charges	300	11% (M: 8%)
Net surplus	350	12% (M: 21%)

Z manages a higher contribution margin than M (90 per cent vs 80 per cent) as the variable costs are lower in percentage terms. However the service fixed costs, and to a lesser extent the fixed administration cost, are a higher percentage leading to lower net surplus percentage margin than M.

Overall, Z appears to perform reasonably, given its target, but we would need to look at other measures, such as the number of external projects sponsored, to give an overall assessment.

174 Exam Practice Kit: Business Strategy

(b) (ii) NPV of Z's proposal:

	$'000	10% DF	PV
t_0	(400)	1	(400.0)
$t_1 - t_6$	105	4.36	457.8
t_6	10	0.56	5.6
		Net present value	63.4

Sensitivity analysis

Original capital: 63.4/400 = 15.85%

The original outlay would have to increase by 15.9 per cent before a negative NPV arose.

Number of units: 63.4/457.8 = 13.8%

The number of units would have to decrease by 13.8 per cent (i.e. 69 units) to create a negative NPV.

Revenue: 63.4/(200 × 4.36) = 7.27%

The revenue per unit would have to decrease by 7.3 per cent to create a negative NPV.

Costs: 63.4/(95 × 4.36) = 15.3%

The costs would have to rise by 15.3 per cent before a negative NPV arose.

	$'000
Impact on ROCE in 2003/04	
Surplus (350 + 105 − 65)	390
Capital (8,000 + 400 − 65)	8,335
ROCE	4.68%

Depreciation = (400 − 10)/6 = 65% per annum

The manager of region Z was managing to achieve 4 per cent before the new proposal. However, most of the income is derived from work for other regions rather than from projects of its own, compared with only 4 per cent of region M's income. Therefore, although it is achieving close to the ROCE required, it may be sensible for the manager to look for more external income opportunities.

The main objective of CG is to provide development funds to organisations around the world and to cover its costs with a return of capital plus 5 per cent ROCE. They would probably be criticised if they made excessive returns. Exactly what constitutes excessive returns is a political question, and partly depends on whether those returns are then re-invested in other projects.

(c) Performance evaluation methods

In a commercial environment, divisions assessed by ROCE are rewarded for any excess return but the divisions must aim for 5 per cent. This is a strange target to have and it reflects the nature of the enterprise which is to help development rather than make a profit. Given this, it would seem odd that the NPV is assessed at 10 per cent and not 5 per cent and that transfers to and from other regions are charged at a marked-up price rather than cost.

Using net book value of assets means that a higher ROCE is recorded as the assets get older and are depreciated more even if the surplus stays the same. Using gross book value would not produce this problem and would also give a result nearer to the 5 per cent required; M which suffers particularly from this would see its predicted ROCE reduce to 6.25 per cent for next year without the new development, or 6.9 per cent with the new development. Continuing to use net book value with a target of 5 per cent is likely to lead to wasteful decisions simply in order to cut the surplus.

The charge from CG headquarters seems to be the same for both regions, and should probably be based on the level of service provided for each region if this can be quantified. Alternative methods of assessment would include considering the surpluses as positive as long as they are then used to fund other projects. Residual income or economic value added could be used as well as incorporating a number of non-financial performance measures. These could be included in a balanced scorecard and targets set for the regional managers relating to learning and growth, internal processes and clients.

Question 8 MW and FS

(a) SWOT analysis

In the rational planning model, objectives are set for an organisation before undertaking a corporate appraisal to identify the strengths and weaknesses and likely opportunities and threats. From these, strategies are designed which help the organisation achieve its objectives by building on strengths and taking advantage of likely opportunities while resolving weaknesses and avoiding or mitigating any threats.

For MW a SWOT might include

Strengths:

- A good secure financial position.
- Increasing profits and a rising share price.
- A good reputation in the north of the country.

Weaknesses:

- Little experience of takeovers or of integrating businesses.
- No presence in the south and limited expansion possibilities in the north.
- Cautious in gearing structure.

Opportunities:

- Possible takeover of FS to expand into the south.
- Increase gearing to reduce overall cost of capital.

Threats:

- Payment in shares will dilute the family shareholding.
- Another competitor may acquire FS leading to a loss of market share.
- Competitors may push up the price of FS.
- Lack of other possibilities for expansion.

In summary, shareholder value can be enhanced through increasing sales, by increasing growth and market share. There are limited opportunities to do this organically, so the potential acquisition of FS offers the best route. However, MW has limited experience of takeover and of integrating businesses, and additional costs in either area would be detrimental to shareholders' interests and achievement of the organisation's objectives.

(b) Rappaport's seven drivers

Rappaport identified seven drivers of shareholder value, which can be applied to MW as follows:

1 Sales growth rate

   A growth in sales will drive profits and cash up; MW has reported an 8 per cent increase in sales this year, but it will be difficult to sustain such growth without an increase in outlets.

2 Operating profit margin

   An increasing profit margin shows costs under control and MW has increased net profits by 15 per cent which is almost double the sales growth. It has therefore become more efficient in its cost management.

3 The planning period

   This relates to the period over which growth can be expected. Given the problems in expanding much more organically, the takeover of FS seems a logical next step.

4 The rate of cash income tax payments

   Although decreasing the tax-rate would help shareholders, companies have only limited control over this. MW has lower debt than could be sustained and a higher gearing ratio would enable more of the finance costs to be tax allowable and hence reduce the tax bill.

5 Incremental fixed capital investment

   Reducing fixed assets without affecting sales would benefit shareholders. However, it is likely that to sustain growth, some investment will have to be made.

6 Working capital investment

   Reducing working capital, without affecting the sales, will benefit shareholders. MW has a high investment in working capital, like any supermarket business, but needs to keep it under control by ensuring it has a very short stock turnover period. This is already lower than that of FS.

7 The cost of capital

   Reducing the cost of capital to a minimum would be efficient for the shareholders. This is because it would enhance cash flows through the cheaper debt finance and the tax saving. Even though shareholders would increase the return required due to the higher risk from the gearing, shareholder value would increase overall. MW would appear to have a lower level of debt than optimal.

(c) REPORT

To: Chairman of MW

From: Management Accountant

Date: xx May 2004

Re: Benefits and Risks of Acquiring FS

Introduction

This report looks at the benefits and risks of acquiring FS, given that our primary aim is to enhance shareholder value. Detailed analysis to support this report is contained in the appendix.

Benefits

There are a number of areas in which MW appears to outperform FS and could therefore improve shareholder value by applying its management techniques.

Gross profit margins are higher at FS but gross profit per square metre is equal to MW or lower, which implies that the higher profit margins are achieved through higher prices. There would therefore appear to be scope for increasing efficiency in store space utilisation to increase the gross profit per square metre.

Stores in the FS group have not managed to achieve the same level of net profits as MW stores despite higher gross profit margins. This indicates that MW have tighter controls of their overheads.

The stock turnover periods show that FS hold their stocks on average for 75 per cent longer than MW, meaning that there is some scope for MW applying more efficient stock management systems.

FS shows a higher sales and gross profit per customer visit, again showing the effect of higher prices, which may have helped to reduce the volume of customers. Again, with MW management, prices could be reduced leading to higher volumes and increased efficiency.

Risks

There is some discrepancy between the salary levels of staff in the two companies. Lower remuneration in FS may have led to a lack of motivation and this should be addressed as soon as possible, as should the disparity in salaries between MW's own two areas. This will, however, have cost implications.

A major risk is that MW will be unable to increase the profit margins in FS or increase efficiency in the operations. However, MW's rising P/E ratio, and FS's falling one, would point to the market's confidence in the MW management.

Finally, the overriding risk is that MW, due to its lack of experience in takeovers, offers too high a price for FS in response to competitive bidding by other supermarket companies. MW must be very careful to consider the likely impact on its own share price and shareholder value before making a bid, and have in place contingency plans to deal with a rejected bid or a counterbid from another competitor.

Conclusion

It would seem a sensible strategic move to bid for FS, as long as MW can manage to acquire it without damaging its own share price. The managers will then need to look closely at increasing both margins and efficiency in order to increase shareholder value. However, it seems unlikely that shareholder value will continue to increase at the rate experienced so far without the takeover.

Appendix

	MW		FS	
	NW	NE	SW	SE
Gross Profit (ex wages)	$6m	$5m	$4m	$3.2m
Gross Profit Margin	60%	62.5%	67%	64%
Net Profit Margin	20%	17.5%	13.3%	10%
Gross Profit/m²	$1,000	$833	$833	$667
Net Profit/m²	$333	$233	$167	$104
Sales/Visit	$33.33	$40	$40	$50
Gross Profit/Visit	$20	$25	$27	$32
Net Profit/Visit	$6.67	$7	$5.3	$5
Salaries/Mgr	$66,700	$83,300	$50,000	$50,000
Wages/Other staff	$18,500	$16,000	$16,700	$15,000
Stock Turnover Period	2 days		3.5 days	
P/E Ratio	4,500/225 = 20		4,000/200 = 20	

Question 9 ACEP

(a) CD Download Proposal

Expected monthly sales = $(10,000 \times 0.4) + (12,000 \times 0.5) + (14,000 \times 0.1) = 11,400$
Contribution per copy = $2.00 - 0.50 - 0.45 = £1.05$
Net monthly fixed costs (at 11,400 sales) = $12,000 + 16,000 - 18,000 = 10,000$
Monthly profits = $50 \times (11,400 \times 1.05 - 10,000) = £98,500$
Annual profits = $98,500 \times 12 = £1,182,000$

However, this has worked on the basis of the expected (or average) sales of 11,400. If we look at each of the three possibilities for sales individually, we find:

Sales Volume	10,000	12,000	14,000
	£	£	£
Contribution at £1.05	10,500	12,600	14,700
Advertising revenue	17,000	18,000	18,000
Fixed costs	(28,000)	(28,000)	(28,000)
Monthly profit per store	(500)	2,600	4,700
Annual store profit	(6,000)	31,200	56,400
Annual profit	(300,000)	1,560,000	2,820,000
Probability	0.4	0.5	0.1

There is therefore a 40% chance that the proposal would make a loss of £300,000. As the music division is already making losses, it would seem too high a risk for the company and its shareholders to take.

These figures have been supplied by the equipment vendor who has an incentive to be optimistic. It has also ignored the impact of competition and substitutes; as downloading at minimal cost from the Internet becomes more widespread, it is likely that sales for downloading for payment in a retail outlet will decline rapidly. It is therefore unlikely, even if it were an acceptable proposal based on these figures, that it would prove viable in the long term.

(b) Portfolio Analysis

Portfolio analysis is helpful in formulating strategy and typically might use the Boston Consulting Group Matrix. This looks at each business unit and examines its market position and market attractiveness. In the BCG matrix, these are measured by the market share of sales and the total market growth.

The business units will be classified as stars (high market growth and high market share), cash cows (low market growth but high market share), problem children (high growth but low market share) or dogs (low market share and low growth). This then dictates the strategic approach to the areas, with stars being invested in, cows being milked for cash generation, problem children being either invested in or disposed of and dogs being disposed of.

In addition, portfolio analysis allows for the comparison of business units to assess the best use of limited resources. It gives a useful overview of the company's operations so that the overall balance of the operations can be easily seen and performance potential can be assessed. Companies often try to have a portfolio of business operations which are at different stages in their respective lifecycles, so that as older businesses become cash cows or dogs, newer ones replace them as stars.

However, the models can be misleading and should be used with caution. It assumes that there is no interdependence between the businesses so that closing down one area will have no effect on another, and assumes that having a low market share (particularly in a low growth market) will inevitably lead to losses. However, smaller players in the market may specialise and be able to protect their sales through differentiation. This shows that the definition of the market and hence the market share is crucial but it is a subjective decision.

As far as ACEP is concerned, both publishing and radio have high market share in markets with low growth, classifying them as cash cows. It is likely that the market for television is only growing slowly while that for music (at least in the area ACEP is involved in) appears to be declining. As they have a low share of each of these markets, they would be classified as dogs.

What is striking is that there are no businesses in markets which are growing rapidly and that under a traditional interpretation of the model both the television and the music businesses should be dropped. However, this ignores any cross marketing opportunities between the businesses, which are likely to be quite strong between television and the publishing and radio divisions.

(c) (i) Risks in European market

A sensible first step in assessing the risks would be to examine the business environment using a PEST analysis:

Political and legal factors

There may be legislation or political concern regarding foreign ownership of media, the content of such media, the sourcing of materials and working practices and language content.

Economic factors

It will be important to understand the likely market and the amount of disposable income that the target customers are likely to have. The cost of inputs such as paper, production costs and rates of pay along with legislation on employment and other company law will also be relevant, as will exchange rates.

Social, cultural and demographic factors

There will be differences in taste and culture and particularly in the younger readers, what is popular in the UK may not be popular in these new markets and reading habits may be different. In addition working practices and organisational culture may well be different.

Technological factors

It will be important to check what technology is available in the editing and printing processes compared to that which is used by ACEP in the UK.

After this review, ACEP may conclude that risks involved in entering the new market include:

Not understanding the business or consumer culture

Not understanding foreign legal restrictions and other regulations

Established players may take action to resist a new entrant to the market.

(ii) Merits of the Two Proposals

Both opportunities are likely to be viable in financial terms. The acquisition would cost £10 m and give a contribution of £3 m per annum and increase fixed costs by £1 m. The joint venture would involve an investment of £20 m but would give contribution of £4 m per annum and an increase in fixed costs of £1 m.

The main considerations in the choice between the two proposals are likely to be non-financial: Joint ventures will generally have huge benefits in overcoming barriers to entry, such as nationalistic legislation and cultural problems as the joint venture partner will already have knowledge of these areas. In addition, in some countries it is required to have a domestic partner in some industries. A joint venture, however, will mean having to agree operational and strategic decisions with an overseas partner, who might have a different management culture and possibly different objectives.

Although a target acquisition has been identified, it is not clear if the owners will be willing sellers. Additionally, although ACEP have a good reputation for post-acquisition rationalisation in the UK publishing industry, it has not attempted this overseas and this is likely to be even more difficult if it is a hostile takeover.

Overall, the joint venture approach would appear to be less risky, even if ACEP's ultimate intention is to acquire its own company in the market.

(d) REPORT

To: Board of Directors

From: Financial Controller

Date: X of X 20XX

CD Downloading, European Expansion and Business Disposals

This report will discuss the CD downloading proposal, the possible European expansion and possible business disposals.

(i) CD Downloading Proposal

Although the equipment supplier shows an annual profit of £1,182,000, this has been based on an average level of sales. Even based on the supplier's own estimates there is a 40% chance that the proposal would lose £300,000 a year. The estimates are likely to be optimistic anyway as the supplier has a vested interest in the proposal being accepted and take no account of the likely downturn in sales as free or cheap downloading form the Internet at home becomes more popular with our target market. In addition, acceptance of this proposal would mean retaining the music division, currently making losses of £14 m, which is discussed below.

(ii) European Expansion

It seems sensible to expand into Europe given the company's position in the UK market. As a leader in consumer magazine publishing and with a leadership position in both teenage and lifestyle magazines, it should exploit this expertise abroad. As culture becomes more global, particularly in the teenager market, it can only increase the opportunity to benefit from such a move.

Of the two alternatives, the safest and quickest approach would be to develop the joint venture with the domestic company. Although this requires more investment than the acquisition, it gives a willing partner who has already in-depth knowledge of the cultural, legal and political framework of the new market. If it is successful, we can use this as a learning exercise in acquiring knowledge of the new environment which will enable us to successfully make further acquisitions or set up other companies.

(iii) Disposal of Businesses

As can be seen in the appendix, the music division has not performed well, with its contribution to company profits dropping and being unable to cover its fixed costs in the last two years. On the assumption that the fixed costs are all related to the music division and that no other division would lose sales or increase costs if the music division was closed down, there would seem to be a good argument for disposal of this division.

The experience of management is primarily in publishing and there would appear to be limited cross marketing between the specialist bands managed and the teenager and lifestyle magazines. Bigger players in the music industry are consolidating while smaller specialist bands are starting to release their music on the Internet rather than using an intermediary. The prospects for the type of business we currently have, therefore, look poor and it is probably best to dispose of it before more losses are incurred.

The television division is also seeing its contribution and profits declining but more slowly, and both are still positive at the moment. It is also likely that greater opportunities exist for cross selling with the radio and publishing divisions. It is recommended that we retain this division for the time being and look for greater opportunities to cross sell through our other divisions.

(iv) Response to Institutional Shareholders

In presenting to the institutional investors, we should make the following points:

- The music division has little synergy with the rest of the company and will be sold as soon as possible. This will increase PBIT by £14 m in terms of 2002 results and possibly provide £10 m (less any disposal costs) of funds for other opportunities.
- Management will then seek to exploit connections and cross marketing opportunities to the full between radio, television and publishing.
- All three divisions have suffered in the last two years from depressed advertising revenue which has been industry wide. However, before this, there was steady growth in all these three divisions and the management expect this to reassert itself.
- The company has decided to exploit its knowledge of the publishing market, and in particular that of teenager and lifestyle magazines, by entering into a joint venture in Europe, thus capitalising on the knowledge of the market and the culture held by its joint venture partner. This will cost £20 m but is expected initially to add £3 m per annum to PBIT.
- Given the size of the market and the company's position in radio and publishing, it is unlikely that further expansion could take place in the UK; the company will, therefore, be looking to expand through expansion overseas where opportunities present themselves.

Appendix

	2002 £m	2001 £m	2000 £m	1999 £m
Contribution				
Publishing	217	275	288	230
Radio	259	281	285	240
Television	53	56	60	52
Music	16	24	32	35
	545	636	665	557
PBIT				
Publishing	56	115	126	75
Radio	109	131	137	112
Television	13	16	20	17
Music	(14)	(6)	0	3
	164	256	283	207
ROCE	18.22%	28.44%	32.53%	25.71%

May 2006 Questions and Answers

12

Strategic Level

Paper P6 – Management Accounting – Business Strategy

Question Paper	185
Examiner's Brief Guide to the Paper	196
Examiner's Answers	198

The answers published here have been written by the Examiner and should provide a helpful guide for both tutors and students.

Published separately on the CIMA website (www.cimaglobal.com/students) from the end of September 2006 will be a Post Examination Guide for this paper, which will provide much valuable and complementary material including indicative mark information.

© 2006 The Chartered Institute of Management Accountants. All rights reserved. No part of this publication may be reproduced, stored in a retrieval system, or transmitted, in any form or by any means, electronic, mechanical, photocopying, recorded or otherwise, without the written permission of the publisher.

Business Management Pillar

Strategic Level

P6 – Management Accounting – Business Strategy

23 May 2006 – Tuesday Morning Session

Instructions to candidates

You are allowed three hours to answer this question paper.
You are allowed 20 minutes reading time **before the examination begins** during which you should read the question paper and, if you wish, make annotations on the question paper. However, you will **not** be allowed, **under any circumstances**, to open the answer book and start writing or use your calculator during this reading time.
You are strongly advised to carefully read ALL the question requirements before attempting the question concerned (that is, all parts and/or sub-questions). The question requirements are contained in a dotted box.
Answer the ONE compulsory question in Section A on pages 186 to 188.
Answer TWO of the four questions in Section B on pages 189 to 192.
Maths Tables and Formulae are provided on pages 193 to 195.
Write your full examination number, paper number and the examination subject title in the spaces provided on the front of the examination answer book. Also write your contact ID and name in the space provided in the right-hand margin and seal to close.
Tick the appropriate boxes on the front of the answer book to indicate which questions you have answered.

SECTION A – 50 MARKS

[the indicative time for answering this section is 90 minutes]

ANSWER THIS QUESTION

❓ Question One

CCC is a specialist car manufacturer, based in Y, a country in Europe. Three ex-employees of a major car manufacturer founded CCC in 1992 as a private limited company. CCC has never required further finance to aid its expansion, and remains a private company owned by the three founders. The three, who are all engineers, decided to leave their former employer in order to establish a business producing hand-built high performance sports cars for wealthy customers. The major car manufacturers are not able to supply such vehicles, as their systems are all based on the assumption that they will produce each car model in sufficient numbers to benefit from significant economies of scale.

CCC has always been profitable, and has grown significantly in recent years. It is now the second largest specialist car manufacturer in Europe and employs 300 staff at its head office and factory near the capital city of Y.

The specialist car industry

The customers who buy specialist cars are very status-conscious, and want a car that is totally unique. They are prepared to pay a very high price for their new car, in comparison to 'top of the range' models from the major manufacturers, but require extremely high quality and service levels in return. At present there are fewer than twenty specialist car manufacturers in Europe, and only six of these (including CCC) produce sports cars. The others specialise in off-road vehicles, armour-plated cars or limousines. As the cars are produced to customer order, there has historically been little price competition between the various specialist sports car manufacturers.

CCC, in common with other specialist car manufacturers, has invested a significant sum in creating the design of its two car models. It also spends a large proportion of its annual budget on sales promotion and marketing. This includes placing expensive advertisements in upmarket car magazines, and attending many car shows and exhibitions. CCC also has a reputation for paying higher than average salaries to its senior designers and production staff. As a result, staff turnover at CCC is virtually non-existent.

Customers, who are often loyal to a particular manufacturer, can specify modifications to the basic design, such as minor changes to the body shape of the car, or major changes to the engine performance and driving characteristics of the car. The directors of CCC have always assumed that their customers are not particularly price-conscious, as they are often wealthy individuals with high disposable incomes. For these customers, the alternative to buying a car from CCC might be to purchase a yacht or go on a round-the-world cruise.

CCC manufactures most of the components of its cars in-house. The main exceptions are electrical and control equipment, wheels and tyres. The only major bought-in component is the car's engine, which CCC buys from a major car manufacturer and then sends to SSS (a subcontractor) for modification and performance upgrades. While the engine is relatively expensive, it is the work of SSS that represents the single most significant cost of producing each car. CCC has, on occasions, paid SSS the equivalent of 25% of the final sales price of a car.

The board meeting

At the most recent board meeting of CCC, the directors discussed the worsening financial position of the organisation. Having spoken to the Sales Manager they came to the conclusion that, with the economies of Y and neighbouring countries in recession, customers had recently become more aggressive in negotiating down the purchase price of their cars. This had put pressure on the profit margin of CCC for the first time in its history. The directors, therefore, felt it was necessary to commission an independent review of their industry.

The Finance Director provided the following summary of CCC's performance:

€million	2005	2004	2003	2002
Revenue	11.75	11.12	10.06	10.10
Pre-tax profit	0.88	1.43	1.55	2.01
Dividend paid	0.08	0.50	0.50	0.50

The directors were particularly alarmed that SSS, the engine modification sub-contractor, seemed to be making almost as much profit on one of the engines as CCC was on the whole car. The Purchasing Manager of CCC said that it was impossible to negotiate a lower price with SSS, as most of CCC's customers specified that their car must have its engine prepared by SSS. The Sales Manager agreed that one of the 'unique selling points' of CCC's cars was the work done by SSS. At present, SSS does not supply engine modification services to any of CCC's competitors, but there is no contractual obligation to prevent it from doing so. The Purchasing Manager reported that CCC has no long-term supply contract with SSS, and the owner-manager of SSS had declined the offer of such a contract, believing that to enter into such an agreement would not be in the best interests of himself and his seven staff.

SSS

The Purchasing Manager has obtained the following information relating to SSS.

Extracts from the financial statements of SSS Ltd:

	2005 €'000
Revenue	2,455
Cost of sales	1,398
Other costs	867
Profit before tax	190
Profit after tax	133
Dividend paid	65

	At 31 Dec 2005 €'000
Non-current assets	894
Inventories	232
Receivables	146
Cash	32
Payables	244
Equity share capital	100
Retained earnings	960

Information obtained from the Motor Trade Association

Automotive component and service suppliers:

Average P/E ratio (for those suppliers with quoted share prices)	7.5
Average annual growth rate in reported post-tax profits (1995–2005)	2.5
Average pre-tax profit margin	4.3%
Average pre-tax return on capital employed	11.2%
Average receivables days	65
Average payables days	28
Average revenue per employee	€128,500

Requirements

(a) Using Porter's "five forces" model as a framework, evaluate the competitive environment in which CCC operates.

(15 marks)

(b) Evaluate the financial position and performance of SSS, as at 31 December 2005.

Note: There are up to 12 marks available for calculations in this part of the question.

(25 marks)

(c) Advise the directors of CCC how the organisation might overcome the bargaining power of SSS.

(10 marks)
(Total for question one = 50 marks)

(Total for Section A = 50 marks)

SECTION B – 50 MARKS

[the indicative time for answering this section is 90 minutes]

ANSWER *TWO* QUESTIONS FROM FOUR

Question Two

2B is a medium-sized retailer of sports equipment and leisure clothing. 2B was established in 1987, and currently operates from three retail shops in town centre locations.

The management team of 2B is very careful about how it recruits staff. In addition to the specific skills required to do the job, any applicant must also have a 'passion' for sport. This has resulted in 2B gaining a reputation for excellent customer service and enthusiastic staff. A large proportion of staff time is also devoted to training, both on the product range and customer service techniques. According to a recent survey conducted by the store managers, the customers believe that 2B employees are 'helpful and knowledgeable'. The customers also praised the 2B shops for being 'well designed' and said that it was 'very easy' to find what they were looking for.

Another feature of 2B that is appreciated by the customers is the range of goods stocked. By developing close relationships with the major manufacturers of sports goods and clothing, 2B is able to stock a far wider range of items than its rivals. Control of this stock was made easier, last year, by the development of a sophisticated computerised stock control system. Using the system, any member of staff can locate any item of stock in any of the shops or the warehouse. If the required item is not 'in stock' at 2B, it is also possible to automatically check the availability of stock with the manufacturer.

At a recent management meeting, one of the store managers suggested that 2B consider developing its very basic website into one capable of e-retailing. At present, the website only gives the location of stores and some very basic details of the range of stock carried. Although the development of the website would be expensive, the managers have decided to give the suggestion serious consideration.

Requirements

(a) Using the value chain model, explain those activities that add value in the 2B organisation, BEFORE the e-retail investment.

(10 marks)

(b) Identify those activities in the value chain of 2B that may be affected by the e-retail investment, explaining whether the value added by each of them may increase or decrease as a result of the e-retail investment.

(15 marks)
(Total for Question Two = 25 marks)

Question Three

3C is a medium-sized pharmaceutical company. It is based in Asia, but distributes and sells its products worldwide.

In common with other pharmaceutical companies, 3C has a large number of products in its portfolio, though most of these are still being developed. The success rate of new drugs is very low, as most fail to complete clinical trials or are believed to be uneconomic to launch. However, the rewards to be gained from a successful new drug are so great that it is only necessary to have a few successful drugs on the market to be very profitable.

At present 3C has 240 drugs at various stages of development; being tested or undergoing clinical trials prior to a decision being made whether to launch the drug. 3C has only three products that are actually 'on the market':

- Epsilon is a drug used in the treatment of heart disease. It has been available for eight months and has achieved significant success. Sales of this drug are not expected to increase from their current level.
- Alpha is a painkiller. It was launched more than ten years ago, and has become one of the leading drugs in its class. In a few months the patent on this drug will expire, and other manufacturers will be allowed to produce generic copies of it. Alpha is expected to survive a further twelve months after it loses its patent, and will then be withdrawn.
- Beta is used in the hospital treatment of serious infections. It is a very specialised drug, and cannot be obtained from a doctor or pharmacist for use outside the hospital environment. It was launched only three months ago, and has yet to generate a significant sales volume.

The directors of 3C meet every month to review the product portfolio and to discuss possible investment opportunities. At their next meeting, they are to be asked to consider three investments. Due to a limited investment budget, the three investments are mutually exclusive (that is, they will only be able to invest in ONE of the options). The options are as follows:

- The directors can invest in a new version of Alpha, Alpha2, which offers improved performance. This will allow 3C to apply for a new patent for Alpha2, and maintain the level of sales achieved by Alpha for an additional five years. Alpha2 has successfully completed all its clinical trials, and can be launched immediately.
- The directors can invest in a major marketing campaign to promote the use of Beta to specialist hospital staff. While this investment should lead to a significant growth in the sales of Beta, 3C is aware that one of its competitors is actively promoting a rival product with similar performance to that of Beta.
- The directors can invest in the final stage of clinical trials for Gamma. This is a 'breakthrough' drug, as it has no near rivals on the market. Gamma is used in the treatment of HIV, and offers significantly better success rates than any treatment currently available. The team of 3C specialists managing the development of Gamma is confident it can successfully complete clinical trials within six months. The team also believes that Gamma should be sold at the lowest price possible, to maximise the benefits of Gamma to society. However, the marketing department of 3C believes that it would be possible to earn very large profits from Gamma due to its success rate and breakthrough status.

Requirements

(a) Briefly explain how the product life cycle model can be used to analyse the current product portfolio of 3C (that is, BEFORE the planned investment).

(8 marks)

(b) Evaluate the potential impact of each of the three investment options (Alpha2, Beta and Gamma) on the product portfolio of 3C, referring to your answer to part (a) above.

(9 marks)

(c) Discuss the social responsibility implications of each of the three investment options, for the directors of 3C.

(8 marks)
(Total for Question Three = 25 marks)

Question Four

4D is a large teaching hospital. While it offers a full range of hospital services to its local community, it also has a large staff of professors and lecturers who teach and train all kinds of medical student. 4D has a very good reputation for clinical excellence.

One of the areas in which 4D is very highly regarded is the training of surgeons. Three of the nine operating theatres in the hospital can be observed from a gallery, though only a limited number of students can watch any operation due to space constraints. This allows the students to watch an experienced surgeon carry out a procedure and then ask questions of their lecturer or the surgeon. Later in their training, students can use the same facilities to carry out operations while being observed by experienced staff and fellow students.

The IT department of 4D has just developed a new Information System for use in operating theatres. This system (OTIS – the Operating Theatre Information System) uses web technology to allow students anywhere in the world to videoconference with a lecturer during an operation. The students can observe the operation and the surgical team, and discuss the procedure with the surgeon and their lecturer. The system also works 'in reverse' so a surgeon at 4D can watch a student perform an operation elsewhere in the world, and provide guidance and support. The OTIS system is currently being tested, prior to introduction.

Requirements

(a)
  (i) Distinguish between Business Process Re-engineering (BPR) and Process Innovation (PI), and explain the role of information technology in each of these techniques.

  (6 marks)

  (ii) Discuss whether, in your opinion, the Operating Theatre Information System (OTIS) implementation is an example of BPR or PI.

  (4 marks)

(b) Evaluate THREE benefits to 4D and TWO benefits to society, of the Operating Theatre Information System (OTIS).

(15 marks)
(Total for Question Four = 25 marks)

? Question Five

5E is a management consultancy practice. It is a limited liability partnership with eight equal partners. Over the past ten years, 5E has invested heavily in the development of knowledge management. It now has a very large knowledgebase, with over half a million documents that have been produced by 5E staff. These range from internal memos, emails and research reports to major client project reports and articles that have been published in professional journals. The knowledgebase is stored on, and accessed through, 5E's Intranet. The Intranet is currently managed by X, a facilities management company which owns all the necessary hardware and software. PCs and laptops are all owned by 5E and maintained by X.

5E also has a website containing contact details for all of 5E's offices, and detailed descriptions of the products and services offered to clients. It also has mini case studies of successful 5E consultancy projects. These case studies have each been approved by the relevant client, as some of the content could have been perceived as commercially sensitive. The website is hosted by an Internet Service Provider (ISP). The same ISP also handles all incoming and outgoing email traffic on behalf of 5E.

Ms Y, the Chief Knowledge Officer (CKO) of 5E, has proposed a major upgrade to the Intranet. This would involve a significant investment, and the major aspects of the planned upgrade are as follows:

- To bring web hosting and the management of the Intranet in-house.
- To redesign the website so it gives clients of 5E password-protected access to the knowledgebase.

Requirements

(a) Recommend the information technology hardware and software that would be required by 5E in order to complete the Intranet upgrade project.

(10 marks)

(b) Using Mendelow's stakeholder mapping model, identify FIVE major stakeholders of the Intranet project. Explain the classification you have given, within the model, to each stakeholder.

(15 marks)
(Total for Question Five = 25 marks)

(Total for Section B = 50 marks)

MATHS TABLES AND FORMULAE

Present value table

Present value of $1, that is $(1 + r)^{-n}$ where r = interest rate; n = number of periods until payment or receipt.

Periods (n)	Interest rates (r)									
	1%	2%	3%	4%	5%	6%	7%	8%	9%	10%
1	0.990	0.980	0.971	0.962	0.952	0.943	0.935	0.926	0.917	0.909
2	0.980	0.961	0.943	0.925	0.907	0.890	0.873	0.857	0.842	0.826
3	0.971	0.942	0.915	0.889	0.864	0.840	0.816	0.794	0.772	0.751
4	0.961	0.924	0.888	0.855	0.823	0.792	0.763	0.735	0.708	0.683
5	0.951	0.906	0.863	0.822	0.784	0.747	0.713	0.681	0.650	0.621
6	0.942	0.888	0.837	0.790	0.746	0.705	0.666	0.630	0.596	0.564
7	0.933	0.871	0.813	0.760	0.711	0.665	0.623	0.583	0.547	0.513
8	0.923	0.853	0.789	0.731	0.677	0.627	0.582	0.540	0.502	0.467
9	0.914	0.837	0.766	0.703	0.645	0.592	0.544	0.500	0.460	0.424
10	0.905	0.820	0.744	0.676	0.614	0.558	0.508	0.463	0.422	0.386
11	0.896	0.804	0.722	0.650	0.585	0.527	0.475	0.429	0.388	0.350
12	0.887	0.788	0.701	0.625	0.557	0.497	0.444	0.397	0.356	0.319
13	0.879	0.773	0.681	0.601	0.530	0.469	0.415	0.368	0.326	0.290
14	0.870	0.758	0.661	0.577	0.505	0.442	0.388	0.340	0.299	0.263
15	0.861	0.743	0.642	0.555	0.481	0.417	0.362	0.315	0.275	0.239
16	0.853	0.728	0.623	0.534	0.458	0.394	0.339	0.292	0.252	0.218
17	0.844	0.714	0.605	0.513	0.436	0.371	0.317	0.270	0.231	0.198
18	0.836	0.700	0.587	0.494	0.416	0.350	0.296	0.250	0.212	0.180
19	0.828	0.686	0.570	0.475	0.396	0.331	0.277	0.232	0.194	0.164
20	0.820	0.673	0.554	0.456	0.377	0.312	0.258	0.215	0.178	0.149

Periods (n)	Interest rates (r)									
	11%	12%	13%	14%	15%	16%	17%	18%	19%	20%
1	0.901	0.893	0.885	0.877	0.870	0.862	0.855	0.847	0.840	0.833
2	0.812	0.797	0.783	0.769	0.756	0.743	0.731	0.718	0.706	0.694
3	0.731	0.712	0.693	0.675	0.658	0.641	0.624	0.609	0.593	0.579
4	0.659	0.636	0.613	0.592	0.572	0.552	0.534	0.516	0.499	0.482
5	0.593	0.567	0.543	0.519	0.497	0.476	0.456	0.437	0.419	0.402
6	0.535	0.507	0.480	0.456	0.432	0.410	0.390	0.370	0.352	0.335
7	0.482	0.452	0.425	0.400	0.376	0.354	0.333	0.314	0.296	0.279
8	0.434	0.404	0.376	0.351	0.327	0.305	0.285	0.266	0.249	0.233
9	0.391	0.361	0.333	0.308	0.284	0.263	0.243	0.225	0.209	0.194
10	0.352	0.322	0.295	0.270	0.247	0.227	0.208	0.191	0.176	0.162
11	0.317	0.287	0.261	0.237	0.215	0.195	0.178	0.162	0.148	0.135
12	0.286	0.257	0.231	0.208	0.187	0.168	0.152	0.137	0.124	0.112
13	0.258	0.229	0.204	0.182	0.163	0.145	0.130	0.116	0.104	0.093
14	0.232	0.205	0.181	0.160	0.141	0.125	0.111	0.099	0.088	0.078
15	0.209	0.183	0.160	0.140	0.123	0.108	0.095	0.084	0.079	0.065
16	0.188	0.163	0.141	0.123	0.107	0.093	0.081	0.071	0.062	0.054
17	0.170	0.146	0.125	0.108	0.093	0.080	0.069	0.060	0.052	0.045
18	0.153	0.130	0.111	0.095	0.081	0.069	0.059	0.051	0.044	0.038
19	0.138	0.116	0.098	0.083	0.070	0.060	0.051	0.043	0.037	0.031
20	0.124	0.104	0.087	0.073	0.061	0.051	0.043	0.037	0.031	0.026

Cumulative present value of $1 per annum, Receivable or Payable at the end of each year for n years $\dfrac{1-(1+r)^{-n}}{r}$

Periods (n)	\multicolumn{10}{c}{Interest rates (r)}									
	1%	2%	3%	4%	5%	6%	7%	8%	9%	10%
1	0.990	0.980	0.971	0.962	0.952	0.943	0.935	0.926	0.917	0.909
2	1.970	1.942	1.913	1.886	1.859	1.833	1.808	1.783	1.759	1.736
3	2.941	2.884	2.829	2.775	2.723	2.673	2.624	2.577	2.531	2.487
4	3.902	3.808	3.717	3.630	3.546	3.465	3.387	3.312	3.240	3.170
5	4.853	4.713	4.580	4.452	4.329	4.212	4.100	3.993	3.890	3.791
6	5.795	5.601	5.417	5.242	5.076	4.917	4.767	4.623	4.486	4.355
7	6.728	6.472	6.230	6.002	5.786	5.582	5.389	5.206	5.033	4.868
8	7.652	7.325	7.020	6.733	6.463	6.210	5.971	5.747	5.535	5.335
9	8.566	8.162	7.786	7.435	7.108	6.802	6.515	6.247	5.995	5.759
10	9.471	8.983	8.530	8.111	7.722	7.360	7.024	6.710	6.418	6.145
11	10.368	9.787	9.253	8.760	8.306	7.887	7.499	7.139	6.805	6.495
12	11.255	10.575	9.954	9.385	8.863	8.384	7.943	7.536	7.161	6.814
13	12.134	11.348	10.635	9.986	9.394	8.853	8.358	7.904	7.487	7.103
14	13.004	12.106	11.296	10.563	9.899	9.295	8.745	8.244	7.786	7.367
15	13.865	12.849	11.938	11.118	10.380	9.712	9.108	8.559	8.061	7.606
16	14.718	13.578	12.561	11.652	10.838	10.106	9.447	8.851	8.313	7.824
17	15.562	14.292	13.166	12.166	11.274	10.477	9.763	9.122	8.544	8.022
18	16.398	14.992	13.754	12.659	11.690	10.828	10.059	9.372	8.756	8.201
19	17.226	15.679	14.324	13.134	12.085	11.158	10.336	9.604	8.950	8.365
20	18.046	16.351	14.878	13.590	12.462	11.470	10.594	9.818	9.129	8.514

Periods (n)	\multicolumn{10}{c}{Interest rates (r)}									
	11%	12%	13%	14%	15%	16%	17%	18%	19%	20%
1	0.901	0.893	0.885	0.877	0.870	0.862	0.855	0.847	0.840	0.833
2	1.713	1.690	1.668	1.647	1.626	1.605	1.585	1.566	1.547	1.528
3	2.444	2.402	2.361	2.322	2.283	2.246	2.210	2.174	2.140	2.106
4	3.102	3.037	2.974	2.914	2.855	2.798	2.743	2.690	2.639	2.589
5	3.696	3.605	3.517	3.433	3.352	3.274	3.199	3.127	3.058	2.991
6	4.231	4.111	3.998	3.889	3.784	3.685	3.589	3.498	3.410	3.326
7	4.712	4.564	4.423	4.288	4.160	4.039	3.922	3.812	3.706	3.605
8	5.146	4.968	4.799	4.639	4.487	4.344	4.207	4.078	3.954	3.837
9	5.537	5.328	5.132	4.946	4.772	4.607	4.451	4.303	4.163	4.031
10	5.889	5.650	5.426	5.216	5.019	4.833	4.659	4.494	4.339	4.192
11	6.207	5.938	5.687	5.453	5.234	5.029	4.836	4.656	4.486	4.327
12	6.492	6.194	5.918	5.660	5.421	5.197	4.988	7.793	4.611	4.439
13	6.750	6.424	6.122	5.842	5.583	5.342	5.118	4.910	4.715	4.533
14	6.982	6.628	6.302	6.002	5.724	5.468	5.229	5.008	4.802	4.611
15	7.191	6.811	6.462	6.142	5.847	5.575	5.324	5.092	4.876	4.675
16	7.379	6.974	6.604	6.265	5.954	5.668	5.405	5.162	4.938	4.730
17	7.549	7.120	6.729	6.373	6.047	5.749	5.475	5.222	4.990	4.775
18	7.702	7.250	6.840	6.467	6.128	5.818	5.534	5.273	5.033	4.812
19	7.839	7.366	6.938	6.550	6.198	5.877	5.584	5.316	5.070	4.843
20	7.963	7.469	7.025	6.623	6.259	5.929	5.628	5.353	5.101	4.870

FORMULAE

Annuity

Present value of an annuity of $1 per annum, receivable or payable for n years, commencing in one year, discounted at r% per annum:

$$PV = \frac{1}{r}\left[1 - \frac{1}{[1+r]^n}\right]$$

Perpetuity

Present value of $1 per annum, payable or receivable in perpetuity, commencing in one year, discounted at r% per annum:

$$PV = \frac{1}{r}$$

The Examiner for Management Accounting – Business Stategy offers to future candidates and to lecturers using this booklet for study purposes, the following background and guidance on the questions included in this examination paper.

Section A – Compulsory

Question one requirement (a) relates to Section A of the syllabus and tests the learning outcome *Evaluate the nature of competitive environments, distinguishing between simple and complicated competitive environments*. It relates to the syllabus content *Porter's Five Forces model and its use for assessing the external environment*. It requires **only the application** of Porter's five Forces model. Requirement (b) relates to syllabus Section D and tests the learning outcome *Evaluate and recommend appropriate control measures*. It relates to the syllabus content *Assessing strategic performance i.e. the use and development of appropriate measures that are sensitive to industry characteristics and environmental factors*. It tests the candidates' ability to **calculate and interpret** ratios. Requirement (c) relates to syllabus Section B and tests the learning outcome *Discuss how suppliers and customers influence the strategy process and recommend how to interact with them*. It relates to syllabus content *Negotiating with customers and suppliers and managing these relationships*. It follows on from requirement (a) in that it requires **application of** the five Forces model, but this time to solve problems.

Section B – Two questions from four

Question two requirement (a) tests learning outcome C(iv) *Identify an organisation's value chain* and the syllabus content *Value chain analysis*. It asks for an **application of** the value chain model. Requirement (b) tests learning outcome B(vi) *Evaluate the strategic and competitive benefits of IS/IT and advise on the development of appropriate strategies* and the syllabus content *The impact of IT (including electronic commerce) on an industry (utilising frameworks such as Porter's Five Forces and the Value Chain) and how organisations can use IT (including the Internet) to enhance competitive position*. It is directly in line with the syllabus content, as it requires the **identification of the impact of** e-commerce on the firm's value chain.

Question three requirement (a) tests learning outcome C(ii) *Evaluate the product portfolio of an organisation and recommend appropriate changes to support the organisation's strategic goals* and the syllabus content *Management of the product portfolio*. Requirement (b) tests the same learning outcomes and syllabus content as requirement (a) but **uses a higher level verb**. Requirement (c) tests the learning outcome C(vii) *Discuss the role and responsibilities of directors in the strategy development process* and the relevant syllabus content. The whole of this question examines the candidates' ability to **apply** the product life cycle model. It takes them through the stages of strategic analysis, strategic choice and strategy implementation.

Question four requirement (a) tests learning outcome C(v) *Evaluate the importance of process innovation and re-engineering* and the syllabus content *The role of IT in innovation and business process re-engineering*. Requirement (b) tests the same learning outcome and syllabus content as (a) but **with a higher level verb**. This question requires candidates to demonstrate a range of skills, beginning with comprehension and ending with evaluation.

Question five requirement (a) tests learning outcome D(v) *Identify and evaluate IS/IT systems appropriate to the organisation's strategic requirements and recommend changes when necessary* and the syllabus content for this requirement is *The concept of knowledge management and its role as a key element in an organisation's success*. Requirement (b) tests learning outcome A(i) *Identify relevant stakeholders in respect of an organisation* and the syllabus content *Interacting with stakeholders and the use of stakeholder mapping*. Even part (a) of this (apparently easy) question **requires a recommendation**, so some justification is warranted. Requirement (b) requires **only the application** of Mendelow's model.

Examiner's Answers

SECTION A

Question One

(a) **Introduction**

The industry of CCC is defined as the specialist sports car industry in Europe. It is analysed below, using the "five forces" model.

Rivalry

Rivalry looks at the number of organisations, within the industry, supplying similar products to the same customers. It also looks at the extent of competitive activity between those organisations. The major car manufacturers are not rivals, as they cannot supply this type of vehicle. There are only six specialist sports car manufacturers in Europe, and these are all assumed to be rivals. There has historically been little price competition; therefore, there has historically been little rivalry. The six appear to have widely differentiated products, and this has led to the current position.

Threat of new entrants

The threat of new entrants is the extent to which the rivals have to divert time and cost to the erection and maintenance of entry barriers. It is assumed that all six rivals, in line with CCC, have significant up-front capital costs invested in design, sales promotion and marketing. This creates a significant barrier to entry. CCC pays high salaries to engender staff loyalty, as must the other rivals to remain competitive, and this creates a further barrier to entry.

Threat of substitutes

A substitute is any product or service that fulfils the same purpose or need. The threat of substitutes is that they will steal away market volume, thus affecting all rivals equally. Substitutes include other 'vanity' purchases such as yachts, powerboats, expensive holidays and even private planes. The product made by CCC and its rivals is not really a car, it is a status symbol and an expensive toy. There are many substitutes for the high disposable income of CCC's customers.

Bargaining power of suppliers

An organisation competes with its suppliers for margin, the most common methods of such competition being arguments over cost/price and quality. Most supplies are relatively minor components, such as wheels and tyres, which could probably be sourced from alternative suppliers without any risk. The engine modification only comes from SSS, which is able to dictate terms. It appears that SSS may earn the same profit on an engine as CCC does on a car. CCC cannot switch from SSS, as customers see value added in the use of SSS engines. SSS is not contracted to supply only CCC. This suggests that, in general terms, the bargaining power of suppliers is low. However, the bargaining power of SSS is very high.

Bargaining power of customers

The organisation competes with its customers in the same ways as with its suppliers. Historically these customers have had little bargaining power, due to the differentiation of the various specialist sports cars, but their power is increasing due, perhaps, to the effects of recession. Customers are now negotiating price down and, until they sign a contract, have few switching costs other than loss of prestige.

Conclusion

Competitive forces have increased recently, driving profit margins down from nearly 20% (2002) to 7.5% (2005). This has forced a drastic reduction in the level of dividend paid, and significantly reduced shareholder value.

(b) **SSS – position and performance**

Ratios	Wkg.	SSS	Ind. Ave.
Revenue per employee	1	€306,875	€128,500
Return on revenue (gross)	2	43.1%	
Return on revenue (pre-tax)	3	7.7%	4.3%
ROCE (gross)	4	99.7%	
ROCE (pre-tax)	5	17.9%	11.2%
Dividend cover	6	2.05x	
Profit per employee (gross)	7	€132,125	
Profit per employee (pre-tax)	8,8a	€23,750	€5,526
Current ratio	9	1.68	
Quick (acid test) ratio	10	0.73	
Non-current assets turnover	11	2.75x	
Inventory days (cost of sales)	12	61	
Receivables days (revenue)	13	22	65
Payables days (cost of sales)	14	64	28

Workings

1 2,455,000/8 = 306,875
2 (2,455 − 1,398)/2,455 = 1,057/2,455 = 43.1%
3 190/2,455 = 7.7%
4 1,057/(100 + 960) = 1,057/1,060 = 99.7%
5 190/1,060 = 17.9%
6 133/65 = 2.05x
7 1,057,000/8 = 132,125
8 190,000/8 = 23,750
8a 128,500 × 4.3% = 5,526
9 (232 + 146 + 32)/244 = 410/244 = 1.68
10 (146 + 32)/244 = 178/244 = 0.73
11 2,455/894 = 2.75x
12 (232/1,398) × 365 = 0.166 × 365 = 61
13 (146/2,455) × 365 = 0.059 × 365 = 22
14 (244/1,398) × 365 = 0.175 × 365 = 64

Commentary

With revenue per employee of 2.4 times the industry average (and likewise, a pre-tax ROCE of 1.6 times the average), SSS appears either very efficient or to charge very high prices. It is unlikely that the reason for this high figure is a high degree of automation (resulting in a low headcount) as the nature of SSS's business is labour-intensive. Pre-tax margin of 1.8 times the average seems to point to higher than average prices. Return on capital employed is similarly high, supporting this conclusion.

Just for comparison, CCC has revenue per employee of €39,166 (€11.75M/300), and pre-tax ROS of 7.5% (compared to SSS – 7.7%). The two companies are, however, in very different business sectors.

It is possible, however, that the pre-tax (after interest) ratios of SSS are all higher than average as a result of the fact that SSS has no debt. Most of the other firms in the industry may be highly geared, thus reducing their pre-tax earnings levels. It has not been possible to calculate operating level ratios for the industry.

A dividend cover of over 2x suggests a reasonably high margin of safety. However, as an owner-managed business, this will be of little importance to the owner.

The pre-tax profit per employee, of €23,750, is a very impressive performance. This figure is over four times the average, underlining the apparent efficiency of SSS. Just for comparison, CCC employees each generate only €2,933 pre-tax profit.

While the current and quick ratios appear low, it is not possible to compare these to the industry average so no conclusions can be drawn. However, it is more likely to be a result of aggressive working capital management (see below) than poor liquidity.

Inventory days of 61 (assumed to consist of raw materials and WIP only, due to the "to order" nature of SSS's business) are quite high, bearing in mind that CCC supplies the engines. However, SSS may be replacing many engine parts with very expensive alternatives.

The low receivables days of 22, far less than one month, suggests that a large proportion of sales are either paid for in cash or by stage payments. This underlines the significant bargaining power that SSS has over its customers, CCC included. It is not known what payment terms CCC takes from SSS.

The high payables days of 64 suggests that SSS also exerts high bargaining power over its suppliers, though there may be a risk of losing some suppliers as a result of such aggressive credit policies.

Other performance indicators

For SSS to have made its service to CCC a unique selling point of CCC's product is an impressive achievement. It is very easy for the providers of sub-contracted services to remain 'invisible' to the end consumer. This suggests that SSS has invested heavily in the "pull" marketing (i.e. to the end consumer) of its services. Further evidence of the strong bargaining power of SSS can be seen in its refusal to negotiate on price, or to sign a sole customer agreement with CCC.

Conclusions

SSS appears to be an extremely efficient and successful organisation. Its only one weak point is its aggressive supplier credit policy.

(c) **Options to defeat SSS**

CCC has four options if it wishes to reduce the bargaining power of SSS:

1 *To exert its own bargaining power.* It is not known what percentage of its business SSS does with CCC, but it must be a significant proportion. This should, theoretically, give CCC an opportunity to be more aggressive in negotiating prices and credit terms with SSS. However, this type of approach has already failed, so is unlikely to succeed in the future. It may also result in a worsening relationship between SSS and CCC, and even worse terms. The worst result might be that SSS decides not to supply CCC in future. This would have a disastrous effect on CCC as the SSS tuned engine is a major USP of its cars.

2 *To avoid dealing with SSS.* CCC could seek an alternative supplier of engine tuning, preferably one with as good a reputation as SSS. However, there would still be significant consequences for CCC, as it would have to invest in developing a new supplier relationship, and in persuading its customers to accept engines that are not prepared by SSS.

3 *To bring tuning services in-house.* This would probably involve recruitment of suitably skilled staff, or possibly 'headhunting' key staff from SSS. In addition to the cost and lead time implications of this strategy, CCC would once again be faced with the problem of persuading its customers to accept cars without SSS tuned engines.

4 *To acquire SSS.* Subject to having funds available, the preferred option would seem to be to acquire SSS. Though this would depend on the willingness of the current owner to sell (but to remain involved), he might be persuaded to take a shareholding in CCC in return for SSS. The price of SSS could be anywhere between €0.7 m and €1 m, (see below), or even more depending on the view of the owner. The P/E-based valuation uses a P/E ratio that is probably not relevant to a small private company like SSS. However, it is included here as indicative of a starting point for negotiation.

The biggest benefit to CCC of acquisition, in addition to the removal of SSS's bargaining power, would be the control it would have over the business. CCC could refuse to provide services from SSS to any of CCC's rivals, effectively giving it a monopoly over the services of SSS.

*Note: It is possible to earn full marks for this requirement **without** valuing SSS*

Valuations
Net asset valuation = 100,000 + 960,000 = **€1.06 M**
P/E valuation = €133,000 × 7.5 = **€1.00 M**

Assumption: P/E valuation may be reduced by up to 1/3 for non-marketability of SSS shares, thus giving a value between about €0.7 m and €1 m.

SECTION B

Question Two

(a)

Note: For a diagram of the value chain model, see page 75 of the official CIMA Study System.

Firm infrastructure: This includes the general nature and fixed assets of the organisation. The location of the shops adds value because it makes them convenient for the customers.

HRM (operations, outbound logistics, or service): This is the way that the organisation uses its staff. Staff training allows customers to deal with 'helpful and knowledgeable staff'. This should allow them to find and buy the products they seek.

Technology development (inbound logistics): This is the use of new technology to support a primary activity. The new stock control system allows 2B to carry a wider range of stock and to 'call off' stock from suppliers. This means that customers are more likely to be able to obtain the right product

Procurement (inbound logistics): This is the acquisition of resources (including staff) to support a direct activity. Good relations with suppliers allow a wider range of goods to be stocked. This also means that customers are more likely to be able to obtain the right product.

Procurement/HRM (operations or service): The recruitment of passionate staff will improve customer service levels.

Outbound logistics: These are the systems and procedures related to getting the finished goods to the customer. Store layout makes it easy for customers to find what they are looking for, so they will buy more.

Note: Some of the above may be "classified" differently, according to interpretation.

(b) The proposed investment in an e-retail Web site will both increase and decrease value added. Reductions in value added assume that some or many of the existing retail customers choose to use the Web site instead of visiting the shops.

Firm infrastructure: The location of the shops may become less important, as many customers may decide to shop from home. This *reduces* the value added by shop location.

HRM (operations, outbound logistics or service): There may be a *reduction* in value added, as customers never deal directly with staff.

Technology development (outbound logistics): The new e-retail Web site will introduce a whole new sales channel, thus *adding* significant value.

Procurement (operations or service): There may be a *reduction* in the value added by recruitment of passionate staff, as e-retail customers may never deal directly with staff.

Outbound logistics: Store layout may be irrelevant to e-retail customers, as they may never visit the stores. Value added in this activity may therefore *reduce*.

Conclusion

The proposed change will probably both increase and decrease value added in the value chain of 2B. This should be considered during the appraisal of the investment project. The managers should ensure that the proposal generates a net increase in value.

Question Three

(a) **Current product portfolio**

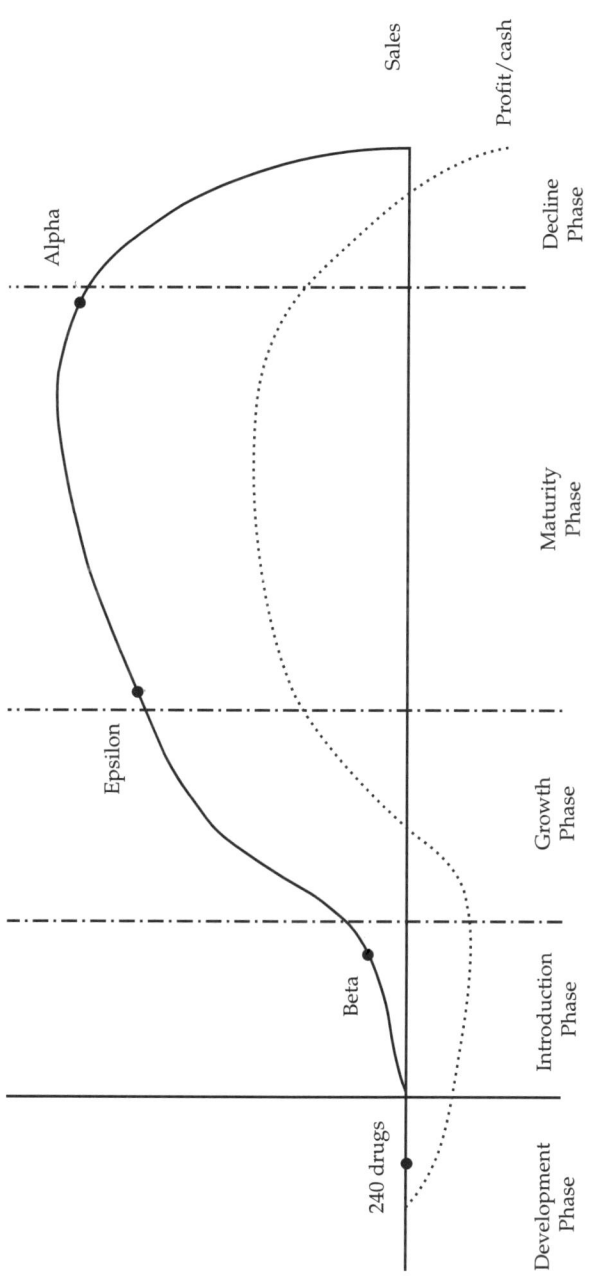

The product life cycle breaks the life of a product down into five phases: development, introduction, growth, maturity and decline. A balanced portfolio of products is one that has products in all stages of the life cycle, and overall generates sufficient profit and cash to meet the organisation's objectives. This means that, as one product enters decline, another is emerging from growth to replace it.

For 3C, the current product portfolio is as follows:

Development – 240 drugs
Introduction/early growth – Beta
Early maturity – Epsilon
Late maturity – Alpha

The product portfolio of 3C appears, at first sight, to be fairly well balanced. In order to make a definitive judgement, it would be necessary to have further information about the likely success rate of development projects and the relative sales and profit/cash profiles of Beta, Epsilon and Alpha.

(b) **Investment options**

The three investments can be evaluated as follows:

Alpha – Investing in Alpha2 will allow 3C to reposition Alpha to the early maturity stage of the product life cycle. As the new product has completed clinical trials, this investment is likely to be low risk. This will have a positive effect on the product portfolio, as it will allow Alpha to continue to generate significant cash flows for a further five years, unless a superior rival product is launched. However, the imminent launch of generic copies of the original Alpha may threaten this drug's market leading position.

Beta – An investment in marketing for Beta should lead to sales growth and therefore take the product from the introduction stage to early maturity. However, there are two major risks. First, the marketing programme may not succeed, and sales revenues may not be significant enough to pay back the investment. Secondly, any investment may be wasted if a rival product is subsequently launched.

Gamma – This drug represents the highest risk investment. Even with the investment, there is no certainty that Gamma will successfully complete its final stage of clinical trials, and reach product launch. However, the returns from any breakthrough drug are likely to be very significant. 3C may also consider the relationship between Gamma and Beta – if Beta is not successful, the portfolio will lack an introduction stage product, thus making an investment in Gamma more important.

(c) **Social Responsibility**

One of the fundamental principles of business is that organisations exist to provide a satisfactory return for their owners at an acceptable level of risk. If this view is taken of the investment decision in 3C, the directors should assess the risk/return characteristics of each of the investments, in the context of the product portfolio, and choose the investment that is most likely to add value to the organisation.

However, it has become increasingly important to consider how companies manage their processes to have an overall positive impact on society. As a drug company, 3C has a product portfolio that directly impacts on the daily lives of individuals and communities. While Epsilon and Beta are fairly specialised drugs, their impact on the respective patient groups is likely to be life-saving, so the social impact of them is still significant. As a general painkiller, Alpha is likely to have a relatively minor impact on a very large number of lives.

The most significant social responsibility issues arise in relation to Gamma. HIV is a very high-profile condition, which affects many millions of individuals and whole communities. The directors of 3C, in evaluating the investment in Gamma, should carry out a full cost-benefit analysis that takes into account the "external" impact of the drug on society.

This is the case not only in deciding whether to invest, but also on deciding pricing. While the potential for profit from Gamma is huge, the directors should also recognise that a drug like Gamma should ideally be priced at a level that makes it affordable to those most in need. From the purely commercial perspective, launching Gamma at a lower price should allow a higher sales volume, and also result in favourable publicity for 3C.

The directors should attempt, in their decision making, to take into account both the commercial factors and their wider responsibility.

Question Four

(a) (i) **Business Process Re-engineering (BPR)**

BPR is essentially about re-designing an activity to make it more efficient and effective. While many of the changes made may be relatively minor and incremental, when viewed collectively they represent a transformation of the organisation. BPR is a company-wide initiative, that looks at all activities in turn. BPR is a culture, rather than a process, as it shares much in common with the continuous improvement doctrine of Kaisen, and should be built into the everyday activity of all staff. The most obvious role of IT in BPR is in the area of automation. By automating a process, we can often have it performed more quickly and more cheaply, and sometimes improve quality and accuracy.

Process Innovation (PI)

PI is a much more fundamental step-change than BPR. PI is about looking for completely new processes or radically different ways of doing things. PI tends to focus on relatively few, key activities or business areas. PI is more closely related to innovation cultures and organisational learning than it is to Kaisen. As such, PI is thought to have a greater potential for competitive advantage than has BPR. In PI, IT is often the change trigger, rather than the enabling tool. Many innovations in processes are only possible because of new technology.

An example to illustrate the difference is the use of IT in bookshops. Computerised stock control (BPR) can improve turnover and reduce costs. The development of the Internet and e-commerce (PI) has revolutionised the way books are sold, and led to the emergence of virtual book retail as a significant sector.

(ii) **4D and OTIS**

The OTIS system may be seen as BPR, as the teaching of medical students has been happening for thousands of years. OTIS simply makes it cheaper and more convenient. However, it could also be argued that the use of videoconferencing allows 4D to carry out processes that were previously impossible. Allowing a lecturer to teach students anywhere in the world would have been infeasable prior to OTIS. Even the use of videotaped lectures would have been far less effective, as there would have been no interaction between lecturer and students. OTIS could, therefore, be viewed as PI. The final decision depends on one's view as to the extent to which the new system has transformed the work of 4D.

(b) **Benefits to 4D** (*Note: only three required*)

1. The OTIS system will significantly reduce the cost of teaching, as a far greater number of students will be able to attend each virtual lecture. While this may not lead to increased 'profit' to 4D, it will allow the organisation to invest funds elsewhere.
2. The system should also lead to a significant increase in revenue to 4D, as a result of the larger student body. Once again, this may not be of importance to increase profitability, but will allow further investment in facilities.
3. The OTIS system may have an effect on the efficiency of the 4D organisation, in terms of shorter courses. It may be possible for students to complete their training in less time and qualify more quickly.
4. There may also be significant reductions in travel costs either for the lecturer or the students.

Benefits to society (*Note: only two required*)

1. The OTIS system should have a major benefit to society in that many more surgeons can be trained. This will improve standards of patient care and shorten waiting lists for operations.
2. The benefits of OTIS will be particularly great in parts of the world where students previously had little or no access to medical teaching. Web technology is relatively cheap, and the OTIS system can be used in many remote or poor areas of the world. In such areas, the impact of OTIS might be very significant indeed.
3. The use of the OTIS system in a number of countries will ensure that consistent levels of care are available in each country. This will mean that patients no longer have to travel to get 'the best' treatment in a country other than their own.

Question Five

(a) **Hardware**

- A Web server, to allow 5E to run its Web site separately from the Intranet and internal systems of the organisation. This will alllow a high level of security to prevent unauthorised access. It will also allow the Web site to be maintained or upgraded without affecting other systems.
- An Intranet server, to hold the knowledgebase, manage traffic and allow all staff to access the knowledgebase. This would be separate from the Web server to prevent unauthorised access, as it will contain confidential material.
- Network cabling, to connect all the 5E PCs and laptops to the servers. Hardware communications devices, such as modems and/or multiplexors, may also be required.

- Broadband communication lines, to allow connection to the Internet. This will allow 5E's customers to access the Web site and also facilitate e-mail within and outside the firm. As 5E has a number of offices, this will also facilitate the establishment of a Virtual Private Network (VPN) for the firm.

Software

- A software package to run the Intranet, probably (in order to avoid re-programming) the same as the one used by X. It may be necessary to negotiate purchase of this, from X, if it is a tailor-made system.
- Security software, to control access to the knowledgebase and prevent hacking and the introduction of viruses. This should also be updated frequently.
- Web design software, to allow the Web site to be updated and re-designed by 5E staff.

(b)

Notes: For a diagram of the Mendelow matrix, see page 4 of the official CIMA Learning System. The following answer is by no means definitive, as the relative power/interest of the stakeholders is a matter of opinion.

1 Staff are in the Low/Low "minimal effort" quadrant. They may be uninterested in the decision because their day-to-day work is unlikely to be affected significantly by the proposed change. They also have little power over the decision, as it will be made by the senior management.
2 Clients are in the High/Low "keep informed" quadrant. They are likely to be very interested in gaining access to the knowledgebase, but have little power individually to influence the decision unless they strongly object collectively to the proposal.
3 Suppliers of IT hardware and software are also in the "keep informed" quadrant. This project may present them with an opportunity to provide the required technology, and they will thus have a relatively high interest. They will, however, be unable to influence the decision to any great extent.
4 The Partners of 5E are in the High/High "key players" quadrant. Their wealth will be directly affected by the success or failure of the strategy, and they will thus be as interested in this project as they would be in any major strategic investment. They are also the final decision makers, thus having high power.
5 X will be directly affected, and therefore interested, as it appears it will lose significant business as a result of the planned change. It is also in a position to make the changeover very problematic if it is not kept satisfied, so has high power. It is, therefore, categorised as a "key player".

Nov 2006 Questions and Answers

13

Strategic Level

Paper P6 – Management Accounting – Business Strategy

Question Paper	209
Examiner's Brief Guide to the Paper	219
Examiner's Answers	220

The answers published here have been written by the Examiner and should provide a helpful guide for both tutors and students.

Published separately on the CIMA website (www.cimaglobal.com/students) from mid-February 2007 is a Post Examination Guide for this paper, which provides much valuable and complementary material including indicative mark information.

© 2006 The Chartered Institute of Management Accountants. All rights reserved. No part of this publication may be reproduced, stored in a retrieval system, or transmitted, in any form or by any means, electronic, mechanical, photocopying, recorded or otherwise, without the written permission of the publisher.

Business Management Pillar

Strategic Level Paper

P6 – Management Accounting – Business Strategy

21 November 2006 - Tuesday Morning Session

Instructions to candidates

You are allowed three hours to answer this question paper.
You are allowed 20 minutes reading time **before the examination begins** during which you should read the question paper and, if you wish, make annotations on the question paper. However, you will **not** be allowed, **under any circumstances,** to open the answer book and start writing or use your calculator during this reading time.
You are strongly advised to carefully read ALL the question requirements before attempting the question concerned (that is, all parts and/or sub-questions). The question requirements are contained in a dotted box.
Answer the ONE compulsory question in Section A on pages 210 to 212.
Answer TWO of the four questions in Section B on pages 213 to 216.
Maths Tables and Formulae are provided on pages 217 and 218.
Write your full examination number, paper number and the examination subject title in the spaces provided on the front of the examination answer book. Also write your contact ID and name in the space provided in the right hand margin and seal to close.
Tick the appropriate boxes on the front of the answer book to indicate which questions you have answered.

SECTION A – 50 MARKS

[the indicative time for answering this section is 90 minutes]

ANSWER THIS QUESTION

Question One

Introduction

AAA is a large manufacturing company that specialises in the design and manufacture of televisions. It was formed in 1985, following the merger of two rival companies, and is now one of the three largest TV manufacturers in Asia. AAA employs over 2000 staff at its head office and four manufacturing plants, which are all in the same Asian country, Jurania. AAA is listed on the Juranian stock exchange.

The production system

TV manufacturing is a mass production industry, with high volumes of identical or similar products being made on a production line basis. The products are generally made to order for customers, who are either other electrical manufacturers (who put their name on the product and re-sell it) or large electrical retailers. The manufacture of televisions is still a relatively labour-intensive process, as many of the components need to be assembled in a precise way. Most of the electrical components used in AAA's process are bought in from suppliers, as is the TV screen and cabinet (the plastic case in which the screen and components are contained). The staff who assemble the components are mainly semi-skilled, and have been trained by AAA to perform fairly simple, repetitive operations. When completed, quality assurance staff test the TV sets, and any that are found faulty are returned to the production line to be re-worked.

Components received from suppliers are also tested by the quality assurance staff of AAA. As they do not have the time to test every component, they test a sample of components from each batch delivered. If they find more than one faulty component in every twenty tested, the whole batch is rejected and returned to the supplier.

Business Performance

The following is a summary of the performance of AAA last year. AAA reports its performance in the currency of its home country, the Juranian dollar (J$):

Financial Performance	Last Year Actual J$ millions	Budget J$ millions
Sales revenue	1,793	1,941
Gross (Factory) profit	1,177	1,320
Pre-tax profit	652	790
Capital employed (average)	2,835	2,550
Cash (closing)	179	485
Finished goods inventory (average)	38·2	20·0
Raw material inventory (average)	11·4	9·5
Work in process (average)	0·8	0·3

	Last year	
Other performance indicators	Actual	Budget
Share price (closing) (J$)	334·50	400·00
Earnings per share (J$)	46·00	50·00
Number of employees (average)	2,259	2,128
Sales (million units)	2·35	2·40
Number of finished units re-worked	54,000	30,000
Percentage of purchases from suppliers rejected (by value)	4·25	3·00
Average production cost of sales per unit (J$)	262	259
Average sales price per unit (J$)	763	809
New product lines developed	12	10
New product lines successfully launched	1	4
Products returned from customers as faulty (per 1,000 units sold)	28	20
Warranty claims (per 1,000 units sold)	56	30
Number of working employee-days lost to industrial disputes	2,500	3,200

The board meeting

At the most recent board meeting of AAA, the Chief Executive Officer asked for suggestions as to how the management of AAA might be improved. One of the non-executive directors suggested that the use of the balanced scorecard might assist in controlling the business, as it had in another company of which she is also a non-executive director. The marketing director mentioned that he had compiled some information about another organisation in the television manufacturing industry, BBB, and asked if that might be of use. The purchasing director mentioned that he had recently been at a conference where a speaker had suggested that the introduction of 'knowledge management' was improving the performance of many organisations. As far as the other directors present at the board meeting were aware, this was not an approach used commonly in their industry.

BBB

BBB is a major rival of AAA, and is based in a neighbouring Asian country, Mesnar. BBB is a private company, owned by a wealthy industrialist. BBB compiles its accounts in the local currency of Mesnar, the Mesnari Riyal (RM). Both the Mesnari Riyal and the Juranian Dollar are freely traded currencies, and the current spot exchange rate between the two is J$1:RM2.50. There is free and unrestricted trade between Jurania and Mesnar.

The following information has been obtained from BBB's filed accounts from last year, and from the trade association of which both AAA and BBB are members.

	Last year
Sales revenue (RM million)	1,400
Total production cost of sales (RM million)	435
Profit before tax (RM million)	557
Capital employed (RM million)	1,589
Closing inventories (RM million)	17
Number of employees (closing)	740
Number of units sold	780,000
Number of warranty claims in the year	19,800

Required

(a) Prepare a balanced scorecard appraisal of the performance of AAA last year.

*Note: There are up to 10 marks available for calculations in this section. You are **not** required to compare the performance of AAA with that of BBB in this section.*

(25 marks)

(b) As the management accountant of AAA, prepare a benchmarking report for the directors that compares the performance of AAA last year with that of BBB for the same period. You should refer to your answer to part (a) in making your comparison.

*Note: There are up to 8 marks available for calculations in this section, and up to 2 marks for the use of an appropriate report format. You are **not** required to reproduce the calculations from your answer to part (a) in this section, but may do so if you wish.*

(15 marks)

(c) Advise the directors of AAA how the introduction of knowledge management might lead to AAA developing a sustainable competitive advantage over BBB.

(10 marks)

(Total for question One = 50 marks)

(Total for Section A = 50 marks)

End of Section A

Section B starts on page 213

SECTION B – 50 MARKS

[the indicative time for answering this section is 90 minutes]

ANSWER *TWO* QUESTIONS FROM FOUR

Question Two

CTC, a telecommunications company, has recently been privatised by the government of C after legislation was passed which removed the state monopoly and opened up the communications market to competition from both national and overseas companies – a process known as deregulation.

Prior to the deregulation, CTC was the sole, protected, supplier of telecommunications and was required to provide 'the best telecommunications service the nation can afford'. At that time the government dictated the performance levels required for CTC, and the level of resources it would be able to bring to bear to meet its objectives.

The shares were floated on the C Stock Exchange with 80% being made available to the population of C and up to 20% being made available to foreign nationals. The government of C retained a 'golden share' to prevent the acquisition of CTC by any foreign company. However, the privatisation meant that many of the traditional ways in which the industry had operated would need to change under the new regulations. Apart from the money received from the flotation, the government privatised CTC in recognition of both the changing global environment for telecommunications companies, and the overseas expansion opportunities that might exist for a privatised company. The government recognises that foreign companies will enter the home market but feels that this increased competition is likely to make CTC more effective in the global market.

You have recently been appointed as the management accountant for CTC and have a background in the commercial sector. The Board of Directors is unchanged from CTC's pre-flotation days.

Required:

(a) Explain to the Board of Directors why the objectives of CTC will need to change as a result of the privatisation of CTC and the deregulation of the market.

(10 marks)

(b) Produce two examples of suitable strategic objectives for CTC, following its privatisation and the deregulation of the market, and explain why each would be an appropriate long term objective.

(4 marks)

(c) Advise the Board of Directors on the stages of an appropriate strategic planning process for CTC in the light of the privatisation and deregulation.

(11 marks)

(Total for Question Two = 25 marks)

Section B continues on the next page

Question Three

DDD is a relatively small, specialist manufacturer of chemicals that are used in the pharmaceutical industry. It does not manufacture any pharmaceutical products itself since these are made by different processes and under different conditions. DDD obtains its raw materials, which are quite simple, from large chemical companies, and modifies them by a number of patented processes before selling them on to a few pharmaceutical companies. DDD makes significantly higher margins than its suppliers, which manufacture in bulk.

Several patents are due to expire in the next three years.

The large pharmaceutical companies, which are DDD's customers, are suffering reduced profits as governments reduce the price they are prepared to pay for drugs. As a result, the pharmaceutical companies are pressuring DDD to reduce its prices.

The majority of the shares are owned by members of the family which started the business some years ago and who still take an active part both as managers of the business and as development chemists. There is a share option scheme for the employees and this is well supported.

Required:

As management accountant for DDD you have been asked to:

(a) Advise the Board of Directors of the possible threats related to the patent expiries;

(10 marks)

(b) Evaluate suitable courses of action that DDD might take to maintain its profits in the face of the threats identified in *(a)*;

(12 marks)

(c) From your analysis recommend, with a brief justification, the most appropriate course of action for DDD.

(3 marks)

(Total for Question Three = 25 marks)

Section B continues on the next page

Question Four

EEE is an established chemical company extracting flavours and oils from plant materials and supplying them to the flavours and fragrances industries. The shareholders include institutional investors (20%), employees and pensioners of the company (20%) and the descendants of the family (30%) who founded the business approximately 100 years ago. The remainder of the shares are in public ownership. The company is reasonably successful but, recently, there has been pressure on margins and its future is not guaranteed.

The majority of the Board of Directors are members of the founding family who have always taken an active part in the management of the business.

When the company was originally started, the surrounding area was mainly used as agricultural land but, over time, a residential area has developed around the factory. Although many of the workers in the factory live locally, some of the housing is quite expensive and has attracted affluent residents from the local city.

The chemical engineers at EEE have recently developed, and patented, a new process which would allow EEE to extract onion oil and garlic oil at far better yields than those obtained by existing processes. The market for these oils is very profitable and presents a significant opportunity for EEE to gain a real competitive advantage in its industry.

Unfortunately, as with all extraction processes, there will be some leakage and, although perfectly safe and compliant with all safety legislation, the smell of the oils will offend some of the more affluent residents who have complained to local government officers.

There is very little other industry in the area and EEE is a large contributor to the local economy. One of the trade union representatives working in EEE is also an elected council member serving in the local government.

Required:

As management accountant you have been asked to:

(a) Advise the Board of Directors of the advantages to EEE of conducting a stakeholder analysis in the context of the proposed investment decision;

(5 marks)

(b) Analyse the principal stakeholders in EEE in the context of the proposed investment in the new process;

(15 marks)

(c) Recommend an acceptable course of action to the Board of Directors in the light of the stakeholder analysis conducted in *(b)*.

(5 marks)

(Total for Question Four = 25 marks)

Section B continues on the next page

Question Five

FFF is a manufacturer of specialist portable communications equipment, which is designed for use in hazardous and dangerous conditions. Developments of new technology in recent years, such as wireless mobile telephony, infra red thermal imaging and global positioning has allowed FFF to create new products.

The market for such equipment has grown significantly over the past five years. The customer base includes fire services, oil and chemical companies and the government. FFF now recognises that, during this period of rapid growth, the market has attracted a number of new entrants and may even be reaching a level of overcapacity.

The directors feel that they do not know as much as they should about the existing, and new, companies in the industry. The market is now maturing and, although FFF is managing to maintain its margins and leading market share (45%), it is likely that the characteristics of the industry will change.

Required

As management accountant you are required to:

(a) Advise the board of the advantages of adopting a formal approach to competitor analysis;

(10 marks)

(b) Advise the directors of the stages in a formal competitor analysis process and identify any information that would need to be gathered at each stage for FFF.

(15 marks)

(Total for Question Five = 25 marks)

(Total for Section B = 50 marks)

End of Question Paper

Maths Tables and Formulae follow on pages 217 and 218

MATHS TABLES AND FORMULAE

Present value table

Present value of $1, that is $(1 + r)^{-n}$ where r = interest rate; n = number of periods until payment or receipt.

Periods (n)	Interest rates (r)									
	1%	2%	3%	4%	5%	6%	7%	8%	9%	10%
1	0.990	0.980	0.971	0.962	0.952	0.943	0.935	0.926	0.917	0.909
2	0.980	0.961	0.943	0.925	0.907	0.890	0.873	0.857	0.842	0.826
3	0.971	0.942	0.915	0.889	0.864	0.840	0.816	0.794	0.772	0.751
4	0.961	0.924	0.888	0.855	0.823	0.792	0.763	0.735	0.708	0.683
5	0.951	0.906	0.863	0.822	0.784	0.747	0.713	0.681	0.650	0.621
6	0.942	0.888	0.837	0.790	0.746	0705	0.666	0.630	0.596	0.564
7	0.933	0.871	0.813	0.760	0.711	0.665	0.623	0.583	0.547	0.513
8	0.923	0.853	0.789	0.731	0.677	0.627	0.582	0.540	0.502	0.467
9	0.914	0.837	0.766	0.703	0.645	0.592	0.544	0.500	0.460	0.424
10	0.905	0.820	0.744	0.676	0.614	0.558	0.508	0.463	0.422	0.386
11	0.896	0.804	0.722	0.650	0.585	0.527	0.475	0.429	0.388	0.350
12	0.887	0.788	0.701	0.625	0.557	0.497	0.444	0.397	0.356	0.319
13	0.879	0.773	0.681	0.601	0.530	0.469	0.415	0.368	0.326	0.290
14	0.870	0.758	0.661	0.577	0.505	0.442	0.388	0.340	0.299	0.263
15	0.861	0.743	0.642	0.555	0.481	0.417	0.362	0.315	0.275	0.239
16	0.853	0.728	0.623	0.534	0.458	0.394	0.339	0.292	0.252	0.218
17	0.844	0.714	0.605	0.513	0.436	0.371	0.317	0.270	0.231	0.198
18	0.836	0.700	0.587	0.494	0.416	0.350	0.296	0.250	0.212	0.180
19	0.828	0.686	0.570	0.475	0.396	0.331	0.277	0.232	0.194	0.164
20	0.820	0.673	0.554	0.456	0.377	0.312	0.258	0.215	0.178	0.149

Periods (n)	Interest rates (r)									
	11%	12%	13%	14%	15%	16%	17%	18%	19%	20%
1	0.901	0.893	0.885	0.877	0.870	0.862	0.855	0.847	0.840	0.833
2	0.812	0.797	0.783	0.769	0.756	0.743	0.731	0.718	0.706	0.694
3	0.731	0.712	0.693	0.675	0.658	0.641	0.624	0.609	0.593	0.579
4	0.659	0.636	0.613	0.592	0.572	0.552	0.534	0.516	0.499	0.482
5	0.593	0.567	0.543	0.519	0.497	0.476	0.456	0.437	0.419	0.402
6	0.535	0.507	0.480	0.456	0.432	0.410	0.390	0.370	0.352	0.335
7	0.482	0.452	0.425	0.400	0.376	0.354	0.333	0.314	0.296	0.279
8	0.434	0.404	0.376	0.351	0.327	0.305	0.285	0.266	0.249	0.233
9	0.391	0.361	0.333	0.308	0.284	0.263	0.243	0.225	0.209	0.194
10	0.352	0.322	0.295	0.270	0.247	0.227	0.208	0.191	0.176	0.162
11	0.317	0.287	0.261	0.237	0.215	0.195	0.178	0.162	0.148	0.135
12	0.286	0.257	0.231	0.208	0.187	0.168	0.152	0.137	0.124	0.112
13	0.258	0.229	0.204	0.182	0.163	0.145	0.130	0.116	0.104	0.093
14	0.232	0.205	0.181	0.160	0.141	0.125	0.111	0.099	0.088	0.078
15	0.209	0.183	0.160	0.140	0.123	0.108	0.095	0.084	0.079	0.065
16	0.188	0.163	0.141	0.123	0.107	0.093	0.081	0.071	0.062	0.054
17	0.170	0.146	0.125	0.108	0.093	0.080	0.069	0.060	0.052	0.045
18	0.153	0.130	0.111	0.095	0.081	0.069	0.059	0.051	0.044	0.038
19	0.138	0.116	0.098	0.083	0.070	0.060	0.051	0.043	0.037	0.031
20	0.124	0.104	0.087	0.073	0.061	0.051	0.043	0.037	0.031	0.026

Cumulative present value of $1 per annum, Receivable or Payable at the end of each year for n years

$$\frac{1-(1+r)^{-n}}{r}$$

Periods (n)	1%	2%	3%	4%	5%	6%	7%	8%	9%	10%
1	0.990	0.980	0.971	0.962	0.952	0.943	0.935	0.926	0.917	0.909
2	1.970	1.942	1.913	1.886	1.859	1.833	1.808	1.783	1.759	1.736
3	2.941	2.884	2.829	2.775	2.723	2.673	2.624	2.577	2.531	2.487
4	3.902	3.808	3.717	3.630	3.546	3.465	3.387	3.312	3.240	3.170
5	4.853	4.713	4.580	4.452	4.329	4.212	4.100	3.993	3.890	3.791
6	5.795	5.601	5.417	5.242	5.076	4.917	4.767	4.623	4.486	4.355
7	6.728	6.472	6.230	6.002	5.786	5.582	5.389	5.206	5.033	4.868
8	7.652	7.325	7.020	6.733	6.463	6.210	5.971	5.747	5.535	5.335
9	8.566	8.162	7.786	7.435	7.108	6.802	6.515	6.247	5.995	5.759
10	9.471	8.983	8.530	8.111	7.722	7.360	7.024	6.710	6.418	6.145
11	10.368	9.787	9.253	8.760	8.306	7.887	7.499	7.139	6.805	6.495
12	11.255	10.575	9.954	9.385	8.863	8.384	7.943	7.536	7.161	6.814
13	12.134	11.348	10.635	9.986	9.394	8.853	8.358	7.904	7.487	7.103
14	13.004	12.106	11.296	10.563	9.899	9.295	8.745	8.244	7.786	7.367
15	13.865	12.849	11.938	11.118	10.380	9.712	9.108	8.559	8.061	7.606
16	14.718	13.578	12.561	11.652	10.838	10.106	9.447	8.851	8.313	7.824
17	15.562	14.292	13.166	12.166	11.274	10.477	9.763	9.122	8.544	8.022
18	16.398	14.992	13.754	12.659	11.690	10.828	10.059	9.372	8.756	8.201
19	17.226	15.679	14.324	13.134	12.085	11.158	10.336	9.604	8.950	8.365
20	18.046	16.351	14.878	13.590	12.462	11.470	10.594	9.818	9.129	8.514

Periods (n)	11%	12%	13%	14%	15%	16%	17%	18%	19%	20%
1	0.901	0.893	0.885	0.877	0.870	0.862	0.855	0.847	0.840	0.833
2	1.713	1.690	1.668	1.647	1.626	1.605	1.585	1.566	1.547	1.528
3	2.444	2.402	2.361	2.322	2.283	2.246	2.210	2.174	2.140	2.106
4	3.102	3.037	2.974	2.914	2.855	2.798	2.743	2.690	2.639	2.589
5	3.696	3.605	3.517	3.433	3.352	3.274	3.199	3.127	3.058	2.991
6	4.231	4.111	3.998	3.889	3.784	3.685	3.589	3.498	3.410	3.326
7	4.712	4.564	4.423	4.288	4.160	4.039	3.922	3.812	3.706	3.605
8	5.146	4.968	4.799	4.639	4.487	4.344	4.207	4.078	3.954	3.837
9	5.537	5.328	5.132	4.946	4.772	4.607	4.451	4.303	4.163	4.031
10	5.889	5.650	5.426	5.216	5.019	4.833	4.659	4.494	4.339	4.192
11	6.207	5.938	5.687	5.453	5.234	5.029	4.836	4.656	4.486	4.327
12	6.492	6.194	5.918	5.660	5.421	5.197	4.988	7.793	4.611	4.439
13	6.750	6.424	6.122	5.842	5.583	5.342	5.118	4.910	4.715	4.533
14	6.982	6.628	6.302	6.002	5.724	5.468	5.229	5.008	4.802	4.611
15	7.191	6.811	6.462	6.142	5.847	5.575	5.324	5.092	4.876	4.675
16	7.379	6.974	6.604	6.265	5.954	5.668	5.405	5.162	4.938	4.730
17	7.549	7.120	6.729	6.373	6.047	5.749	5.475	5.222	4.990	4.775
18	7.702	7.250	6.840	6.467	6.128	5.818	5.534	5.273	5.033	4.812
19	7.839	7.366	6.938	6.550	6.198	5.877	5.584	5.316	5.070	4.843
20	7.963	7.469	7.025	6.623	6.259	5.929	5.628	5.353	5.101	4.870

FORMULAE

Annuity

Present value of an annuity of $1 per annum, receivable or payable for n years, commencing in one year, discounted at r% per annum:

$$PV = \frac{1}{r}\left[1 - \frac{1}{[1+r]^n}\right]$$

Perpetuity

Present value of $1 per annum, payable or receivable in perpetuity, commencing in one year, discounted at r% per annum:

$$PV = \frac{1}{r}$$

The Examiner for Management Accounting – Business Strategy offers to future candidates and to lecturers using this booklet for study purposes, the following background and guidance on the questions included in this examination paper.

Section A – compulsory

Question one requirement *(a)* tests learning outcome D(ii) *"Prepare and evaluate multidimensional models of performance measurement"* and the syllabus content *"Multidimensional models of performance (e.g. the balanced scorecard..."*. It requires **only the application** of the Balanced Scorecard model. Requirement *(b)* tests learning outcome C(iii) *"Prepare a benchmarking exercise and evaluate the results"* and the syllabus content *"Benchmarking performance with the best organisations"*. It tests the candidates' ability to **calculate and interpret** ratios and other financial information. Requirement *(c)* tests learning outcome D(iv) *"Evaluate and advise managers on the development of strategies for knowledge management..."* and the syllabus content *"The concept of knowledge management and ..."*. This is a fairly tough requirement, as it asks for the **application** of two pieces of theory at the same time.

Section B – two questions from four

Question two requirement *(a)* tests the learning outcome A(ii) *"Evaluate the impact of regulatory regimes on strategic planning and implementation"* and the syllabus content *"regulation in major markets"*. It asks for an **application of** stakeholder analysis to the organisation's changing relationship with government. Requirement *(b)* tests learning outcome D(i) *"Evaluate and recommend appropriate control measures'* and the syllabus content *'assessing strategic performance"*. It requires the **application** of knowledge relating to performance objectives. Requirement (c) tests the learning outcome A(ii) *"Evaluate the impact of regulatory regimes on strategic planning and implementation"* and a variety of content from throughout the syllabus. It asks candidates to **advise** management.

Question three requirement *(a)* tests learning outcome B(iv) *"Discuss how suppliers and customers influence the strategy process and recommend how to interact with them"* and the syllabus content *"negotiating with suppliers and customers and managing these relationships"* Requirement *(b)* tests learning outcome C(i) *"Evaluate strategic options"* and the syllabus content *"strategic options generation"* and *"acquisition and divestment strategies"*. Requirement *(c)* tests the learning outcome C(i) *"Evaluate strategic options"* and the syllabus content *"strategic options generation"* and *"acquisition and divestment strategies"*. The whole of this question examines the candidates' ability to **evaluate** strategic options and to **advise** management.

Question four requirement *(a)* tests learning outcome B(iii) *"Discuss how stakeholder groups work and how they affect the organisation"* and the syllabus content *"stakeholder management"*. Requirement *(b)* tests learning outcome B(iii) *"Discuss how stakeholder groups work and how they affect the organisation"*, and the syllabus content *"stakeholder management"*. Requirement (c) tests learning outcome B(ii) *'recommend pro-active and reactive approaches to business / government relations and to relations with civil society.'* and the syllabus content *'approaches to business government relations and with civil society'*. The whole of this question examines the candidates' ability to **evaluate** strategic position and to **advise** management.

Question five requirement *(a)* tests learning outcome A(v) *"Evaluate strategies for response to competition"* and the syllabus content *"competitor analysis and competitive strategies"*. Requirement *(b)* tests learning outcome A(v) *"Evaluate strategies for response to competition"* and the syllabus content *"competitor analysis and competitive strategies"*. The whole of this question examines the candidates' ability to **advise** management.

The Examiner's Answers for P6 - Management Accounting – Business Strategy

SECTION A

Answer to Question One

Requirement (a)

The Balanced Scorecard looks at the performance of an entity from four different perspectives; financial, customer, internal business process, and innovation & learning.

Workings

Sales as a percentage of budgeted	1,793/1,941 x 100	92%
Return on sales (gross margin)	1,177/1,793 x 100	66%
Budgeted ROS (gross margin)	1,320/1,941 x 100	68%
Budgeted re-work	30,000 x 2·35/2·40	29,375
Staff numbers variance	((2,259 – 2,128)/2,128) x 100	6% adverse
EPS variance	((50 – 46)/46) x 100	9% adverse
Change in market capitalisation	((400 – 334·5)/400) x 100	16% lower
Sales price variance	((809 – 763)/809) x 100	6% adverse

Note: These are a selection of calculations and there are many other equally valid calculations available

Financial perspective

- Sales, at J$1·8bn were only 92% of budget. While this may have been due to externalities, it is more likely (due to the other evidence discussed below) to be due to a combination of poor quality, high price and poor marketing.
- AAA generated a gross margin of 66%, compared with budget of 68%. This implies poor control of direct costs. Other factors (see below) suggest that this applies to both labour and materials.
- Some of the shortfall in margin is due to excessive re-work. For sales of 2·35 million units, re-work (in line with budget) should have been 29,375 units. It was actually 54,000 – an increase of 24,625 units (or, 1% of production) and an "adverse operational variance" of over 80% (24,625/29,375).
- A pre-tax ROS of 36%, compared to a budget of 41%, suggests poor control of indirect costs. This may partly be attributable to excessive manpower numbers, as the average staff level was 6% over budget. Once again, adjusting for lower activity levels makes the operational element of this variance much greater.

- An EPS figure that is almost 9% lower than budget implies a loss of shareholder value. This has contributed to a reduction in market capitalisation (assuming no change in the number of shares issued) of 16%.

Customer perspective
- The average sales price of each unit is 6% down against budget. This may be due either to conditions in the market, or to customer perception. Evidence relating to quality suggests the latter.
- Warranties and returns of 84 units per 000, equates to 197,400 dissatisfied customers (84 x 2,350). Although this seems a relatively small rate of returns, it represents a very large absolute number, and implies very poor quality in the production process or components used. It is also significantly over budget, suggesting that a serious problem exists.

Internal business process perspective
- The closing cash balance is much lower than budgeted. Assuming capital expenditure was in line with budget, some of the shortfall is attributable to the reduction in pre-tax profit (790 – 652 = 138m) but the remainder of the 306m shortfall is likely to be due to poor working capital management.
- Inventory is high, in comparison to budget: finished goods inventories represent 23 days cost of sales (budgeted 12), raw materials 7 days (budgeted 6). This implies poor control over (particularly finished goods) inventory, and/or poor production planning.
- WIP of 0·5 days cost of sales (against a budget of 0·2) is very high, implying poor control over the production process and possible bottlenecks in production. A high volume assembly operation should have little or no WIP, if run on JIT principles.
- Re-work represented 2·3% of production (against a budget of 1·2) but a further 2·8% of units sold were returned as faulty this means that over 5% of production was initially faulty, and less than half of these were identified before despatch. This implies major failures, both in the control of production, and quality inspection. (Note – all of this assumes that sales and production are roughly equal.)
- There is a distinction between production staff and quality inspectors, so the production staff have not taken ownership of the quality of their products.
- Just over 1 day per employee lost due to disputes (against a budget of about 1·5) suggests that industrial relations are good.
- A sales per employee figure of 1,040 units (against a budget of 1,128) implies that either production or sales efficiency is down.

Innovation and learning perspective
- 12 new product lines were developed (against a budget of 10), but only 1 was successfully launched (budget 4). This implies poor management of R&D and/or poor management of marketing, as AAA is either developing product lines that nobody wants to buy, or the new lines are not being effectively promoted.

Conclusion
While performance is reasonably good overall, there are some significant issues that need to be addressed.

Requirement (b)

To: Directors
From: Management Accountant
Date: Today

Benchmarking performance – AAA vs. BBB

Terms of reference
This report will compare the financial performance of AAA with BBB. Limited information relating to BBB is available, and what was provided is assumed to be accurate for the purposes of this report.

Analysis

	Working (BBB)	BBB	AAA
Turnover (J$ million)	1,400/2·5	560	1,793
Sales per employee	780,000/740	1,054	1,040
Average price achieved (J$)	560,000,000/780,000	718	763
ROS (gross margin) %	((1,400 – 435)/1,400) x 100	69	66
ROS (pre-tax) %	(557/1,400) x 100	40	36
ROCE (pre-tax) %	(557/1,589) x 100	35	23
Inventory days (cost of sales)	(17/435) x 365	14	30
Warranty claims per thousand	19,800/780	25	56

In terms of both turnover and manpower numbers, we (AAA) are about three times the size of BBB. It is interesting to note that, despite the differences between the two organisations, unit sales per employee are quite similar. One would, however, expect there to be efficiencies of scale in production, so BBB has achieved a much higher efficiency level than AAA despite its smaller size.

In the balanced scorecard I raised concerns that our products are over-priced. While there might be differences in the generic strategies being pursued by BBB and AAA (cost leadership vs. differentiation, for example) it is noticeable that the average unit price of BBB's TVs was $718 compared to ours of $763. BBB's products are obviously priced much more competitively than ours.

Despite the lower price per unit, BBB's profitability (at both the gross and pre-tax levels) was better than ours. This suggests that BBB is more efficient in its control and management of both direct and indirect costs. While there might be differences in labour and overhead costs between Jurania and Mesnar, this analysis is not available.

A ROCE of 35%, compared with our 23%, simply underlines the efficiency advantages that BBB seems to have. While this figure may be distorted by age of assets or accounting policies, it still implies a far more effective creation of shareholder value.

A great deal of comment was made in the balanced scorecard analysis about inventory levels. Ours is a mass production industry, with high volumes of identical or similar products, made to order for customers. This suggests that we should hold very little raw material inventory, and virtually no WIP or finished goods. Our total inventory level runs at about 30 days (cost of sales), whereas BBB manages to be more profitable than us while maintaining only about 14 days inventory.

While we do not know the extent to which BBB controls quality or re-works defective output, we can see that its rate of warranty returns is less than half ours. This implies a far higher quality level, and should be a cause for concern.

Conclusions
While we do not have detailed information about the operations of BBB, the financial information provided suggests BBB to be a more efficient and profitable organisation than AAA. We must find some way to improve our performance level, if we wish to compete with BBB.

Requirement (c)

Competitive advantage is the position where a firm exerts more competitive force on its rivals than they do on it. A firm can achieve a competitive advantage by the pursuit of cost leadership, differentiation (having a product that is believed to be better, different or unique) or focus (tailoring the products to perfectly meet customer needs).

Knowledge management is a deliberate strategy, by an organisation, to record the knowledge of its employees and encourage knowledge sharing. It normally involves cultural change within the organisation, and the development of an Intranet.

In AAA, knowledge management could lead to a competitive advantage over BBB in a number of different ways:

- If employees shared knowledge and experience of procurement and production techniques, it might be possible for AAA to significantly reduce the unit cost of production to a level below that of BBB. We know that BBB is more efficient, as it has a lower selling price but delivers a higher operating margin than AAA. It may be that AAA employs staff who have previously worked for BBB, and could explain what they do and how they do it.

- If staff were willing to share knowledge relating to improvements in quality, either through better manufacturing or the use of better raw materials, it may be possible to differentiate the AAA televisions in the marketplace. Such action would, of course, require marketing strategy to be modified, to ensure that any improvements in quality were recognised by the customer. We believe that product quality is an area where BBB currently has competitive advantage over us.

- If staff share knowledge relating to customer needs, this can be used to re-design and re-position the products to 'focus' AAA's televisions. It may be, for example, that some customers want high technology televisions, while others look for a wide range of features, or compatibility with PC or gaming equipment. AAA might be able to position products against each of these niche markets, and be perceived as the only manufacturer to do so.

In conclusion, there are very many opportunities for AAA to use knowledge management to achieve a competitive advantage over BBB.

SECTION B

Answer to Question Two

Requirement (a)

Prior to the deregulation, the principal stakeholder was the government of C and it had set a requirement relating to the quality of service within a budget. The emphasis would have been on economy, efficiency and effectiveness. Any objectives set would, therefore, have been based on level of service and/or cost efficiency.

The board of directors will also need to be aware of the corporate governance issues that it will now face. The stock market of C will almost certainly have a code of practice which must be followed for listed companies.

Now that CTC is owned by shareholders it will be necessary for it to meet objectives addressing the values of those shareholders whilst still complying with the regulations imposed by the government. Since the telecommunications industry in C has become deregulated it is possible that foreign companies could enter the market and offer a rival service. With this in mind CTC will need to consider the customers as an important stakeholder group whose values must also be addressed. Failure to do this might lead to a significant loss of market share.

Although the relationship with CTC is now 'at arms length' it is likely that the government will want CTC to capitalise on the opportunities offered by overseas expansion and to generate significant tax revenue for the good of C. The shareholders are more likely to want CTC to demonstrate significant, profitable, growth and a reward in terms of both dividend and share price increases. This may lead to a conflict of stakeholder objectives that must be managed by the directors.

The customers will still want to receive a level of service at, in their perception, a cost effective price. This will also lead to a conflict with the interests of shareholders, who will necessarily seek a growth in profitability. Increasing prices may be one of the ways to achieve higher profits.

Now that CTC has become privatised it will be subject to the full range of regulation that commercial organisations have to deal with in addition to any industry specific regulation that the government has created in the light of the privatisation. This may mean that CTC is required to provide some unprofitable services, or be prohibited from providing some profitable ones.

The objectives that CTC sets from now on must address the areas of profitability and reward for the shareholders, customer satisfaction, the competitive position of CTC with respect to any new entrants to the market, overseas expansion and compliance with the new regulatory regime.

Requirement (b)

There are a number of areas in which CTC could specify strategic objectives but these must be SMART – Specific, Measurable, Attainable, Relevant and Timed. With the principal stakeholders of shareholders, government and customers, appropriate objectives could be:

1. To increase shareholder value, measured according to an agreed formula, by 10% per annum.

2. To increase the percentage of shareholder value derived from overseas business to 25% within 5 years.

The first of these would address the needs of the shareholders and would focus on the longer term rather than a short term measure such as ROCE. Additionally as shareholder value increases, so does the tax revenue of the government.

The second would address the needs of the government and its desire for overseas expansion whilst increasing the growth opportunities for the shareholders.

Requirement (c)

An appropriate strategic planning process for CTC would consist of the following stages:

1. Environmental analysis – the analysis of the issues external to CTC which may impact upon its business. This will involve a PEST (or similar acronym) analysis and an analysis of Porter's five forces for the industry. CTC should also, at this stage, conduct an analysis of potential competitors for the market in C and existing competitors in any foreign market into which it is considering expanding. This analysis should be done on a continuous basis and should 'drive' the strategy-making process. CTC should be seeking a 'good fit' with its new dynamic market.

2. Having carefully considered the stakeholders of the company, CTC should clarify the mission and objectives of the company. Any actual or potential conflicts should be identified and resolved. The use of 'stakeholder mapping' might be beneficial at this stage.

3. A position audit should be conducted to determine the competitive position and core competencies of CTC. This should provide the board of directors with a clear analysis of the strengths and weaknesses of the company. This will almost certainly involve the use of value chain analysis to determine whether CTC is likely to enjoy a cost-, or differentiation-based, advantage compared to the rest of the industry.

4. CTC should then identify the strategic issues that face the company over the coming planning period. These will be derived from both the internal and external appraisal. In order to summarise these issues, a SWOT analysis might be prepared. This shows both internal and external issues, and allows strategic options to be identified.

5. Having identified the issues a creative phase of generating strategic options that may be appropriate to address the issues that it has identified, should be undertaken. Although companies are often better served by innovative approaches, in most instances the options generated will fall into the generic strategies proposed by Michael Porter. If CTC wants to be more innovative, and to satisfy the government's expectations, it might consider the 'market development' or 'product development' strategies proposed by Ansoff.

6. The options that have been generated should then be formally evaluated using appropriate criteria such as suitability – will the option actually contribute to the desired objective, acceptability – will the option gain the support of the principal stakeholders and feasibility – does CTC have the resources to actually carry out the strategy successfully? Additionally CTC should seek to adopt options which will contribute to the long term competitive advantage of the company and so a test of sustainability should be applied.

7. CTC should then determine how the selected options will be implemented. This may be by organic growth, joint venture or possibly by acquisition. Since CTC has been controlled by the government for some considerable time there are likely to be significant change management issues that will need to be addressed within the company. An implementation plan needs to be developed with clear recognition of roles, responsibilities and milestones. An important component of the implementation plan will be to create the performance measurement criteria which will be used for the last stage of the planning process.

8. Monitor and control of the results and adjustments to the strategies to keep the organisation on track. A periodic review of the strategic plan will also be necessary, as there are likely to be further changes in CTC's environment, which will necessitate some strategic response.

CTC will need to recognise that this deliberate strategic planning process described here is unlikely to deliver exactly what they plan. As time passes, modified strategies will emerge and it will be those which the company follows.

Answer to Question Three

Requirement (a)

At the present time DDD is in a favoured position compared to both its suppliers and its customers. With regards to its suppliers, it is making higher margins than the suppliers using processes which are protected by patents. The fact that the majority of shares are held by members of the family protects it from hostile takeover. With regards to its customers, the large pharmaceutical companies, the same situation is true. There is patent protection and, as a family business, the threat of takeover is limited. The patent protection also prevents other manufacturers from entering DDD's market and competing directly with it, and will allow DDD to charge reasonably high prices.

Once the patent protection expires this situation will change and will become worse. Other companies could enter the industry offering the same products as DDD or the larger chemical companies from whom DDD obtains its supplies could forward integrate and manufacture the same products as DDD, most probably at a lower cost.

It is unlikely that DDD will be able to build any differentiation advantage for the chemical intermediaries it is manufacturing. With that in mind, the only advantage possible for DDD is one of cost leadership – particularly with the pressure currently being exerted by the pharmaceutical companies. It is unlikely that the pharmaceutical companies will wish to backward integrate into DDD's industry since the processes are most probably different.

It may be the case that DDD is able to operate at higher margins than its suppliers because of a lower overhead cost structure due to its relative size. However, if the large chemical companies wish to enter this market because the margins are better there would be little to stop them charging DDD a premium price for the intermediates. This would put pressure on the margins that DDD could charge and eventually force it out of business or make the prospect of takeover more attractive to the family. Alternatively the chemical companies may just put up the price and look for a 'fairer' split of the profit that DDD makes by modifying the chemicals for use by the pharmaceutical companies. Due to the difference in the process used it is unlikely that the chemical companies would want to enter DDD's market by organic growth.

In summary the threats facing DDD are:

- Margins squeezed by pharmaceutical companies;
- Margins squeezed by suppliers;
- Threat of forward integration and takeover by suppliers;
- Threat of new entrants to the market.

Requirement (b)

There are a number of options which DDD might choose to adopt in the face of the changes to the market and these should be evaluated using the tests of suitability, acceptability and feasibility and sustainability.

First, it may decide to do nothing and hope that the situation will not be as bad as it expects. This is not a suitable option since it does not remedy the situation. Similarly it is not likely to be acceptable to the family or the employees who would wish the business to continue profitably. It is, however, feasible, in that no action is necessary. The option offers no sustainable advantage.

A second option might be to develop new processes to replace those that are due to go 'off patent' in the near future. This option would be suitable in that the new processes would be patent protected, and would be acceptable to both the family and the employees. The feasibility of doing so would depend upon the expertise of the development chemists within the firm and the funds that are available for R&D. In terms of sustainability, this option would be viable since, if a steady stream of new products and patents could be developed, the firm could maintain the current situation.

A third option would be to look for alternative markets for its existing products. If this were successful it would expand its market and increase its revenue but would do little to prevent both the suppliers and customers squeezing its margins. Therefore, although it may be feasible it fails the suitability and acceptability and sustainability tests.

A fourth option would be to form a joint venture with one of the suppliers seeking to gain the protection of a large partner to keep other suppliers at arms length. To some extent this would prevent the pharmaceutical companies squeezing margins excessively but would involve DDD sacrificing some margin to its new partners. There would be the risk, however, that the partner would know an increasing amount about DDD's business and this might make eventual takeover, or substitution, a bigger threat. Although this does not fail the suitability test it is not the most suitable option and may not be completely acceptable to the family or the employees since it could be seen as a loss of some independence. The option is feasible but offers little in the way of sustainable advantage.

A fifth option would be to decide now to be taken over by one of the chemical suppliers since DDD could command a higher asking price whilst its processes are still under patent. While this is feasible it will not be acceptable to the family or the employees and is not suitable in terms of the long term future of the company. The option offers no sustainable advantage to DDD.

Requirement (c)

Of the options identified the most suitable would be to develop new, patented, products to sell. As long as DDD has the skills necessary to do this it will be able to maintain the current situation. However, the current situation is not ideal. DDD should also seek to spread its customer base so that the buyer power of its few customers is reduced.

Answer to Question Four

Requirement (a)

EEE has a diverse group of stakeholders and it would be in the interests of the board of directors to determine both the power and interest of each group in the future of the organisation, particularly when strategic decisions are to be made. Any strategy that EEE tries to pursue must have the agreement and, preferably, the active support of the more powerful stakeholders. It is unlikely that a chosen strategy will satisfy, equally, all groups of stakeholders so such an analysis will help EEE determine who will be more able to disrupt the plans made by the organisation. Similarly some stakeholders may be in favour of a particular course of action and, depending on their power, may be used by the board in convincing those who are against any changes. In this particular instance, there is potential for conflict between some of the residents and EEE over the new process. However, there will be others, such as the employees and other shareholders who will be in favour of the changes. EEE will need to establish the power and interests of the various groups so that it can decide whether to accommodate, negotiate, manipulate or resist the claims of the various groups.

Requirement (b)

The principal stakeholders of EEE can be classified by their power and interest in the organisation according to the work of Mendelow.

Powerful and interested and who are key players

1. The local government is powerful in that it can make life difficult for EEE. Although the proposed process complies with safety legislation, it has the potential to upset some of the residents and future development work may be jeopardised if this stakeholder is alienated. The local government will have a strong interest in EEE since it is a contributor to the local economy. Its interest can be described as benevolent since, on balance, it would want EEE to prosper.

2. The founding family is a powerful shareholder since it collectively owns 30% of the shares and forms the majority of the board of directors. Its interest will be strong since it is dependent on the business for its living and most probably has strong loyalties to 'its' business.

3. The employees are in a similar position in that their interests lie in continuing employment which is likely to be more secure if the new processs is implemented and, as they collectively own or can influence 20% of the shares, will be quite powerful as well.

Powerful and with low interest who should be kept satisfied

1. The institutional shareholders are a relatively powerful group with a 20% shareholding in EEE. However, their interest in the particular issue is not likely to be so strong. As long as EEE is making a satisfactory return then they will not be so interested in the 'local' difficulties that EEE is experiencing with its neighbours.

Low power and low interest – minimal effort

1. The general shareholders are also unlikely to have a particular interest in the 'local' issues that EEE has with the residents and, unlike the institutional shareholders, are not so powerful since they are unlikely to act as a group.

Low power but high interest – keep informed

1. The affluent residents are very interested in what is going on with the new process and the perceived nuisance. However, their power to influence the situation is dependent on the local government giving more attention to them than to the impact that EEE has on the local economy and as a local employer. They do have the ability to make a lot of noise and protest, but whether this will have an impact on the current development is debateable. They could, however, make it difficult for EEE in the future and, as such, they should be treated as well as possible.

2. The other residents living in the area have a similar level of interest and power but are more likely to agree, possibly grudgingly, with what EEE is doing, since a number of members of their families may be working at the factory.

Requirement (c)

EEE finds itself in a difficult situation in its attempt to balance the interests of all of its stakeholders. As the company has been in the area for many years it will want to take a long term view in the situation in which it finds itself. It will want to carry on with the new process because of the effect on the profitability. While it would be easy, and very short term, to ignore the affluent local residents and just carry on with the new process, this would be storing up resentment and difficulties for the future. Although the other residents are not likely to be so openly opposed to the smell coming from the factory since some of them may depend upon the factory for their livelihood, they would also prefer the smell not to be there. If they protest too much to the local government it is likely that the local government officers will look more closely at any developments that EEE proposes and will be more inclined to refuse permission in the future. EEE must engage in a 'charm offensive' with the local government and, as best it can, with the local residents in an attempt to be a good neighbour. The trades union official who also serves as a local government elected officer is an ideal champion of the company's cause and should be encouraged to convince his fellow officers of the importance of EEE to the local economy and local community. Members of the local government should be invited into the factory to see the process and should be kept fully informed and engaged.

Similarly EEE should hold a number of events to engage with the local community and its families in a public relations exercise. Sponsorship of the local sports team, grants towards local events, and even financial assistance to local schools for books and sporting equipment are some of the possibilities. Open days to show how the company works and where its products are used, particularly as EEE is supplying the flavours and fragrances industry, might also be used to good effect.

Answer to Question Five

Requirement (a)

Competitor analysis should provide a comprehensive picture of the strengths and weaknesses of current and potential rivals in the company's marketplace.

As the market matures and competition becomes fiercer, it is important that FFF knows as much as possible about the other companies competing in its market.

The advantages of a formal approach to competitor analysis would be:

1. To help management understand their competitive advantages or disadvantages compared to the other players in the industry. FFF is, presumably, an innovative company which has gained its market share by first mover advantage and maintained it by continuing to conduct R&D on the particular products.

2. To find out if other players are pursuing a similar strategy or if their particular skills are in process engineering, allowing them to copy the products FFF offers more cost effectively? Alternatively the competitors may be more skilled in marketing than FFF.

3. To help provide insights into the present and future strategies that the competition might adopt. If FFF is able to determine what the competition is currently doing, this may well help FFF to decide what the competitors are likely to do in the future. It is unlikely that all players in the industry are currently following the same strategy, or that they are likely to do so in the future. Knowing that competitors intend to leave the market or the basis on which they intend to stay will be a significant advantage when it comes to deciding which approach FFF should take.

4. To provide an informed basis on which defensive or offensive strategies can be developed to maintain both the market share and profitability of FFF. It will always be easier for FFF to make decisions if it is aware of the likely reaction to those decisions.

5. To provide part of the basis on which rational decisions can be made to choose between alternatives strategies that FFF should be considering at this time to maintain its present competitive advantage.

Requirement (b)

Having identified the close competitors in the industry, the stages in a competitor analysis are as follows:

1. *Identify their current strategy.* This should be based on what a competitor says and does. What a competitor does is far more important than what it says. FFF should be looking to establish whether competitors are seeking a differentiated advantage or whether they are attempting to be cost leaders in the industry.

2. *Identify each competitor's objectives.* It is important to understand the competitors' goals if FFF is to accurately predict their behaviour. FFF needs to know whether its competitors are happy with their current level of achievement. If the competitors appear happy with their current level of performance, there are unlikely to be any changes in their behaviour.

3. *Identify competitors' assumptions about the industry.* It will be useful for FFF to know whether the other companies in the market are as concerned as FFF itself about the possibility of overcapacity and other features of a maturing industry. The perceptions of the competitors will often be based on the views and values of the senior management and, wherever possible, those senior managers should be psychologically profiled.

4. *Identify the competitors' resources and capabilities.* It is impossible to assess the seriousness of a challenge from a competitor without a rigorous analysis of its capability. Ideally a company should know as much about its competitors as it knows about itself. Since FFF capitalised on the new technology which made this industry

possible, an assessment of the innovative capabilities of the competition would be particularly important.

5. *Prediction of competitor behaviour.* The information gathered in the first four stages should be used to predict the behaviour of the principal competitors under different scenarios. Those scenarios might be related to the potential growth, or lack of growth, of the market foreseen by FFF. FFF would need to make decisions regarding the likelihood of competitors leaving the market or entering into a price war as a reaction to any strategic decision that FFF might make.

6. The results of the predictions should be presented in the most user-friendly form possible to those who will make decisions about future strategy.

7. Once this has been done, the behaviour and performance of the competitors should be continuously monitored for evidence of changed activity, and the environment screened for indications that there are new entrants to the market.